No More Masterpieces

Short Prose by New Writers

Collected and Edited by Guy Allen
with Arnie Achtman Tim Kitagawa Pauline Stanley

Canadian Scholars' Press Inc.

Toronto, Canada

No More Masterpieces

First published by
**Canadian Scholars' Press Inc.
211 Grenadier Road
Toronto, M6R 1R9
Canada**

Introduction © copyright Guy Allen. Stories © copyright by the individual authors.

All rights reserved. No copy, reproduction or transmission of this material may be made without written permission.

Canadian Cataloguing in Publication Data

Main entry under title:

No more masterpieces: short prose by new writers

ISBN 0-921627-21-1

1. Short stories, Canadian (English).*
2. Canadian fiction (English) — 20th century.*
3. College prose, Canadian (English) — Ontario — Toronto.*
4. University of Toronto. I. Allen, Guy, 1947- .

PS8321.N6 1989   C813'.54'08   C89-094817-8
PR9197.32.N6 1989

No More Masterpieces

For
Bob Forcier, Richard Van Fossen, Dorothy Weirich
in appreciation for support

Contents

Preface		1
Introduction		5

Chapter One — *The Child* — 17

Gina Barbosa Tousignant	*Sixty-Six Hail Marys on an Air Mattress*	19
Tim Kitagawa	*The Birthday Party*	21
G.F. Ricketts	*Mr. Bong's Variety*	22
Maria Lausmaa	*Why I Never Went to School*	24
Jim Kelly	*Angels With Dirty Faces*	25
Laura Szostak	*Dandelions*	28
Gordon Scott	*The Wind*	29
Pauline Stanley	*Up in the Clubhouse*	30
Mary Tomaz	*Going My Way*	32
Tim Kitagawa	*Tryout Day*	33
Marian Van der Meeren	*Stretchie*	36

Chapter Two — *School* — 39

Mary Lou C. DeBassige	*Lakeview Indian Day School*	41
Ed Caissie	*The Tipton Zone*	43
Marian Van der Meeren	*Mr. V*	44
Danielle Cohen	*Doggie, Doggie, Who Brought The Bone?*	47
Carol Allen	*The Report Card*	49
Tina Reyes	*Tea Time*	51
Sandra McKenzie	*Math 30*	55
Gord McGuire	*Leaving*	56
Acalla Ng	*Someone New*	58
Tim Vesely	*Me And Mill*	59
Janice Uba	*Too Many Worries*	62
Bruce G. Tavender	*The Defeat*	63

Chapter Three — *Places* — 65

Aline Burke	*Terre de Caïn*	67
Ieva Martin	*Where My World Began*	71
Stephen Kamachi	*The Swamp*	72
Tieho Masinga	*The Mirror, The Thing*	74
Steve Richards	*My World*	75
Paula Peters	*My First Day at St. Patrick's Anglican*	78
Sybil C. Horton	*My India Rubber Ball*	79

Chapter Four

	People	83
Titus Cheong	*Who Was Henry?*	85
Alison Rasmussen	*Dan The Man*	87
Sharon F. Yee	*Marilyn*	90
Debra Antrobus Bruce	*Angie*	92
Grace Abelarde	*Papa*	94
Brian Cartwright	*Apt. 314*	95
Lisa Oki	*Gramma*	97
Gordon Scott	*You Never Visit*	99
Jennifer Sealy	*Martha*	102
Tina Reyes	*William*	103

Chapter Five

	Jobs	105
Gordon Scott	*Trust Me*	107
Patricia Muiser	*Max*	108
Nic Disanto	*Kodaklone*	110
Charles Helawa	*The Job*	112
Brad Littleproud	*The Jungle Line*	114
Sybil C. Horton	*The First Day*	115
Pat Haramis	*Jackson's Shell*	118
Heather Mathys	*The End Of The Road*	120
Marilyn Major	*Room 601*	123
Ann Porter	*The Lawn Shop*	124
Bruce G. Tavender	*The Arrest*	127

Chapter Six

	Women and Men	129
Fook Ho	*The Decision*	131
Ingrid Babjak	*The Dump*	132
Neveen Howard	*Crilly*	134
Tim Kitagawa	*Legs on the Bus*	137
Nigel McInnis	*On the Way Home*	138
Pauline Stanley	*Mick and I*	139
Irene M. Dutton	*Miss Wood's Advice to Girls*	142
Mary Alilovic	*Okay*	143
Lynn MacKenzie	*My Story About Men and Women*	146
M. Nakamura	*Dreamer*	148
Jennifer Brown	*In Morning*	149
Ieva Martin	*Manville*	150

Chapter Six	***Women and Men*** *continued*	
Jeff Robins	*Real Soon*	153
Saudade Gaspar	*The Day After*	155
Jane Anthony	*The Steak*	156
Hugh Bancroft	*The Happy Wanderer*	158
Jennifer Brown	*Those Grey Eyes*	160
Rosamund Elwin	*The Wedding Dress*	162
Chapter Seven	***The Family***	165
Jill Watson	*Best of Friends*	167
Charmaine Browne	*Parental Guidance*	168
Mary Beth Shickluna	*You'll Have To Ask Your Father*	171
Bonnie-Jayne Errett	*The Weekend Mom Came To Town*	173
Saudade Gaspar	*Papa*	175
Ieva Martin	*The Motherhood Myth and Me*	176
Linda Tompkins	*The New Kid in School*	179
Jordin Neumann	*My Father, Football and Me*	182
Roger Pires	*Visiting Home*	184
Rick Alexander	*Goodbye*	186
Laura D. Rubino	*Cindy*	188
Emilio Sinopoli	*Wrong Room*	189
Anne Markey	*Laura*	191
Chapter Eight	***Wild Cards***	195
M. Nakamura	*M.M.N.*	197
Jennifer Sealy	*The Boyfriend and the Albatross*	198
Pauline Stanley	*So Many Things*	201
Suzanne Ponikowski	*LTD*	202
Emilio Sinopoli	*Animal Lovers*	205
Linda Tompkins	*Spring Rolls and Beer*	207
Laura D. Rubino	*Change*	208

Chapter Nine — Interviews — 211

Nancy Nieuweboer	Growing Up in Beirut	213
Alison Rasmussen	Personality and Goodwill	214
Scott McDonald	Bill Bates	218
Anne Markey	Bob	220
Michelle Faultless	Scum	223
Lorraine Storr	I Love A Good Party	224
Aline Burke	A Pregnant Lesbian Talks About Her Pregnancy	225
Diane Salter	The Ecuadorean Endurance Test	227
Ted Bialowas	From Russia Without Love	232
Lynn MacKenzie	Innocent Victims: An Account of a Parental Abduction	234
Laura Szostak	Carl, An Ex-Gambler	237
M. Nakamura	Mr. William Long	239
Karin A. Treml	Love and Guns	242

Chapter Ten — Arguments — 247

Diane J. Salter	Trouble in Paradise	249
Brian Cartwright	House #39 and Why I Should Get Into It	250
Ed Ogibowski	Police Power	252

Chapter Eleven — Evaluations — 255

Julia Compton	Chief Elison	257
Jo-Anne Timmins	Fun In The Sun	259

Chapter Twelve — Murders — 261

Bruce Parker	Sergeant Banks	263
Karen Bush	The Bridge	265
Mandy Irvine	Another World	267
Sylvia Stiglic	As I Stand Here. . .	269

Preface

No More Masterpieces is a collection of 111 short prose pieces *by* new writers *for* new writers. Although several of these authors have gone on to have work published and presented in public readings, none had substantial experience in prose before taking the introductory course where these pieces were handed in as assignments. Almost none of the authors in this book had ever thought to call themselves writers.

Even though this collection has been put together with an academic setting in mind, anyone can enjoy the work. The writing is vital, bold, entertaining and new. The voices are fresh. Readers will find a range of experience in these stories not commonly represented in writing because "writers" tend to lead lives apart.

No More Masterpieces reinforces my feeling that most of the expressive potential in our society remains unvoiced. Given opportunity and support, there are many among us who can create moving, sensitive, funny, shocking, sad, courageous writing. There is no good reason why a few should monopolize the pleasure, the power, and the release available through expression. The people who worked on this collection dream that it will provoke others to take up their pens and break the silence.

The editing and selection task posed by this project has been enormous and would have been unthinkable without the energy of many skilled people, mostly former students.

Laura Szostak and Irene Dutton selected and edited work at a time when the project had little focus. They helped find its centre.

Jeanne Perrault helped me understand that what I was doing had important implications for new writers and those who work with them. She was the first teacher outside of myself to use some of this work in her classes. Her positive reports gave me the confidence to continue.

Susan Swan read some of these pieces to her classes at York University and offered more evidence about their stimulating effect on new writers. She convinced me there was a book here. Her certainty eventually became mine.

Beverley Biggs and Aline Burke, new writers, read the manuscript and offered sensitive critiques.

Dick Van Fossen, my professor twenty-two years ago at Cornell College and ten years ago Associate Dean of Humanities at Erindale College, appointed me to teach the course where the experiment and research that led to this collection began. He has encouraged and supported this project for a long time.

June Woods at Erindale College did much of the early entering. Her love for the pieces reassured me about them.

This project would not have gone forward without many many hours of editing, discussion and organizing by the co-editors, who made hard work fun.

Tim Kitagawa entered about a hundred pieces on the computer before we knew there would be a book. He helped shape the idea.

Arnie Achtman read, edited, entered many pieces. He used early versions of the work in his writing classes at George Brown College and reported an encouraging response by the students there.

Pauline Stanley, a skilled writer, editor, and project overseer/organizer, has given most of her evenings and weekends for the last six months to orchestrate the finish. She has brought it together with amazing patience and perseverance.

Thanks to the writers for contributing their work.

Thanks to Janet Fotheringham, Lena Spoke and John Ormsby for advice on type design.

Thanks to Jack Wayne and Shelagh Ross, patient publishers.

I couldn't believe this voice was mine. I stood up.

From Laura Szostak, "Dandelions,"
in Chapter One, *The Child*

> *Past masterpieces are good for the past. They are not good for us. We have the right to say what has been said and even what has not been said in a style that belongs to us, reacting in a direct, immediate way to present-day feelings everybody can understand. . . . [It] is our adulation of what has already been done, however beautiful and valuable it may be, that paralyses us and keeps us from connecting with the underlying power in us. . . .*
>
> Translated from Antonin Artaud, "En finir avec les chefs-d'oeuvre," (No More Masterpieces)[1]

---

[1] In *Le Théâtre et Son Double* (Paris: Gallimard, 1938; rpt. 1964), pp. 114-127. I owe this reference and the title of this collection to students John Massey and Tim Kitagawa, who published a now-defunct magazine called *No More Masterpieces*.

Introduction

Expressive Writing

No More Masterpieces is a collection of expressive writing, a form that shuns the appearance of form. Expressive writing, I contend, offers a powerful and seldom used medium for people learning to write.

Expressive does not mean literary. Literary writing often contains contrivance and cultivated sophistication that expressive writing does not.

Expressive writing is hard to define precisely because, when it is successful, its content and its style evolve naturally from the personality and experience of the writer. The form calls little attention to itself. Instead, the form recedes into an intimate, spontaneous union with the writer's content. It is almost the opposite of the expository essay, where form is primary, or so it seems to students, who feel that the most immediate demand on them is to get the form right. Meaning slides into the background.

It is the direct relationship between meaning and form that makes expressive writing ideal for people learning prose skills. The expressive writer realizes and communicates the experience of the self in the world. Expression shows the self to the self and the self to others. Experience becomes real, ponderable, knowable. One of the first acts of groups seeking change is to seize expression, to validate their experience in writing. Consider the importance of expressive writing in the liberation movements of women and blacks in the last thirty years.

Many people have almost no experience with *conscious* expression. For them, expression is for the "the gifted". Their lives are a busy silence.

There are many reasons for silences.[2] Prominent among them is simple absence of opportunity and encouragement. When we allow others to monopolize expression, we surrender the power to make meaning, or more precisely, to be conscious of making meaning.

It is at once surprising and commonplace that expression is not a priority in university and college writing courses. As James L. Kinneavy wrote eighteen years ago in his comprehensive *Theory of Discourse*, expressive discourse is all but ignored in schools even though it is "psychologically prior to all other uses of language." Kinneavy felt that the neglect of the kind of writing where people express personal and social experience is a symptom of "the impersonality of the university machines of the present day. The high schools," he wrote, "are even more culpable in this regard."[3]

Models

The expressive writing in this collection has been done by students taking their first writing course after high school. These pieces replace the masterpiece models used in college and university courses. New writers find this work by their peers accessible, provocative and encouraging.

These pieces illustrate attainable writing virtues: honesty, clarity, simplicity, directness, vividness and originality. These writers use language that belongs to them and write about the world they care about.

My intention is not to offer models for imitation but to suggest possibilities by showing people what others working in the same circumstances, at the same level of experience, have accomplished.

---

[2] For a thoughtful consideration of silenced people, see Tillie Olsen, *Silences* (New York: Delacorte Press, 1965).

[3] James L. Kinneavy, *A Theory of Discourse* (New York: Norton, 1971), p. 396. I am grateful to Professor Peter Saunders for the reference.

Here are messages I intend this collection to communicate to new writers:

1) Writing is a form of caring—caring about yourself, caring about your reader, caring about life and the world.

2) Good style is style appropriate to content and situation. There is no "correct" style. Correctness by itself is sterile. Good style is style that works, that expresses your meaning.

3) Simple, direct, natural style in your voice is acceptable and usually preferable. It is a mistake to shift into contrived voices that speak unfamiliar, complicated or ornate language just because you are *writing*.

4) A natural style expresses the personality and experience of the writer. Content and style fuse to express you and your experience.

5) Your world and your experience, whatever they are, are valid, interesting subjects for writing. Treat your experience as though it matters, and your attitude will probably influence your readers: they too will believe it matters.

6) Precise detail brings writing alive and allows readers to participate in your observations. Instead of *telling* your readers how you see the world, *show* them the world you see. Detail accomplishes this.

7) Honesty is compelling and sometimes threatening and dangerous. The truth has power. You honour your reader when you write the truth. Honest writing engages the reader's trust. Writing is a way of coming to know your truth. Good teachers respect this and will support and encourage your effort to reveal yourself to yourself and others.

How This Collection Is Arranged

The twelve chapters of *No More Masterpieces* are organized around topics I suggest to new writers. A synopsis of each assignment appears on the first page of its chapter.

The first eight chapters contain simple expressive narratives where people convey some aspect of their experience or observation. Chapter Nine, Interviews, involves the same writing objectives, but here people go outside of their own experience (or they create an experience with another) for source material.

The final three chapters, relatively short, are examples of people adapting expressive narrative to more specialized purposes such as persuasive argument (Chapter Ten), evaluation (Chapter Eleven), and fantasy/fiction (Chapter Twelve—Murders). These last chapters show how expressive elements underlie forms shaped by particular practical or creative objectives.

Criteria for Selection

I collected more than a thousand pieces produced in my classes over six years. Other writing instructors contributed some work by their students. The editorial committee, consisting of myself, Arnie Achtman (a writer and writing teacher), and Pauline Stanley and Tim Kitagawa (former students) made the final selections.

Our judgments about the quality of the writing and our belief that the collection should offer diverse examples were basic criteria. We favoured spirit, vitality and risk over perfection, control and caution.

The demonstrated ability of these pieces to encourage and stimulate new writers was paramount. Five teachers including myself used the work collected in classes. One teaches "creative" writing; the rest teach "practical" prose skills. Expressive writing transcends the artificial separation of the practical and the creative. Expression is the foundation of both.

The Backgrounds of the Writers

Diversity is important. People respond more intensely to writing that reflects their own experience in the world. Writing transforms experience and validates it to ourselves and others. Here expression becomes power.

Canada is a collection of cultures, and we sought to represent as many as possible. The presence of distinct immigrant and exile communities in Canada, and specifically around Toronto, has enhanced the diversity of this collection. *No More Masterpieces* includes immigrant writers, political exiles, visa students, and second generation Canadians from many places: Antigua, Dominica, Grenada, Jamaica, and Trinidad in the West Indies; Japan, China, Hong Kong, Malaysia, and the Philippines in the east; the Ukraine, Poland, Russia, Latvia, Yugoslavia in eastern Europe; Italy, Portugal, Germany, Britain, and Ireland in Europe; South Africa (Soweto Township). Native peoples, underrepresented in universities, have but one piece to speak for them. This and other imbalances I plan to address in future anthologies.

The youngest writers here are in their teens, the oldest in their sixties. Most are in their twenties.

Sixty-five percent of the writers are from classes I taught at Erindale College, a suburban campus of the University of Toronto. Most of the balance come from the Transitional Year Programme, a progressive one-year upgrading programme on the University of Toronto's downtown campus. Readers will recognize urban, suburban, rural and small-town voices.

The Evolution of New Procedures

Ten years ago, when I taught my first writing course, I followed conventional procedures—among them, the use of *The Norton Reader*, a classic collection of prose by masters of the craft, popular enough to spawn several versions of itself and to inspire numerous nearly identical imitations. Indifferent results led me to experiment.

I found that peer models work where masterpiece models do not. Where the masterpiece models seem to handcuff new writers, the peer models inspire and animate them. The more I rely on peer models, the more students see themselves as participants in, rather than observers of, the writing process.

I also found that expressive writing facilitates rapid and thorough development in new writers. People's skills appear to shift suddenly in a positive direction. I say *appears* because the rate and degree of change suggests dormant capacity. It seems the ability awaits release or stimulus.

Teaching expressive writing means creating conditions where people's natural urge to express themselves through language is allowed and encouraged. People's consciousness of language as an expressive instrument develops, and within four to six weeks I observe a dramatic change in students' ability to write concise, original, detailed prose. Most report a change in their writing habits. Spontaneous first drafts coupled with systematic revisions replace the labourious struggle of "figuring out what to write" and worrying about correctness.

Students say they feel more relaxed, more confident and that they are able to put more of themselves into their work. "I just wrote and wrote and wrote, and then I cut out extra words and clichés" is a typical comment. Or, "I never realized I could write like that before; I thought I had to use big words and long sentences. Now I think about what I want to say. It's harder because I have to say something, but I like it better."

The changes include improvements in formal style. Grammar breakdowns diminish without direct grammar instruction. Where people seem resistant to grammar as a matter of "correct" usage, they respond easily to matters of meaning. Grammar matters because it involves meaning.

The most surprising effect of using expressive narrative as a foundation in the introductory writing course is its impact on people's handling of more structured formats: academic essays, lab reports, legal opinions, or business communications. Most students report striking improvements in their grade results on writing submitted for regular academic courses. The average increase is about one letter grade. Professors in sciences, social sciences, humanities, management studies, and law comment specifically and favourably on the changes in peoples' writing styles, changes that occur after six weeks of intensive work with expressive narrative. This improvement occurs whether or not I give direct attention to formal, structured writing in my teaching. The seemingly automatic transference of skills to other forms points to the power of expressive writing to activate or release latent ability. The changes I observe are too rapid and too complete to account for by learning alone.

Introduction

Alienation and Writing in the Schools

How can people's practice of expressive writing enhance their ability to work in other modes? I will venture a hypothesis. Expressive writing offers scant opportunity for a retreat into forms and conventions. It forces the issue of meaning.

The connection of writing to meaning should be obvious, but for many students practiced at mimicking or reproducing the conventional forms, it is not.

People are accustomed to the disengagement of meaning from writing in school settings. Of course, students do communicate a meaning even if their writing appears to mean nothing. Alienation becomes the unintended meaning. This estrangement is rooted in students' belief that schools are places where their meanings are unacceptable. Some tell me they have no meaning to offer, that they have nothing to say about themselves or their lives. The demands of expressive writing frighten them—until they are shown how others like them have dealt with these demands.

The negativity surrounding writing yields further evidence of alienation. "What's wrong with it?" is a question I hear frequently when people show me their work for the first time. Writing assignments are seen not as opportunities to express or accomplish something but as submissions to frowning judgment. There are exceptions, but there can be no doubt about the negative atmosphere around writing in schools. The people coming into my courses feel they have had almost no helpful instruction about writing; they see it as a skill often demanded and rarely taught. Asked to describe their writing, more than a few say only that they make mistakes when they do it. Good writing, they believe, is grammatically correct.

The main experience most people have with writing comes in high-school English courses. There they labour to articulate respectful understandings of meanings others have made—in masterpieces. The appreciation of extraordinary works is valuable, but it does not develop people's capacity to write. The customary treatment of writing as a subsidiary of English leads many to assume a connection between the skills of literary analysis and writing process. People without aptitude or interest in literary discourse sometimes conclude they are deficient writers.

These people, if they are to prosper in school, learn how to parrot interest. They make the sounds without the thoughts. This is an often repeated and reinforced activity. Writing becomes dissociated from caring.

Yet care is essential. Reading the prose of writers who do not care is like eating sawdust. Writing without caring is a hollow struggle to fill an emptiness with nothing, and sawdust is useful for this. Teachers know the flavour well, and since they are products of the same institutions they teach in, they have themselves developed some taste for it. I have savoured, and served, my share.

The serving-up of prose sawdust may be passing the course or surviving university, but it is not making meaning. It is the negation of meaning, and yet this negation, the correct form filled with something that is very nearly nothing, is so widespread that we have grown accustomed to writing not meaning much. This experience in the academic setting reinforces the degenerate no-meaning use of language in politics, advertising and the popular media. In this context, connecting writing to the expression of meaning becomes a radical act.

No More Masterpieces addresses this alienation of writing from meaning. That may be why peer models of expressive writing prove effective. I do not want to comment on the pieces in this collection. They should speak for themselves. But I will say that in all of them I see caring and I see form growing directly out of the meanings the writers have chosen to express.

Expression: The Positive Message of Theory

A number of modern theorists have recognized and tried to explain the power of expression in language. Discussions of expression in various disciplines perceive in language evidence of the miraculous human capacity to change through consciousness. These positive messages, while they permeate theoretical discussions, have not had much effect on educational practices, especially in the field of writing. I will mention briefly a few ideas.

Jean-Paul Sartre's assertion of the importance of reflective consciousness has been a primary influence on my conception of my task as a teacher of writing. According to Sartre, we define ourselves through our choices about who we are and who we want to be. These choices are affected by our consciousness of ourselves. Sartre asserts that we are "condemned to be free."[4] We face a void, and we alone are responsible for filling it. There is no meaning there but the meaning we choose. Our aloneness and our responsibility produce anguish. Writers sit before the void of the empty page feeling the anxiety of lonely responsibility for the meaning they inevitably express on that page. Even to put nothing there expresses a meaning the writer cannot avoid.

If this describes the terrible vulnerability of writing, it also speaks to the powerful experience of filling that page with the meaning the writer chooses to put into the world. Here the writer becomes conscious of consciousness and at once defines and transcends a situation. Sartre's idea of freedom and responsibility suggests the role to be played by the teacher of writing. I try to confront people with their freedom to choose their meaning and with their responsibility for what they express. Students will often say, "What do you want me to write?" I say, "What do you want to say?"

Maurice Merleau-Ponty adds to Sartre's analysis of freedom by emphasizing the role played by expression in our definition of ourselves and our world. Words are powerful tools because we "can make them say something they have never said."[5]

Merleau-Ponty rejects any distinction between meaning and language. Language *is* meaning. Our thoughts are not really thoughts until they are put into words. Expression gives new meanings to ourselves and to the world. Language "like a wave, gathers and poises itself to hurtle beyond its own limits."[6]

Expression *makes* meaning, according to Merleau-Ponty. The tools of expression are the tools of life. Language is

---

[4] Jean-Paul Sartre, *Being and Nothingness*, trans. Hazel E. Barnes (New York: Washington Square Press, 1956), p. 707.

[5] Maurice Merleau-Ponty, "On the Phenomenology of Language," in *Signs*, trans. Richard C. McCleary (Evanston: Northwestern University Press, 1964), p. 91.

[6] Merleau-Ponty, *Phenomenology of Perception*, trans. Colin Smith (London: Routledge and Kegan Paul, 1962), p. 197.

dynamic, ever-changing as it makes and responds to new meaning. New writers must have the sense of writing as life activity. Too many students dread writing because they have come to know it as an anti-life struggle to reproduce conventional (for them, dead) forms. New writers must have the opportunity to use the flexibility of the language and to see form arising from the act of expression.

Linguistics is another field where we find testimony to the positive dynamism of language. Noam Chomsky's important study of language structures yields a possibility-oriented conception of grammar. Grammar offers evidence of the capacities of the human mind. The miracle of grammar is our ability to generate and understand infinite new meanings.[7]

Chomsky writes:

> ... [In] normal speech one does not merely repeat what one has heard but produces new linguistic forms—often new in one's experience or even in the history of language—and there are no limits to such innovation. . . . The normal use of language is thus free and undetermined but yet *appropriate to situations*, and it is recognized as appropriate by other participants in the discourse situation. . . .[8]

Since human language capacity is responsive to situation, our schools, if they are to be places where people develop their power to express meanings in language, must present situations where the free and undetermined character of language use is confronted by students. If the learning situation is rigid and restrictive, then people's language will express the conformity and obedience that the situation demands—and little else.

Chomsky's analysis of generative grammar is important because it shows that human beings have as a property of their humanness the capacity to make meaning through language. The educated, the talented, the powerful have no spe-

---

[7] Noam Chomsky, *Aspects of the Theory of Syntax* (Cambridge, Mass.: The M.I.T. Press, 1965), pp. 56-59.

[8] *Language and Problems of Knowledge: The Managua Lectures* (Cambridge, Mass.: The MIT Press, 1988), p.5. The emphasis is mine.

cial claim on this capacity. Expression through language will flourish where it is nurtured, and often where it is simply allowed. Where confined or suppressed, it will remain unseen as though in hiding—and eventually wither. Capacities are not taught. They must simply be allowed to function and develop. Chomsky observes, "It is a traditional insight, which merits more attention than it receives, that teaching should not be compared to filling a bottle with water but rather to helping a flower to grow in its own way."[9]

If my experience is any indication, few students have a positive sense of grammar or their language system. Students associate grammar with rules, limitations and penalties, not with its evidence of the capacity of the human mind to express and comprehend new meanings.

Finally, the post-Freudian psychoanalytic tradition validates expression and chronicles the damage of suppression. Through expression, this tradition tells us, people realize their freedom. Barriers to expression, taboos, bind people to their past. Alice Miller, in her sensitive critique of psychoanalysis, *Thou Shalt Not Be Aware: Society's Betrayal of the Child,* makes clear the paramount importance of people expressing their experience, no matter how difficult. Miller's criticism is specifically aimed at psychoanalytic procedures and the danger of following form (the predictions of Freudian doctrine) at the expense of substance (people's actual experience). Miller's message applies to the teaching of writing in our schools, especially to the restrictive concern for order and correctness.

> The more one-sided a society's observance of strict moral principles such as orderliness, cleanliness, and hostility toward instinctual drives, and the more deep-seated its fear of the other side of human nature—vitality, spontaneity, sensuality, critical judgment, and inner independence—the more strenuous

---

[9] *Language and Problems of Knowledge,* p. 135.

will be its efforts to isolate this hidden territory, to surround it with silence or institutionalize it.[10]

Too often, students are driven into a kind of institutionalized silence by a system that associates writing with restriction and convention.

Miller makes clear the conditions necessary to enable the vulnerable act of expression. They are conditions a teacher can create. Respect, acceptance, interest and care are attitudes teachers need to show if they expect students to express their thoughts and feelings. If we are to confront people with their freedom to express meaning, we have to be completely ready to hear what they are going to say. The teacher must become an empathetic advocate for people who brave the frightening, exciting business of defining and realizing themselves through language. People will not engage this process if they feel they will be penalized or scorned. For honest expression to take place, people must know it will be met with appreciation and understanding, not judgment or criticism.

I hope *No More Masterpieces* will encourage new writers to explore the capacity in themselves and in language to make meaning.

Guy Allen

University of Toronto
June 1989

---

[10] Alice Miller, *Thou Shalt Not Be Aware: Society's Betrayal of the Child*, trans. Hildegarde and Hunter Hannum (Toronto: Collins, 1984), p. 190.

Chapter One

The Child

Present a short, detailed account of an experience you had as a child.

Gina Barbosa Tousignant

Sixty-Six Hail Marys on an Air Mattress

Pray sixty-six Hail Marys on an air mattress. Sweep the four fingers on your right hand from your forehead down to your belly-button. "In the name of the Father, the Son. . . ." Sweep the four fingers from the left end of your chest to the right, "and the Holy Spirit. Hail Mary, full of grace."

My parents are separated. I live with my mother in Providence, Rhode Island. The shingles covering the house on 66 Sheldon Street are dry, brittle, weak. The veranda is pale green with paint chipping off. In front of the house, three steps lead down from the veranda to a sidewalk. The sidewalk slants where a tree grows out from the pavement.

The house isn't ours. My mother's sister, my Aunt Mary, and my grandma are letting us stay here for a while. My mom doesn't have much money and she doesn't want to live with my dad. So we're staying here. Mom has two jobs. She sleeps a lot. Pete and Luis, my younger brothers, and I sleep on air mattresses. The plastic feels soft and cool. But when I'm hot, the wet plastic sticks to my legs and pulls my skin when I move. If it's too hot, I place the sheet between my skin and the plastic, but by morning I have kicked the sheet off.

Mom bought Pete a new Zenith colour television. She left the black and white my dad bought Pete for his communion at home. Pete won't let anyone touch his new TV. He says he'll break their arms first. After school we watch *Get Smart* and *Gilligan's Island*. If I ask to watch *The Saint*, Pete tells me to shut up or get out. Sometimes he just shakes his head.

Anne, my cousin—she lives in the same house—borrows my Barbies without asking. She strips my Barbies—Love, Flower, Ken and Barbie—and changes their clothes without my permission. I tell her she'd better not, or else. My mother yells at me. I have to be nice to Anne because my aunt lets us stay here.

My grandmother is nice—most of the time. She lets me have the face towels that come in the detergent boxes. I use them for my Barbies' beds. Sometimes she yells at me. It wasn't my fault the toilet paper fell into the toilet when I lifted the seat. It was an accident. She won't stop yelling. When she yells, she looks like a witch—old, wrinkled, pointed, and squeaky.

I hate Fox Point Elementary School. I don't understand latitude and longitude. What exactly is an equator? Can you actually see the line? I'm good in math—that's all. I want to go back to St. Mary's school in Brampton. I want to go home.

Daddy isn't allowed to call here. My mom doesn't want to hear his voice. He calls us at school. I miss him—a lot. At home, I have my own room—pink—and my own veranda. At home, we're a family—even Saturdays when Mom and Dad argue about laundry. I don't like living here: I can't watch "The Saint," Anne takes my Barbies, I'm not sure what an equator is, Mommy sleeps all the time, and grandma yells a lot. I want to go home.

"Hail Mary, full of grace, blessed art thou among women. . . ." Lying down on the air mattress, with your hands folded tightly over your chest, repeat the Hail Marys sixty-six times. I pray Pete will let me watch "The Saint." I pray that you punish grandma. I didn't mean to wet the toilet paper. Help me understand latitude and longitude, and what an equator is. Please make sure my dad calls during Geography. Punish Anne. Don't let her touch my Barbie case. Bring us home. Get my parents together again. Please God, make us one family again. Let everything be okay.

"In the name of the Father, the Son, and the Holy Spirit." Make an invisible cross with your right hand. Kiss the four fingers on your right hand six times: one for Pete, one for Luis, one for Mommy, one for Daddy, one for me, and one for everyone. Go to sleep. Everything is going to be okay.

Tim Kitagawa

The Birthday Party

I really looked forward to that birthday party. Peter Barfield, the guy in my grade-one class who was having it, lived on Glen Rutley, one street over.

Peter told us in school about all the things they were going to have at the party. Peter was the only guy I knew who had a swimming pool in his backyard. We would swim, he told us. His mom bought a bingo game for the party, and they had good prizes. Peter wouldn't tell us what the prizes were, probably because his mom wouldn't tell him. I was really looking forward to that party.

Until noon that Saturday, I was happy. My brother Mitch and I played hockey in the driveway. It didn't matter that it was mid-June and the temperature near seventy-five degrees. Mitch always played in goal. I was almost two years older and could talk him into just about anything. Mitch and I were having so much fun playing hockey we almost forgot about the party.

"Tim! Mitch! Come in for your bath!" Mom yelled from her bedroom window. We stopped for a few seconds and resumed play.

I had to take baths with my brother. He never wanted the water hot. That bugged me. Mitch always wanted me to wash his back. That bugged me too. And once, (this really bugged me) he urinated in the bathtub just as he was getting out. He said he couldn't hold it. I never believed him.

"Come in here, now!" She was getting angry. We went inside.

The water was lukewarm, and Mitch asked me to wash his back. I did it only because Mom watched us. She made sure we cleaned ourselves properly. Mitch didn't urinate in the tub, though I feared it when he stood up to get out.

After, Mom dried our hair (she rubbed us with the towel too hard, and it hurt) and pushed us naked into the bedroom. Our clothes were ready. I put on my underwear and itchy blue socks. The pants (the only good pair I had) were navy and my long-sleeved shirt was light blue and flowery. Mitch had a similar brown outfit. My good shoes were black with a fairly high heel. I agreed to wear them because I didn't feel like walking around stores looking anymore. Mom said they were "funky." I hated that.

I hoped no one was on the street when we left. Mom handed us a wrapped present and a card. We signed the card while she combed our hair. Mitch and I walked together along Chiplow towards Glen Rutley and Peter's house.

"Hey! Are you guys going to a party or something?" It was Jan Simpson, who lived across the street. She was older.

"Yeah! A birthday party!" Mitch called back. I wanted to tell him to shut up, but he would tell Mom and I'd be in trouble. I put my head down and pulled him along.

We approached Peter's house. The worst part was over and I felt excited again.

The front door was closed. I rang the doorbell. After a minute, Mrs. Barfield came to the door. She seemed surprised. It must be because we looked so good, I thought.

"Tim, Mitch. . . ."

"Hi! We're here for the birthday party." Mitch was smiling.

"You must be mistaken. Today is the tenth. The party is next week. The seventeenth." She laughed.

We didn't.

G.F. Ricketts

Mr. Bong's Variety

There is a very small store behind our house crammed with a department store worth of household necessities and junky goodies. As a child, I went there every day after school. I spent the thirty-five cents my mother gave me for milk on a licorice twist and six pieces of Mr. Chuckle's bubble gum.

The owners of Bong's Variety were Mr. and Mrs. Bong. Mr. Bong was a short, bad-tempered man.

Mr. Bong charged out of the back room as if the store were on fire every time he heard the tinkling of the four small silver bells that hung on the back of the store's heavy wooden doors. He stood beside the old metal cash register. It was so large it took up nearly half of the sales counter. Mr. Bong watched closely as I went up and down the over-stuffed aisles. He stood there until I had my purchase and let the heavy wooden door tinkle shut behind me.

At fourteen, I began to shoplift. At first, I stole only Smarties and gum from the unattended candy counter at the nearby Zellers. After a few successful raids, I began to think of more challenging heists. Twice I stole right under the nose of Mrs. Ellis, the three-hundred-pound attendant at the candy counter. After a week I was bored. My mind worked on the ultimate crime: stealing the little silver bells from Bong's Variety.

My plan was simple but expensive. The only way to elude Mr. Bong's ever-watching eyes was to have four or five decoys roaming the over-packed aisles. I offered to buy the whole outfield of my ball team a cold pop after a five-to-three win over the previously unbeaten Bramalea Legion.

Four of us swarmed into Bong's Variety wearing dirty red and white uniforms with "Burlington Midget Bears" stencilled across the front. The four silver bells tinkled, and Mr. Bong assumed his usual position. His eyes darted back and forth from one intruder to the next.

I watched Mike Fass, the skinny centre fielder, reach in the refrigerator for a Coke. Mr. Bong's eyes took in Mike's reaching hand, and I grabbed the four silver bells. I stuffed them into my pocket. Within minutes, the outfielders had selected their drinks, and the heavy wooden doors closed silently behind us.

The next day, Mrs. Ellis caught me taking two packs of Smarties from the candy counter at Zellers.

Maria Lausmaa
Why I Never Went to School

I was fourteen and having a relationship with a man of twenty-six. Sometimes I went to my parents' house in the mornings before school. Sometimes I just couldn't stand going to school and went to my parents' house to sleep all day. My mother couldn't get me to go to school, and she didn't try anymore.

One morning, I entered the house, and my mother told me to please leave her alone, that she couldn't stand to have anyone in the house right then.

"Just get out of here. Go someplace and leave me alone. Why are you here anyway?"

Her eyes bulged out of her head. I knew this look well. Her hands shook. Many papers with her handwriting on them were scattered around the table. She had spilled coffee over everything. The coffee was beginning to dry on her papers. She had been up all night, writing and drinking and taking her drugs. She was about to do something terrible, I could tell. Seconds were like hours in her struggle to maintain herself.

I hate insanity!

My stomach was ice, and the ice froze into the rest of my body. I knew how horrible this could be because I felt just like her whenever she fell apart. I couldn't help it.

I asked if I could do anything for her and she told me again to leave the house. I left the house and went to the park and sat in the grass all morning.

"Oh, well."

I went back in the afternoon. This time I saw my mother's blood splattered about the sink and counter top. Her glasses lay on the floor, but she wasn't there. I had no way of knowing what she'd done, so I just sat by the phone. My little sister called from the hospital and said, "Mommy tried to cut off her nose." I went to the hospital, and there was my mom sitting on a stretcher in the busy hallway with bandages on her face.

"Dear sweet Maria," she said, "you were always so good. Suck on my titties, will you? Please?"

"No, Mom. I don't want to."

"Maria! Please?"

"I can't!"

My sister and I waited until another ambulance came and took her back to the Queen Street Mental Health Centre—again. I let my sister go home alone. I couldn't bear that house anymore. I went to my boyfriend's place. I got very stoned, and, as usual, he fucked me very violently. I didn't go to school the next day either.

Jim Kelly
Angels With Dirty Faces

Father Campbell raised his arms and held the chalice over his head. "Amen."

I pulled the cord, and the bell rang through Italy Saviour Church, Marathon, Ontario. Ray Lapierre smiled across the altar at me. His red altar boy gown barely covered his knees. I tripped on my cloak. I usually stole Robitaille's puny cloak before mass. He had a nice square collar that didn't itch.

"Bingo will be at 7:30 this Thursday in the basement. All are welcome. Peace be with you. Amen."

Father Campbell stepped away from the podium. His massive green gown trailed along the tile floor, and I followed Father Campbell through the door into the vestibule. Ray followed me.

The work calendar hung beside the closet. Ray Lapierre and Rusty Robitaille had signed up for Thursday. I pencilled in my name alongside theirs. We served pop, potato chips and nut bars at the bingos.

I walked out to the altar and collected the chalice, water glass and the wine. Father Campbell never put water in the wine. The water glass always remained full after offertory.

"Who served 8:30 mass this morning, Father?" I asked.

"Rusty Robitaille, and he was late again!"

"What did he do with his robe?"

"I told him to bring it home so his mother could wash it. It's wrinkled and dirty." No wonder I couldn't find it in the closet.

"Jim, you and Raymond please load the fridge with pop for Thursday's Bingo. Here's the key."

Ray and I left the vestibule and raced down the stairs to the basement. Ray collected the dolly and followed me to the cold room. We loaded cases of Coke, Orange Crush and Sprite. Ray wheeled four cases on the dolly. I carried two. We loaded the pop into the fridge in the basement kitchen.

"See that?"

"What?" I asked.

Ray knelt down and pointed to an opening under the sink.

"See where the water pipe goes through the wall? Robitaille discovered that hole last Thursday. You can see right into the ladies' washroom."

"Does anyone know about it?"

"No. Just you, me and Robitaille. Rusty broke a pop bottle last Thursday. He was cleaning it up when he saw the hole."

We heard footsteps. We glared at each other.

"Father Campbell!" Ray and I leapt from the cement floor and loaded the empty cartons onto the dolly.

"G - 58." Mr. Tremblay, head of the Knights of Columbus, barked out numbers. I walked down to the kitchen. The radio blared.

"What's the score, Ray?"

"Still tied. Yah, Dryden's great in the nets."

"What's the jackpot tonight, Ray?"

"I think it's 57 numbers. Father Campbell will cry if it goes. He loves his money."

Rusty Robitaille wheeled the cart into the kitchen.

"Fill 'er up. More Coke. The old bats are putting it away tonight. Hey, look! Debbie Moran! She's going into the washroom!" Robitaille abandoned his cart and crawled beneath the sink.

"Keep an eye on Father Campbell. I don't want to get caught." Robitaille stuck a straw in his mouth and poked it through the hole. He pulled the straw from the hole and stuck it into his Coke bottle. He pulled Coke into his straw and blew it through the hole. Ray and I broke out laughing.

"Are you crazy, Rusty?"

"Come down here. Take a look. She's got nice curly hair."

Ray and I choked. The toilet flushed. Father Campbell stood over Robitaille.

"What are you doing down there, Rusty?"

"I'm just picking up bottle caps." Robitaille picked up a Pepsi cap and crawled from under the sink.

"Make sure all you boys attend confession on Saturday. I haven't heard from you lately."

I slipped into the confessional. I knelt on the wooden stool. A tiny bright light lit the bottom corner of the cubicle. I heard Father Campbell whisper to the confessor on his other side. Father shut the screen of the far confessional and opened mine.

"In the name of the Father, the Son, and the Holy Spirit."

"Bless me Father for I have sinned. It has been three months since my last confession and these are my sins. I swear, I lie, I argue with my brothers and sister all the time."

"What else, Jim? What were you doing at the Bingo on Thursday?"

"Nothing, honest! Well, okay, Rusty was looking at the girls through the hole under the sink. Did you know the hole was there, Father?"

"Yes."

Rusty had confessed.

"Say ten Hail Marys and the act of Contrition. Peace be with you. In the name of the Father, the Son, and the Holy Spirit. Amen."

I opened the door of the confessional. Ten Hail Marys. A stiff sentence. He usually gave me three.

I spotted Rusty Robitaille in the far pew by the altar. I walked up the aisle and tapped him on the shoulder. "Hey, Robitaille, let's play ball hockey in the basement after confession. Ray, Blanch, and those guys are coming over at four."

Laura Szostak

Dandelions

It was June. I was twelve. I rang the doorbell at 9 Brandon Avenue. Mrs. Sittick answered.

"Come in," she said. "I've been waiting for you for half an hour. George usually does the garden. He's away. It's in terrible condition. George and me, we're old now. Time is almost gone. Time flies."

Mrs. Sittick drifted into another world.

"The gardening," I said.

"What? Oh yes." Mrs. Sittick never seemed to accept that her husband was dead.

Mrs. Sittick hobbled down the long dingy corridor. The photographs on the left wall were faded. The Sitticks' wedding picture was the only picture free of dust.

I followed her into the garden. I saw the dandelions.

"It will be twenty-five cents an hour, right?"

"Twenty-five cents! Well! I remember how I worked damn hard for five cents! George won't like this."

"Twenty-five, right?" Mrs. Sittick nodded.

I pulled a knife out of my red knapsack. The sun was hot. I made myself select a corner in the yard. I sighed. There were so many dandelions. She glared at me from the porch. Why didn't she go away into the house?

I pushed the knife into the earth. I carefully cut around the dandelion. I pulled the weed with one hand. It wouldn't come. I dug both heels into the ground. I gripped the weed and tugged. The dark green weed came out along with a huge clump of soil. It had taken me ten minutes to free the grass of this one weed. There were still at least fifty heads.

Mrs. Sittick hobbled back out.

"What are you doing? Are you trying to cheat me? You take half an hour to weed one dandelion. I watched you from the house. You trying to get my money? What's the matter with you?"

I didn't know what to say. My father told me to weed this way. Remove the entire weed. Why was this woman yelling at me? She had probably hexed her garden. My friend Anna said Mrs. Sittick was a witch—she poisoned her husband.

I was scared. She stared into my face. I had to speak.

"I am trying my best," I said. I couldn't believe this voice was mine. I stood up.

"Bigger kids ask for fifty cents. They just want the money. I want the job. I want to save for a bike. I'm not cheating you. If you don't like my work, I'll leave." I stood up and dusted my hands.

"Wait," she said. "I don't want to yell anymore." Mrs. Sittick cried.

I stood there. I felt like an idiot. I made her cry. I fidgeted with my knife.

"I'm sorry." She sniffed. "George, my husband, he made me so hard. I loved him."

"I'm sorry," I said. "I'll come back another day."

Mrs. Sittick continued to cry.

"Bye, Mrs. Sittick," I whispered. She didn't hear me. I took one last look at her. She was very old.

A week later, an ambulance drove up to Mrs. Sittick's house. I watched as they wheeled her covered body from the house.

The yellow dandelion heads changed into white puff balls. Their heads rippled in the breeze.

Gordon Scott

The Wind

I was ten. So it must have been 1971 that the only hurricane to hit Cobequid Bay, Nova Scotia, during my life there, was coming.

It was September. My brother David and I were bored.

"Come on Marie. What kind of sister are you? Just try it!"

She agreed.

We placed her into an old steamer trunk and locked it. David and I hauled it into the yard.

We went into the house and looked out at the trunk. The wind came up. The trunk hit a tree, spun around, hit the tree again and smashed into the house.

David laughed. The wind died. We raced for the trunk, now beaten and torn. We unlocked it. Marie was crying. Her tooth had gone through her lip. We pulled her out. We helped her into the house. The wind blew hard. We watched from inside as the trunk blew into the woods.

Marie looked at the spinning trunk, looked at the blood on her dress, looked at us, ran and yelled for our mother.

David and I looked at each other.

Pauline Stanley

Up in the Clubhouse

Dad built a room in the beams of our garage. The walls were two-by-fours, and the floor had a new, rubbery-smelling carpet. In the summer the walls were hot to the touch, and sun poured in through the roof bubble.

I liked to show off my clubhouse. I numbered my Nancy Drews like a library so people could check them out. My friends were not much liked and neither was I.

Trudy, my best friend, played volleyball and ran on the track team. Everybody hated her. She had buckteeth, braces, freckles, and hairy arms and legs. She took an hour blow-drying and flipping her hair every morning.

One day, Betty Stone, one of the toughest girls in grade five, Brendan Clark and his friend Todd wanted to see the clubhouse. Betty was skinny, her features sharp like a rat's, her eyes green and flinty grey. Todd was a clown.

Brendan lived down the street. I'd seen him a few times when I biked by his house. Brendan was scrawny and bird-boned, but he had dreamy brown eyes, and I was obsessed with him. He ignored me.

I wrenched up the garage door, and they filed up the ladder to the clubhouse with me at the tail.

"Are these your books?" Betty said.

"Yeah, they are."

She turned her back on them and sat on the wall bench. "So what do you want to do?" she asked Brendan, who sat beside her. I stood at the ladder hoping they would leave.

Brendan shrugged and stared at the dartboard.

"I saw some beer cases in the garage. Let's play spin-the-bottle!" Betty said. "Go and get a bottle."

I climbed down the ladder.

I felt sweaty and ugly. I had allergies and my nose dripped. What if I had to kiss Brendan?

I got a bottle. When I poked my head up through the entrance, they looked bored. Betty said, "What took so long?"

Betty took the bottle and placed it on the floor. Todd spun first, and the bottle stopped pointing at Betty. They whooped, and Brendan said, "We should turn out the light for thirty seconds!"

Todd moved over and sat beside Betty, while Brendan grabbed the light string and counted, "One, two . . . THREE!"

The light went out and he counted, "Thirty, twenty-nine, twenty-eight, twenty-seven. . . ."

At twenty, he flashed the light on and flicked it off again. The flash revealed Betty and Todd in each other's arms.

"Three, two . . ONE!" The light clicked on.

Betty smiled and flipped back her hair. "You next, Brendan," she said.

"I can work the lights," Todd said.

Brendan spun the bottle. It stopped at me. I looked at Brendan. He smiled.

"Well?" Betty said. It was sweltering.

"Well?" she said again.

"What?" I yelled down the ladder. "What, Dad?" I started down, "Let me see what he wants."

I stood at the base of the ladder. I hated myself. I had no guts.

I climbed up. I was about to say, "My dad's gotta use the garage."

Betty spoke first. She stretched and said, "I gotta go." They climbed down and left without looking back.

Mary Tomaz

Going My Way

Death is difficult—especially slow death. My grandfather's aunt was as old as anyone could be. Aunt Julia had reached the end of her time in life. I was young. Death had never entered my mind until I saw my Aunt Julia for the last time.

Aunt Julia lived next to my grandmother's house. Their homes shared a garden. I was playing in the garden.

The nurse came out of the house and announced to my grandmother that Aunt Julia was awake. Grandmother told me I was to go and see her for a while.

Aunt Julia was never alone. She had people visiting her at all times. Most of the time they came in groups. They told each other neighbourhood gossip every time they visited her. But Aunt Julia was so senile it seemed she was always alone at home.

I went into the house. It was empty. No one was there except Aunt Julia. I entered her room and I immediately sat down. I stared at her. Her gentle blue eyes were fixed on the ceiling. She turned to look at me, then she looked back up at the ceiling. She did not say a word.

I didn't like those visits. The silence. The emptiness. The house seemed hollow. I just stared at my aunt. I waited for her next reaction toward me. I was really waiting for someone to call me away. I tried not to move. I did not want to disturb her. She had always pretended she liked children. I think she thought children were a menace. She could never keep her garden because of me and my friends.

I grew impatient. I did not want to be there. I knew she was in agony though she looked serene. I didn't want to watch. It frightened me.

Suddenly, she shrieked and shook. At that moment, I heard her breathe. But it stopped. She stopped. I could tell she was dead. I didn't know what to do. Her cold blue eyes were still open. Her lifeless face looked white. I was frightened.

After a few moments of immobility, I caught my breath. I stood up and left the room.

As I walked down the hallway, I felt a terrible weight on my back. I thought it was her following me. I did not want to run out. I might upset her, since she was leaving the house, just as I was. She was only going my way.

Tim Kitagawa

Tryout Day

Every Saturday night, I watched the Toronto Maple Leafs on TV. The games didn't start until 8:00, so I had to go to bed after the first period. I told Dad I wanted to play hockey. He took me to Dixie Arena to sign up. Dad got a list of what I needed and found out when Tryout Day was. I didn't have equipment, so we went to Eaton's.

It took a long while to put all the pads on. I could hardly move. The skates were Bauer, shiny brown leather. It was hard to stand in them. Dad and the sports guy asked me how I felt every time they put a piece of equipment on my legs or arms or shoulders. I said everything was okay. I didn't know how anything was supposed to feel.

Dad let me pick the stick I wanted, a Louisville Slugger bigger than I was. Dad said he would cut it at home.

The sports guy at Eaton's made jokes about how I looked like Dave Keon or George Armstrong. They played for the Leafs. I didn't want to look like those guys. I wanted to look like Jim Neilson, who played for the New York Rangers. He looked Japanese, like me.

I was excited when we got home. Tryout Day wasn't for two weeks, but I wanted to try on the equipment. Dad helped me and told me I'd have to remember how to put on all the stuff on my own. Dad worked shift, so he might not be able to help me at all my games. That scared me.

I practised dressing all day but kept forgetting to put my jock on. Dad said it was the most important thing. I didn't have a sweater. Dad said I could use one of his. His sweater was maroon and white. Number 23. No one wore number 23. Dad's sweater came down to my knees and looked like a dress.

Dad cut my stick and showed me how to hold it. He had played hockey so he knew. He put my white CCM helmet on my head. Jim Neilson didn't wear a helmet. Dad said all kids had to wear them. Mom came to take a picture of me.

I asked Dad to buy me a puck so I could practise in the basement. Mom didn't like that because the puck made black marks on the baseboards. She told me to use a tennis ball. She bought three. I lost them.

I had never skated before. Dad took me to the big outdoor rink at Centennial Park. He put my skates on me and did them up tight. The laces were long and he wrapped them around my ankles. The skates hurt. Dad unwrapped the laces and did them up again. They were too loose. He untied them. The next time Dad tied them I said they were all right even though they were tight again.

Dad carried me from the car to the ice. He sat down and did up his own skates. I had my elbow pads and my CCM helmet on. I fell a lot, but Dad said it was okay because it was only my first time. I tried to chase him, but he was too fast. Mom made hot chocolate when we got home.

My skates were scratched. Dad said I could polish them. He gave me a brush. He put shoe polish on the skates and told me to brush them. They got shiny again, but they weren't like new. We polished Dad's skates too. His were too scratched and didn't shine.

I was anxious on Tryout Day. I was glad the tryout was early. Dad didn't think 8:00 a.m. was a good time to play hockey. I put my equipment on before Dad and Mom got up. I remembered everything. But I still had a sweater that came to my knees.

When he got up, Dad told me to take the sweater off. He said he had something better, and he gave me a box. When I opened it, there was a New York Rangers sweater: number 15, Jim Neilson's number. It was hard to hug Dad and Mom with all the equipment on. I put on the sweater. It fit better than Dad's. Mom took my picture and said good luck. Dad and I left.

Dad carried my skates. I wore everything else. I had a hard time getting into the car with my stick. Dad put it in the backseat. When we got to the arena, we realized I had left the stick in the car. Dad had to run back and get it.

There were lots of people in the rink. Most kids were dressed in their equipment. Most had Montreal Canadiens and Toronto Maple Leafs sweaters. Some kids skated around the rink. I worried I'd be late. Dad said it wasn't supposed to start for ten minutes. He told me to relax. I was nervous.

It was cold. We sat beside the ice on a wooden bench. Dad put my skates on me and tightened them. I could see my breath.

"Some of those guys look pretty good, Dad."

"You don't worry about those guys. Just go out there and have fun. Do what the coaches tell you. Are these laces tight enough?"

"Yes." They were too tight. I wanted to skate.

Dad carried me over to a gate and said good luck. I went the wrong way and almost smashed into a guy. I got turned around and went the whole length of the rink before falling. Dad laughed when I looked at him in the stands. Lots of guys fell. I wasn't the only one. I felt better.

I was the only player with a New York Rangers sweater on, and I had the newest sweater. Theirs were dirty. Soon the ice was full. We ran into each other. The parents laughed. Most of the other kids were taller than I was. They could skate better, but I had the shiniest skates.

A coach on the ice blew a whistle. Everyone stopped and looked at him.

"Okay, you guys! Just skate around until one of us comes and tells you what dressing room to go to. Each dressing room will be a team. A coach will come in and tell you when your practice is and everything else. Your parents can go in too."

Everyone skated. I hoped I wouldn't be the last one left. Coaches grabbed kids and sent them off the ice. I skated for a long time. Soon there were only a few players left. I was tired. A man came from behind and picked me up. He carried me to a gate. "Room number six, son." Where were the dressing rooms? I didn't know.

I walked into the tunnel in front of me. There was a "3" on the door at the end of the tunnel. I turned left and fell. I got up and saw a "2" on the next door. I turned around and watched doors until I reached dressing room "6."

There were many kids in the room. They sat on the benches against the walls. Some parents stood around. They had coffee in white cups. Some kids had cans of Pepsi. I looked around at the other players. The only space left on the benches was next to the door. I sat down. I took off my CCM helmet. I looked at my skates. They were scratched again. I'd have to polish them when we got home.

A blonde kid on the other side of the door saw me. "Hey, Dad, look. A Jap. We don't need any Japs on our team." His father looked at me and told the kid to be quiet.

I wanted Dad to come and get me. I wanted to go home.

Marian Van der Meeren

Stretchie

Angela had been my best friend since first grade. We had just finished seventh grade. In the previous year or two, we spent more time fighting than being friends. She was changing. She hung around more popular kids. I was quiet, a goody-two-shoes, the kind of kid it was easy to make fun of.

I knew ways of getting in with them. I could smoke with them in the washrooms. I could hang out with them at the mall. That would mean lying to my mother. I didn't want to do those things. I especially didn't want to start hanging around with boys.

Angela stood around corners with the popular girls like Ellen and Maureen. They talked about which girls brought their purses to school for a few days every month. We all knew what that meant.

Sometimes, just to look good in front of her new friends, Angela made fun of me. She always came back though. She didn't apologize. She just asked if we were still friends and promised things would be different.

When Angela asked me to her big summer bash, I didn't want to go. She planned to have girls and boys come over for a pool party. The girls would sleep over. I had this sick feeling in my stomach. Something would go wrong. I told Angela I didn't want to go. She promised she wouldn't let anything bad happen to me. I believed her.

The pool party was kind of fun. One of the girls threw cotton in the air when I jumped in the pool. Nobody understood the joke. By the time she explained that it was meant to look like I stuffed my training bra, she looked the bigger fool.

Eventually, the boys went home. We pigged out on pizza and watched a Late Night Thriller Chiller. Then we got ready for bed. We slept in a large colonial-style den with the furniture cleared from the room. I put my sleeping bag in the corner farthest from the door. I was anxious about changing in front of everyone, so I did it when most of the girls were out of the room. We—there were about fifteen of us—arranged our sleeping bags in a circle with our heads facing the middle. I relaxed and started to have fun.

Ellen put her clothes away right in front of me. "Don't look at my bra just because you don't have one," she said. I didn't know what to say. I got out of my sleeping bag and went to the washroom. When I walked back, the room was silent. Everyone watched me. As I crossed the room there were muffled giggles. Ellen told me to get into my sleeping bag. I opened it.

"Hey, look what Stretchie got!" Angela yelled. Everyone laughed. Someone had poured tomato juice in the centre of my sleeping bag. I looked down, speechless. I forced a long blink to hold back tears. I looked up and met Angela's eyes. It seemed like we were the only ones in the room. She looked down. I walked out of the room.

I dialed my parents' number. I didn't know how I was going to explain wanting to come home at 2:00 a.m. Angela came up behind me and clicked the receiver. "It was only a joke," she said. "Can't you take a joke?"

My throat felt like there was a baseball in it. I thought I was going to choke.

"You promised," I whispered. My body shook. I couldn't talk.

We didn't speak for weeks. Then Angela came back. She asked if we were still friends.

I said no.

Chapter Two

School

Present a short, detailed account of an experience you had in school.

Mary Lou C. DeBassige
Lakeview Indian Day School

Real fast, I turn around in my desk to look at my cousin. He says something in our Odawa and Ojibwe language. This is a mistake.

The teacher, Miss McNulty, walks with a limp. She uses a cane. We all jump when she hits a desk with it. I'm sure the cane would cry if it had feelings. She doesn't need her cane this time. She stands in front of me waving a new yardstick.

Another yardstick. How many did she break so far, on someone or on the blackboard? Crack! Across my knuckles. It happens fast. I half cry out. I try to hold it in. A big lump rises from inside, pauses at my throat, stops briefly at my nose. My eyes hurt. Tears roll down my face. My nose drips.

"Mary Louise, you must never speak that whatever language again! Never! Never! It is not a proper language. You must forget it totally! Speak English only. Hear me?" She shakes me by the shoulders.

"Yes ma'am."

She glares at me. "Repeat after me. I will not speak Indian ever again."

I chokingly speak every word after her because I am scared she will hit me with her yardstick. But my habit is to speak *anishinabe* and English together. I don't understand why speaking *anishinabe* is wrong. Miss McNulty makes my mother language sound evil and ugly.

Catechism begins another day at this Indian Day School. Miss McNulty asks, "Who made you, Jane?"

Jane looks around and says, "God made me."

"Dick, where is God?"

Dick answers fast. "God is everywhere." I look at Dick in wonder. He is smart.

"Mary Louise, say The Hail Mary in front of the class."

I get up in front of the classroom trying to keep my eyes straight ahead. I'm ready to die. Miss McNulty will kill me if I forget a word or a line of this English prayer. She tells me to fold my hands.

I start.

> *Hail Mary, full of Grace*
> *the Lord is with Thee.*
> *Blessed art thou amongst women,*
> *Blessed is the fruit of . . .*

I wish I could say this prayer in *anishinabe*. *N'mishomiss*, my grandfather and the chief of the West Bay Reservation for many years, taught me to pray in *anishinabe*. *N'mishomiss* is a devoted Roman Catholic.

This morning, I feel scared as I try to remember. I've said this prayer at The Legion of Mary, the religious group on the reservation. There, we pray together. I am not forced to say every word or sentence. I feel safe and happy there. This morning, my mind empties and I forget. Nobody is allowed to help me. I have to say this prayer by myself. For sure, this is doomsday.

"Mary Louise, stay after school and write The Hail Mary on all the blackboards and then stand in the cloak room and repeat it until I return."

I write until my arm feels like falling off. At last, the blackboards are full with Hail Marys. I say them aloud over and over again in the cloakroom. I am alone. I feel weird and sick. Miss McNulty does not come back. Maybe she forgets I am still here. I need her permission to go home. I have chores to do. I have to bring in firewood and feed the pigs.

I knock on Miss McNulty's kitchen door. I almost picture her eyeballs rolling. I am not used to her loud, screechy voice. She sounds like the pigs we kill on our farm. The door finally opens and out comes Miss McNulty almost pushing me down. Straight for the classroom goes bent-over Miss McNulty, like "the crooked man who walked a crooked mile." Her legs or whatever must be bothering her again. She checks the blackboard carefully. She orders me to sweep the steps.

"Make sure you sweep the corners properly. Then you may go."

I run all the way home without stopping. I'm going to tell someone what happened at school today. I know my mother does not like to hear something like this. One of her rules is "Children should be seen and not heard." She nearly always listens to other people's sayings. Like Miss McNulty, she hits me, except she uses long branches off trees. I try to stay away from her, not tell her anything, even when I know it's the truth.

N'mishomiss is different. His rule is to always tell the truth.

"*Mishomiss! Mishomiss!* Where are you?"

I run to the barn and find him in his workshop. He is fixing Queen's harness. Queen is one of his ponies. *Mishomiss* looks at me with a question in his eyes. He sits himself down, takes his pipe out, fills it with tobacco. He points to the glass bottle filled with sweet tea. I fill two cups with tea. He reaches out his hand to take one cup; I keep the other and sit in front of him in one of his handmade chairs made out of tree stumps. *N'mishomiss* looks at me, stays quiet while I tell him my day at school. When I finish talking, he quietly puffs his pipe. He is in deep thought. I wait for him to finish thinking. He takes his pipe out of his mouth.

"Are you telling me the truth, Brother (his nickname for me)?"

"*Aehn* (yes), Mishomiss." This time he does not laugh or smile as he does when he catches me telling him big or funny stories.

Soon, a younger, kinder teacher takes Miss McNulty's place at Lakeview Indian Day School.

Ed Caissie
The Tipton Zone

Stafford Tipton sat at the back of my grade seven class at Camilla Senior Public School. Every morning at 9:00, Mrs. Whitlock told us to begin Undisturbed Solitary Silent Reading. Stafford seldom brought anything to read. Playboy and Penthouse weren't allowed. He usually talked to the people around him, or threw paper wads at them.

One day, Stafford turned to fantasy. He got comfortable in his "midnight blue Barracuda." The people in the class turned to the back to see what was happening. He screeched out of his parking slot while sitting at his desk.

Stafford pulled a few fast corners. He squealed his tires. He stopped at a red light. "Hey! Hey, you! Yeah, you! You wanna drag?" He revved the engine and peeled out. "Shit, man! The cops!" Stafford stomped on the accelerator and leaned back.

Stafford slid into an A&W. He rolled down the window and ordered, "Yeah, I'll have a Poppa-Burger, onion rings, no, make that fries, and a large root beer. Oh, can you have the bear bring it out to me?" He lit a joint and swallowed it as the waitress approached. Stafford grabbed the girl and rolled up the window, catching her arm.

He screamed out of the parking lot, "Aaiiiiiiiyy!"

"Oh, well. So much for the waitress."

Mrs. Whitlock put down her copy of *War and Peace* and said that Undisturbed Solitary Silent Reading was over. It was time to leave the Tipton Zone and open our physics books.

Marian Van der Meeren

Mr. V

I sat in the chair, my back straight, my right arm stiff on the arm rest, my left clutching the coat on my lap, my feet square on the floor. I was in an office, more like a closet than an office, barely big enough for the chair I sat in and an old desk. One small, dirty window looked out on some bare branches and a sidewalk covered in slushy snow and ice. Long Island, New York, had had a wet, cold winter.

Paper, files, a stapler, a pen, a phone book, a softball, a broken badminton racquet, and a needle to inflate basketballs covered the desk. This was the office of Mr. V, the gym teacher at St. Hugh of Lincoln School, where I attended my eighth and final year. I was thirteen years old.

I couldn't figure out why Mr. V wanted to see me. He asked Grace to tell me to come down to his office during recess and to bring my coat. Grace, a plain-looking, shy girl, usually kept to herself. I was one of her few friends. The message confused me. Why hadn't Mr. V told my homeroom teacher he wanted to see me? That's how the teachers normally did things.

The door opened and Mr. V came in. A big man in his early thirties, he had black curly hair and an Italian-New York accent. He wore a grey sweatsuit and beat-up sneakers. His name was Mr. Violante, but he liked it better when we called him Mr. V.

Mr. V. closed the door behind him and said, "Hi." I whimpered a nervous, "Hello."

"Relax, you're not in any kind of trouble," he said grinning. He cleared a place on his desk and sat on the edge.

"Listen," he said, "I know friends can put a lot of pressure on you. I remember some dumb things I did in school for that reason."

He must know about the knife, I thought. I had to hide it for Angela. She had ways of getting me to do things. She could turn the whole eighth grade against me if she felt like it. Angela used to be my best friend. She was afraid someone would tell on her. She figured no one would suspect me.

"Well. Anyway, I um. . . ." It seemed Mr. V didn't know how to get to the point. "I heard something about, um, you hiding something. Is it true?" His voice was soft and warm.

I hesitated.

"It's okay," he said, "I want to help you. This is just between us."

"Yeah, it's true," I answered quietly.

"Is it a switchblade?"

"No. I've only got a camping knife. Angela wanted me to hide a switchblade too, but I said no."

"Oh," he sounded surprised. "I thought you had the switchblade. But, in any case, do you have it on you?"

I felt more comfortable now. I had nothing left to hide.

"No. It's in my book-bag, in the classroom."

"Well, I asked you to bring your coat because that's where I thought you'd hide it. I was going to ask you to let me help you get rid of it." He spoke more fluently now. "Your teachers suspect something's going on and I don't want you to get caught. You're a good kid and you deserve better than that." He talked about doing the right thing and how it shouldn't matter to be accepted by the wrong people.

I felt my eyes getting wet. I looked to the floor. One tear sat on my cheek. I wiped it away. Mr. V pretended not to notice. All day, I'd felt pressured and scared. I couldn't believe someone was talking to me this way. He understood me. Before I left, Mr. V asked me not to let the other teachers know I'd seen him.

Later, I sat in the principal's office. One of the kids had told. "Do you realize the seriousness of what you've done?" Sister Carol, dressed in her white and black nun's habit, stood behind her desk. "This will be on your school record for the rest of your life."

To avoid her glare, I looked down at her desk. On it were a matching desk mat and pen holder, and a calendar. It looked like a display in a furniture store.

"You'll have to sign this form that states you understand the reason for your suspension." Her office was big and bright. She sat down. My eyes drifted to the large, clean windows behind her.

"I also have a list of assignments you are to do." I saw that the parking lot and walkways were plowed and dry on this side of the school.

"Go wait outside while I call your mother." I left the room without having said a word.

I returned to school a week later. Things were different. On the bus, Mike Sullivan asked if I was going to stab him to get the back seat. As I got off the bus, I saw a group of girls talking and laughing. As soon as they saw me they shut up and watched in silence as I walked by. I saw the little grey window of Mr. V's office. I forgot I was being watched and smiled to myself. Slush squished under my feet. The ice was melting.

Danielle Cohen

Doggie, Doggie, Who Brought The Bone?

Welcome to the temple of doom, Homelands Senior Public School. Please have a seat. You'll need it.

MONDAY, 7 SEPTEMBER 1976. All is quiet on the new frontier. I bide my time and sidestep dirty looks. I maintain myself by knowing I have to survive only three hours of this—today. Nothing happens. Phew. Only the rest of the school year to go.

THURSDAY, 12 NOVEMBER, 1976. Chris Kanski has started a rumour. He says I stuff my bra. He came up to me today and asked if I wanted a kleenex. I had my first fit. I screamed, "If I was gonna stuff my bra, at least I'd stuff it so it looked like there was something in it!"

Hey, I'm a thirty-two double A. Phone Guinness.

MONDAY, 22 JANUARY, 1977. I'm hurt. I'm upset. But I can't say I'm surprised. Today, when I came into class, there were three presents on my desk: a can of dog food, a Milkbone, and a drawing. The drawing was entitled "Dani the Dog." The drawing showed me in a T-shirt. The T-shirt had written on it: "I am flat." Anyone with half an eyeball could see that. I know Glenda did the drawing. Christ! What a bunch of jerks! I don't want to go back to school. I hate it there. Besides, I'm flunking out. I skip as much as possible. My only friend is Laura Wishart, and she never goes to school either. We go over to her place, watch TV, and steal booze, if there is any.

FRIDAY, 28 JUNE, 1977. Well, holy shit! You'll never believe what happened. All year long, I've put up with this crud at school. Anyway, to make a short story long, today we had science. It's my favourite class. Mr. Richardson's a super-cool teacher. At least, I thought he was.

Since it was our last class, he asked us to tell our "most memorable experience of the year." I was just trying to forget, so I opted for shutting up and drawing. Things were fairly groovy until Chris Kanski opened his fat face.

Out it all came: "My most memorable experience was the time we put a dog bone on Dani's desk." I turned various shades of red, finally ending up a candidate for the part of the Blueberry Girl in Willie Wonka's Chocolate Factory. Everyone else in the class was in the midst of obtaining hernias, including Mr. Richardson.

I'd had enough. I stood up and screamed: "You make me sick! Does it make you feel good to centre out one person? And Mr. Richardson, you're the worst of all. How could you allow this to go on?"

I forget exactly what was said, except that as my tangent built my vocabulary diminished, until I was spewing an array of four-letter words. When I was finished, or exhausted—I'm not sure which—I looked around, and then I told Mr. Richardson I could see myself to the office. I stomped off. In the hallway, I was cut-off from my rendezvous with Mr. Cantor, the principal, by Mr. Richardson. He told me there was no need for me to go to the office. He apologized. Nice, but I still had to go back to that slimy classroom.

I opened the door and bit down on my lip. Chris and a bunch of people were huddled in a circle. I was scared. Chris came up to me. Dumb as it was, I tried not to notice. Do you know what he said?

"I'd like to apologize for the whole class, and especially myself. I put the bone on your desk. It was my idea. I'm very sorry."

I, being my usual composed self, attempted to say something or other. I couldn't say anything.

Carol Allen
The Report Card

These were the last days of spring. It was 1975, and I was sixteen. In homeroom we received our third semester report cards. I was nervous. I thought I had done well, but I had been wrong before.

Mr. Cook called our names in alphabetical order. I was first. I was always first. I walked up the aisle past Mike, Lyn and Pat, my friends. They and the rest of the class watched me. Mr. Cook handed me the envelope and smiled. I took it back to my desk and just held it. I decided to wait until after class to look. If the news was bad, nobody would see my reaction.

After class, I walked to my locker. There I met Karen, my best friend. She was upset and scared. Her marks were not good. Her father would be angry tonight.

I thought going for a walk and talking might help her, so we walked across Morningstar Drive to the park opposite the school. A small creek runs the length of the park. We walked beside it and talked—that is, Karen talked, and I listened. There was nothing I could say to help her. My father did not yell at me all the time, and he never hit me. I wanted to find words to make Karen feel better. I loved Karen, and I felt helpless.

We sat down by the creek. I leaned back on the grass, closed my eyes, and tried to think of something to say. We had only a forty-minute spare so after a while I sat up to say we should start back.

My eyes met Karen's, then traced a line from her eyes to her right hand. She held a broken coke bottle. She dragged the jagged edge methodically along her left wrist. She didn't look as if this caused her any pain. I wanted to scream, grab the glass away from her, but I sat paralyzed and no sound came out of my mouth.

Then, after what seemed like minutes but was, I am sure, only seconds, I asked Karen to stop. She did not. She did not seem to hear my voice. I ran.

I ran across Morningstar Drive and into the school. I needed to find Mrs. Shepherd. We trusted her. She was our friend.

Mrs. Shepherd looked up as I walked in. She ate a sandwich. In a calm, unhurried voice that I did not recognize I said, "Karen is in trouble."

Mrs. Shepherd ran with me across Morningstar Drive and into the park. We sat down beside Karen. Mrs. Shepherd did not take the glass away from Karen. I was surprised.

Mrs. Shepherd said in a soft voice, "Give me the glass." Tears ran down Karen's face. She continued to cut long vertical lines down the centre of her left wrist. Blood ran straight down her arm, then changed course to drip off the side of her hand into the creek. Blood hit the water, dispersed, and was gone.

Karen stopped. She gave the glass to Mrs. Shepherd. The three of us walked back across Morningstar Drive and into the school. The bell rang. People poured out of classes in a rush. They all talked at the same time. We threaded through them to the nurse's office.

Mrs. Shepherd closed the door and led Karen to the bed, one of those white metal hospital beds. Karen looked small and pale against all that white. Mrs. Shepherd filled a bowl with water, and she poured in antiseptic. She cleaned Karen's wrist and talked in a soft, calm voice.

I watched. They seemed to talk from far away. I couldn't hear what Mrs. Shepherd said.

I had to get away. I needed to think. There was a tiny room just off the one we were in, a little office with a desk. I crawled under that desk. I curled as tightly as I could into the far corner underneath that desk. I felt cold. I pulled my jacket tightly around me. There was something in the pocket. I took it out. It was my report card. I looked at the envelope, still unopened, and quietly, so that Mrs. Shepherd and Karen could not hear me, I cried.

Tina Reyes
Tea Time

The teachers at St. Mary the Virgin consider their high school a breeding ground for young scientists. Our principal, Sister Josephine, came on the P.A. almost every morning to congratulate "one of our fine young ladies" for winning some prize in a science fair somewhere. Terri Lombardi even discovered a new protein and went to Hawaii for an international competition. It was only natural, then, for Mr. Chiu, the head of St. Mary's science department, to expect his team of grade-thirteen science students to once again win recognition for the school in the University of Toronto's Second Annual Science Olympics.

A few days before the Olympics, Mr. Chiu called us up to his classroom. He scurried in, handed each of us a set of stapled photocopied papers, and scurried out. He had to go to a meeting. He said he had to attend another meeting on the day of the Olympics, so he wouldn't be with us. Mr. Chiu always had meetings.

The papers he gave us included a map showing the way to the University of Toronto and all the details about the Olympics. They also described the events that would take place. We had to prepare for two of them: we had to construct a giant yo-yo, and, in an event called Tea Time, we were to heat one cup of water from room temperature for three minutes, using "purely mechanical means," to make an "acceptable cup of tea."

We were supposed to work on these during the rest of activity period, but we talked about arranging car pools until it was almost time to leave.

We decided to make the yo-yo out of cookie tins and fishing line. We didn't know what to do about Tea Time.

Joanne, one of our friends, popped her head into the room. "It's three-thirty. Are you coming?"

"Yeah. Just a minute."

"What'll we do about this stuff?" asked Rasa, waving her paper around.

Joanne looked at the instructions for Tea Time. "We did something like this in camp. You put the water in a deep container," she said, gesticulating wildly. "It would help if it's insulated. You take a wire whisk and put some string around it and move it back and forth with the wires in the water. It heats up because of the friction."

"Say that again," said Debbie.

Joanne started her explanation again. She spoke more slowly this time, scrawling a strange little diagram on the chalkboard.

"Oh, no! I'm gonna miss the bus!"

We scrambled to gather our books and purses and coats. Joanne promised to finish her explanation sometime soon. Debbie said she'd bring the whisk and insulated cup.

On the day of The Science Olympics my dad drove Debbie, Dorota and me to the University of Toronto. Maria, Judy, and Kathryn were already there. While we waited for the rest of our team to arrive, the room filled with students carrying bicycles, copper tubes, and other contraptions that looked stolen from Dr. Frankenstein's lab. Tea Time was the first event.

"Did you bring the whisk?" asked Kathryn.

Debbie reached inside her coat, pulled out the whisk, held it up, and stuffed it back. "I'm keeping it warm. We should keep the cup warm too." She fumbled into her purse and pulled out a styrofoam-lined mug with Ronald McDonald's face on the side.

Dorota stared at it. Her mouth fell open. "You've got to be kidding."

Debbie shrugged. "It's insulated."

"What are we supposed to do with all this?" I asked.

"I don't know," Judy replied. "Didn't you talk to Joanne?"

"No. I thought you were going to."

"I didn't."

"Neither did I."

"We need string. Do we have any string?"

"It's all in the yo-yo."

A loud voice interrupted. "All teams to your stations."

"What are we going to do? We don't have any string."

"We wouldn't know what to do with it anyways."

"We can use our hands instead."

"We're going to beat the water?"

"Do we really have to do this?"

"It could be fun."

"It could also be embarrassing."

"We have to at least give it a try. We can't not do anything."

A balding man with glasses poked his head into our little circle. "Hurry up, girls." We dragged ourselves and our Ronald McDonald mug to the only empty station—next to a group of guys wrapping thick ropes around a tall, gleaming copper tube. I rubbed the egg beater's wires against my sleeve, trying to warm them.

A man with a microphone walked around the room. Behind him walked another man with a video camera with a CBC logo. They said they were filming this for the eleven o'clock news.

"Oh my God—we can't go through with this," said Dorota. "We're going to make complete fools of ourselves."

It was too late to back out. An official placed a 250ml beaker of water in front of us.

"The water is presently at twenty degrees Celsius. You will be given three minutes to heat it. At the end of the three minutes, the temperature will be taken. The team with the highest final temperature wins. On your marks, get set, go!"

Kathryn dumped the water into the Ronald McDonald mug. Debbie plunged the whisk in and rolled the handle furiously between her hands. The cup wobbled and water swirled up and over the rim. I put my hands around the bottom half of the mug and Judy grabbed the top half. We tried to keep it warm while holding it still.

"Someone take over. I'm getting tired," called Debbie. Kathryn worked her way through our tangle of arms and took the whisk. Maria and I switched places with Rasa and Dorota. I blew on my cold, wet hands and rubbed them together briskly, trying to warm them for the next shift.

Judy pointed to the team next to us. "Look at them!" Their locks of thick rope whipped around their tall copper tube as they pulled the ends from side to side. Steam rose from the top of the tube.

I dipped a finger in our cup. It was freezing.

Debbie whipped off her fuzzy pink woolen scarf, looped it around the middle of our cup the way the ropes looped around the tube, and pulled back and forth. The styrofoam cracked and water trickled out.

The CBC men stopped at our station. The man with the mike smirked.

"We're—uh—attempting," Dorota explained, "to heat this water using the most basic equipment available. Using basic principles. Friction and—um—body heat."

They walked off. They could have at least tried to stifle their grins.

That did it. We broke down. We laughed so hard our sides hurt. Water was everywhere—on the table, on our hands, on our clothes. Debbie's scarf stretched to twice its length.

"Time's up."

Everybody poured their water back into their beakers. We only had about a half cup left.

The guys from the team beside us, with their red and sweaty faces, looked like they had just run a marathon. Steam curled out of their beaker of water. The judge dipped a thermometer in. "Eighty-three degrees." They cheered and patted each other on the back.

The judge came to our station. "St. Mary the Virgin. Twenty-two degrees." Snickers rose from various parts of the room. We snickered too.

"Maybe they'll give us a consolation prize."

The rest of the events passed the same way. All day long, people whispered about "those girls from St. Mary—the ones who made iced tea with an egg beater, the ones who put cherry lip gloss on their yo-yo (Rasa forgot to bring the grease), the ones who answered only one question in Reach for the Top.

We decided not to answer any questions. Then we wouldn't lose any points. We wouldn't gain any either, but so what?

Strategy pays. We came in third place.

Sandra McKenzie
Math 30

The subject, Math; the grade, twelve; the time, 8:35 a.m., and I prepare for the conics exam. It counts for thirty percent of our next report card. I bombed both my trig and quadratics tests so this is my last chance. I detest every class and fear every mark. The course is two-thirds over. It is my final year and I will not come back to upgrade.

Mr. Gagnon, a little Frenchman about forty with big ears, a turned up nose, and dyed black hair, follows every move with cat-like eyes. He looks busy over his desk, but he really watches over his glasses. He has a quick eye and a bionic ear. Rattling paper is an alarm to him. Here I sit, third row from the door and four seats from Mr. Gagnon.

My cheat sheet, approximately two inches by three, holds four hundred and twenty-three letters and numbers and includes ten formulas. I pull the sheet from my binder and slide it under my test booklet. I keep one eye up and I check to my left. I know people who do this bi-monthly and pull off A's. I think I can do it.

Half of the eighty-minute class goes by. I look only two times because I'm afraid.

I ask myself if this is worth the risk. My nerves wear. Mr. Gagnon stands. I bite my lower lip, and my body heats. He walks to the sixth row. He is careful not to take his eyes off the rest of the class. He searches the calculators of three students. He quietly picks up Chris Levang's test paper, tears it in half, and throws the pieces in the trash. I sit stunned, chewing the end of my pen.

There he is. He gets closer every second. Sweat pours down my forehead as he stops at the desk in front of me. I make myself look down at the test and attempt to work out problems on my scrap paper. I want to confess before I get caught. I want to say I'm sorry. He steps towards me. He looks at my desk. His hand slides over the surface. I hold my breath. My stomach turns. Mr. Gagnon walks down the last two rows and sits back at his desk. I stop shaking.

There are twenty minutes left. I want to leave. With five minutes to go, I hand in my exam. I walk back to my desk and pick up my cheat sheet, crumple it with my scrap paper, and drop it into the garbage. As I walk through the door, I close my eyes and vow never to cheat again.

A month passes before I use another cheat sheet to pass my chemistry final.

Gord McGuire
Leaving

Another school day. "What a joke," I thought when the alarm went off. I rarely attended Ancaster High, and when I did, I didn't pay attention or take notes. High school was just a way to be on the football team.

Mom went to work at 8:30, so the house was wide open for the rest of the day. We had a pool table. Steve Tharme and I sat in the field by the highway, waited for Mom's car to go by, then went back to the house to shoot pool.

Absence excuses were easy. Grade thirteen students were allowed to write their own notes. Part of the fun was to create an unbelievable and untraceable excuse for missing school. Some of the best excuses were legal aid appointments and clinical check-ups, because, being confidential, these excuses couldn't be traced.

This was my second try at grade thirteen. The previous year, I dropped out after football season. My marks that term were lower than my days absent. I had managed to pass grade twelve. I knew that I would never attend university, so twelve was all I needed.

My girlfriend of three years left to live in northern British Columbia. That summer I lost all interest in school. I had gone to school to be with her. Now that she was gone, there was nothing pushing me through those doors. I failed my first try at grade thirteen badly. My football performance, fueled by my bitterness and loneliness, was strong that year. I landed a starting linebacker spot.

I dropped out at the end of the season and went to work in the laundry department of a retirement home where many residents had bowel and bladder problems. "A little shit on your hands is good luck," Al Stone, an old laundry hand, told me. I was determined to do better.

Back at Ancaster the next year, my attitude was unchanged. I was dedicated to football and attended classes rarely. In a small town, you know everyone and everyone knows you. I was making a bad name for myself and my family. Tough shit. Early in my second year of grade thirteen, the vice principal, Mr. Elliot, called me into his office.

Mr. Elliot lived close to me and knew my family. He gave me a pep talk. He told me absence without excuse would result in my note-writing privilege being revoked. Any other misbehaviour would not be tolerated. My football was not enough to carry me through school. It was shape up or ship out. I wasn't worried. I was eighteen, my own boss.

I had been absent frequently in the month of September. I got cold stares in the office when I did show. My notes were scrutinized. I knew how to play the game. I was still enrolled. I missed few practices. I wanted a starting spot.

One day, I went to school after I had slept through my morning classes. It was a glorious afternoon—cool, crisp, clear, made for football. In my head I heard the pop of the pads and the grunts of exertion. I felt good that day.

I went to the smoking area to meet my friends. Some were smoking a joint and passed it to me. I put it to my mouth. I felt a rap on the shoulder. I turned, the joint poised. It was Mr. Elliot. "Gord," he spat, "my office in ten minutes." He turned on his heel and left.

Ten minutes? Why not right away? It hit me. He was giving me time to dispose of dope I had on me or in my locker. That wasn't like him, but this was a serious offence.

I went to the office. Adrenalin pumped. I heard the blood rushing in my ears. Mr. Elliot had some papers on his desk—official dismissal slips. He explained them. He watched as I signed. He smiled and took the papers.

On the walk home, I cried. My mind raced. I felt a strange relief. I wondered where to go, what to do.

Acalla Ng
Someone New

"Who is she?" "Is she new here?" "Is she going to stay?" Some people whispered and some people stared. A four foot eleven, red-headed, lean boy walked toward me. He asked, "Are you the new student?"

I couldn't understand him. "Wha...at?"

He repeated, "Are you new here?"

"Yeah . . . yes." He asked me a few more questions but I couldn't understand. He was annoyed and walked away. I felt stupid. I wanted to leave.

Mr. Fehren walked into the classroom. He was my grade seven teacher. The students in class didn't have to stand up and greet the teacher. Mr. Fehren said, "Hi," to everybody and introduced me. "We have a new student in class. Her name is Jean." Everybody in class looked at me. "Today we're going to have a spelling quiz. . . ." Tension eased. Everybody got ready to write the quiz. Some were busy looking for a pen and others were busy looking for a piece of paper.

I didn't bring a pen with me. Gord, the one who asked me the questions, lent me his pen. I thought, what a nice guy. Donna, who sat beside me, kept talking to me. I didn't understand a word she said.

At lunch time, I walked home by myself. I didn't know anybody.

Speaking English was a problem for me, but I didn't have trouble with school work. I had learned how to read and write before I came to Canada. Since I couldn't speak fluently, many students ignored me. But they were interested in me because I was the only Chinese in school.

I walked home by myself for the first few days. Then, I found out Lauren and Stacey lived close to me. From then on, we walked to school together.

One afternoon, I was waiting for Lauren to walk home. She didn't show up. When I went back to school, I asked her what happened. She said, "I had something to do, I couldn't go home for lunch."

"Oh, I see." I went to class.

Next day, I waited for Lauren again. She didn't show up, but Stacey did. She said, "Why don't you go ahead, Lauren is going to be a while." I walked slowly by myself. Lauren and Stacey caught up to me. They didn't stop. They said, "Hi," and walked past. I had a clear picture of what was going on.

On my way back to school, I saw Linda and Lisa walking in front of me. I walked faster and tried to catch up.

"She is strange." I overheard.

"Not really. She is not strange but she has slanted eyes." They both laughed.

"Lauren told me she doesn't want to be close with her," said Lisa.

"I can understand that, who wants to hang around with a chink!"

I felt like hitting them. I walked very fast. I passed them. I didn't look at them.

Maybe I can't speak this language clearly, I thought, but I don't have problems with my hearing. These people are not being fair to me. I hated them.

Tim Vesely

Me And Mill

It got to be a habit. After dinner Tuesday night, I took a break from my reading of John Stuart Mill's *On Liberty* for Political Science. I drove my mother's Volvo over to Joe's apartment for some coffee.

After a four-hour discussion about sex, religion, and bass guitars, we left. Jumpy from two pots of coffee, we felt like going to "Gordie's" park for fresh air. Long stretches of field and forest follow the winding Humber River. It was slightly cold, raining lightly. There were no people around. Joe wore his fedora. I found a piece of a white cotton sheet in the back of the car and wrapped it around my head the same way my mother does with a towel when she gets out of the shower.

Following the bike path, we walked upstream towards the sloping cement banks and bridges. The wet cement reflected light from the street lamps of Eglinton Avenue. I dragged on my Camel cigarette to keep it burning in the rain. On the way to the car, we noticed worms crawling on the bike path. With every step I crushed living creatures beneath my feet. I walked on the grass for the rest of the way. My eyelids felt heavy and my mind wasn't working sharply. I knew that if I didn't go home then, I would never read about liberty.

I dropped Joe off and pulled into my driveway at 1:30. Slowly, I eased the front door open and closed it behind me. I listened for my mother. I heard heavy snoring. I removed my cold desert boots, placed them on the shoe mat, turned off the dining room light, and went into my bedroom. I thought of what one of my Public School teachers once said: "A messy room reflects a messy mind."

Cassettes and cassette cases lay scattered on the floor in front of the stereo. Coats, jackets, pants, shirts, hats, underwear and socks lay on or around the coat rack in the corner. I stumbled over underwear, socks and T-shirts near the door. My foot slammed into the body of the acoustic guitar on the floor. The National Hockey League waste basket, spray-painted red, gold and green, the colours of the Ethiopian flag, overflowed with Kleenexes from the cold I had the previous week.

Before I could read Mill, I had to work on the atmosphere of my room. I turned off the main light and turned on the small, adjustable, yellow reading lamp suspended over the mattress on the floor.

I removed a ragged quilt from the tangled mess of covers at the foot of the mattress and spread it out on the floor. Its pattern in shades of wine, brown and gold made me think of court jester costumes in the Middle Ages. I picked up a box of wooden matches from the floor and lit a fat, orange candle on top of the pine chest of drawers. Shadows from the leaves of the tall umbrella plant spread out on the ceiling and the walls.

With another match, I lit a cone of sandalwood incense and set it in the gold container that my mother bought in Busch Gardens, Florida, when I was ten. I lit another match and watched the red sulphur tip flare. It fell from my hand and rolled along a blank piece of paper. As I blew out the flame, I noticed the brown pattern it left on the paper. I examined it more closely. It looked like a distant horizon of mountain ridges and peaks.

Inspired, I took a piece of white paper from a pile on the bookshelf and rolled a burning match on it. It stopped in the middle of the paper and went out. It left a hazy brown line that looked like a stick-figure person.

I left the room and went downstairs to my father's collection of Tremclad rust-proof paint he used on the nineteen-seventy-three Dodge van parked in our driveway since last winter.

In my arms, I cradled small cans of green, brown, yellow, and silver, and in one hand I held a screwdriver to open the cans. Beside my right foot, I saw a golf ball. I picked it up and went back to my room. I sat on the quilt and spread the cans of paint, the screwdriver, the golf ball, and the white paper on the floor in front of me. I opened the can of silver paint, dipped the golf ball in it, and rolled it three times across the bottom of the page.

I opened the green paint. I needed a brush. I looked in the can of pens and pencils on the bookshelf. It contained a thin, yellow brush. Things didn't usually go this well. I painted three green trees—they looked more like cacti—emerging from the silver patterns. With the brown paint I filled in the spaces around the silver paint. It resembled a landscape. I thought of how well a thin, even black line would define the horizon between the silver-brown land and the white sky, empty except for the stick-person hovering in it.

I went back downstairs, found a can of gloss-black paint, and came back into my room. The smells of sandalwood incense, sulphur from the matches, and fumes from the paint came to me. I painted the black outline of the horizon. I poured yellow paint in the centre of the sky and let it run off the side of the paper, creating a sun. Finally, I set fire to the top edge of the paper and burned an uneven border along the top.

I stepped back to admire this little world. I put my Mozart record on the stereo, turned off the lights, crawled into bed and wondered what Mill had to say about liberty.

Janice Uba
Too Many Worries

November 12, 1983. Graduation tickets went on sale. Posters hung in the cafeteria and in the halls of the second and third floors. Announcements at the end of the day reminded students to buy their tickets. The grad wasn't until June 22. We had eight months to find a date.

As it was the year before, the grad was to be at the Harbour Castle. Tickets were twenty-five dollars for a single and forty for a couple. Nobody went stag. You either went with a date or not at all.

Grad dates were hard to find at Holy Name of Mary, a girls' school. From 8:30 in the morning until 2:30 in the afternoon, we did not see a boy. There were male teachers, but they were teachers. Social life was difficult.

I had a wonderful time at my grade-twelve graduation. I had a boyfriend in grade twelve. I met Mike at the St. Francis of Assisi Church Youth Group. Mike escorted me to my grad. He wore a tux and I wore the dress I finally bought after months of searching.

I wanted to go to my grade-thirteen graduation, but I didn't have a boyfriend. Neither did a lot of my friends. Three days remained for purchasing grad tickets. Jane and Kim bought theirs. After eight months, they were still determined to find dates. Sheila and I hesitated before buying. We remembered Kim's date last year, thirty-two-year-old Mario. Kim and Mario were late for cocktails because Mario had to drop off his ex-wife's alimony cheque. I bought my tickets; Sheila did not. I wanted to ask Jason.

January 2, 1984. School has resumed after Christmas holidays. Jane returned with a date for the grad. She met Bruce at a New Year's Eve party. Kim and I were still looking.

After March break, Bruce was no longer escorting Jane. Jane met David in Florida. He would be her escort. Kim still didn't have a grad date, but she bought a dress. I had neither a dress nor a date. I wanted to ask Jason.

By May, Kim had a date. She asked her paperboy, Tom. He was sixteen and male. I still needed a date. I would ask Jason.

May 12, 1976. I dialed the phone. Jason answered. We talked about the weather, we talked about school, we talked about his job, then we talked about my grad. I asked him if he would escort me. I had waited too long. Jason had plans for June 22.

One month before graduation. No one special had walked into my life. Sheila met a guy, a friend of her brother's. She wanted grad tickets. I had waited long enough. I sold Sheila my tickets. I didn't need a dress, a boutonniere or a pair of shoes. My worries were over.

Bruce G. Tavender

The Defeat

We boarded the bus. I sat in the middle across from my new friend Tom. Coach Avery and Coach Light were last on board. They sat at the front, where coaches always sat. At three o'clock sharp, Coach Avery stood up and gazed over the occupants of the bus.

"Hope everyone is here," he said. The bus rolled out of the parking lot.

We missed our last class that afternoon. This was one of the privileges wrestling team members had on tournament days.

Tom and I were new guys on the team. Everyone else had wrestled for at least a year. I was nervous. Getting beat up by my own team members the first month didn't help. Despite this, Coach Avery and Coach Light encouraged me.

We arrived. Strange faces stared as we made our way to the visitors' change room. Getting into my wrestling uniform was a challenge. It was two sizes too small. I felt naked.

"Remember what you learned, guys, and look mean," were the closing words of Coach Avery's pep talk. George, our meanest fighter, sat on a bench with his eyes closed and smashed his head against the cement wall.

We left the change room and went to the mats. The Trojans were warming up. We walked past them to the open mat. We didn't look at them. They didn't look at us.

"Everyone do your stretches," Coach Light yelled.

I did my stretches and eyed the Trojans. They all looked big.

"Stretch it, Tavender. Stretch it," Coach Light hissed.

The lightest weight category started. Thank God I wasn't first. Fourth was bad enough. The ref started the match. We were all cheerleaders. Nobody screamed louder than Coach Avery.

It was my turn. We had won two matches and lost one. I knelt beside Coach Avery.

"Keep your head up. Watch for single- and double-leg takedowns."

"One minute," the ref announced.

Coach Avery grabbed my hair and shook my head up and down.

"You got to look meaner, Tavender." He pushed me onto the mat.

My opponent walked onto the mat. His arms looked bigger than my waist. We were both supposed to weigh 120 pounds. He probably did, but he was five feet two and I was six feet. My thoughts changed from winning to survival.

"Wrestle!" the ref commanded.

We locked arms and heads. He grunted. I grunted back. He went for a single-leg takedown. He got the single-leg takedown.

"One for the blue," said the ref.

I fell right next to my bench. Coach Avery's face was blue.

"Get up, Tavender! Get up!" he screamed. Suddenly I was on my back. He had me in the chicken-wing. My arm was bent out of shape.

"Bridge, Tavender! Bridge!" Coach Avery screamed.

The ref's hand hit the mat. It was over. My opponent gave me back my arm and shook my hand.

"Good fight," he said.

I watched him walk back to his bench. He wasn't so big. He was just mean.

Chapter Three

Places

Write about a place where you realized important things about the world and about yourself. Present details of incidents, people and landscape to show the special character of the place.

Aline Burke

Terre de Caïn

1. On the Map

Out across the water are Alloby and Patsy's Islands. Southeast of Alloby and Patsy's are the blue hills of Newfoundland. South of the islands is water to the border of the sky. From a ledge of rock on the hills behind the village, Terre de Caïn feels like the neverland of the world.

Tomorrow, I will leave these forty-eight houses and 313 people. I will leave because there is no high school and I am fourteen.

Yesterday, the last of the wolf-huskies was shot. In the past fourteen years, Terre de Caïn has gotten electricity, telephones, ski-doos, a police station and CBC.

Today, I take Terre de Caïn inside me. I carry the rocks, brooks, marshes, the people and their houses. I carry the reels and jigs, the boats and sleigh dogs. I store the sea and the sky.

2. Uncle Lo

Uncle Lo was the best singer in Terre de Caïn. He sat children on his knees and sang "The Rose in June" and "The Star of Logie's Bay."

Uncle Lo was the village drunk. He beat Aunt Jeanne and walked the road singing out, "Ye're all fucking frogs. Ye got not a decent cocksucking woman among ye."

Uncle Lo went on a spree a few times a year. Every wedding, Christmas, Easter and Terre de Caïn time, he went to church, someone's house, or the town hall, sang old Irish, Newfoundland tunes, got drunk and stayed drunk for a week.

Uncle Lo hated Terre de Caïn. He called the village, "a Quebec hell-hole." But he had to live there because he was married to a Terre de Caïn girl and he had been kicked out of his own village, Savage Cove, Newfoundland.

3. Howard

No one, except his mother, ever saw much of Howard. Howard was caught once, crouched out of sight behind Mickle's Knob.

He cleared a patch of ground. Old Saul said Howard made a chain of dandelions, buttercups and bluebells and wound them around the rock pile on Mickle's Knob.

One Christmas, Howard went to a party. He played the accordion. He looked dazed when he played. His jaw moved around with the reels and jigs. He beat his feet on the floor like a drum.

Howard did dirty things to the Terre de Caïn girls. He caught Mary one day, knocked her down, pissed in her face.

Another time, he caught Annie, dragged her into his father's shed. He tied her up, hung her up by her feet, tore off her hospital uniform, swung her back and forth, held an ax to her head, told her to be quiet or she was dead.

Annie screamed, just once.

Sebastian heard. He broke down the door.

Howard went for Sebastian with the ax. Sebastian knocked Howard out. Sebastian cut Annie down, helped her up the rocks to her mother's house. Annie's mother took her in, put her straight to bed, yelled at Annie's brothers and sisters to shut up and get out.

Annie's father came home from work in his overalls without his tools.

Annie's mother called him up the stairs.

Annie cried, "Howard hurt me. Howard hurt me."

Annie's father left her room, walked down the stairs, pushed one of his sons out of the way. He stomped down the rocks, shook his fist at Howard's window.

Howard's mother locked Howard in his room. She faced Annie's father, told him, "Howard is sorry. I punished him."

Annie's father yelled, "You keep that animal in." He turned around and stomped back home.

4. The Teacher from Montreal

Mr. O'Reilly, our grades four and five teacher, came from Montreal. "He's a weird one," people said. He walked by himself on the beach at night. With his easel, he stood up on the hill, where the back of everyone's house was turned against the north, and painted Terre de Caïn from behind. Everyone was suspicious of him. People called him a sissy.

Mr. O'Reilly left our classroom in tears. Stunned, we heard him slap the double doors downstairs open. The doors creaked back and snapped shut. We ran to the windows and watched him walk to the post office where his flat was.

At the back of our classroom, his paintings were stabbed with dozens of jagged staples.

Vera flew into Jake. "You bastard," she hissed and kicked him. "Now he'll think we're nothing but a bunch of wild animals."

"That's exactly what you are," said the principal, who walked into the room. "Get to your seats."

We scurried to our desks. Stupid tears fell on my drawings of princesses. The principal plucked the drawings from the wall. "I want you all to know," he said, "Mr. O'Reilly leaves on the mail plane tomorrow. He heard last night his mother is dying."

5. Early Magic

The foghorn from Patsy's Island lets out a thick moan. I get up before my brothers, sisters, parents and grandmother and sneak outdoors. The world is a salty shadow. Fog whiffs in from the sea. Inward and north it goes, over the hills where the rocks stick out. The rocks are jagged and threaten to fall on the houses below.

I watch from my cave in the sandbank. I breathe in deep. I must be eating ghost dust. I might grow fat and white, become a cloud. Or I could splash like soggy ashes into the water.

Nothing happens.

The houses lean at my back. I creep past them. I fly down the sand dunes, into clouds on the pink sandy shore. Little gusts of wind follow me: sheer pale grey angels. I swoop and glide; arms outstretched, I slice the wet chilly air.

A voice trails to me. My magic fades. My jacket wings fall damp and limp to my sides. The sea sucks back its wave. I cannot move.

"Eileeeeeen?"

"Dear God it's the sea witch. Sweet Jesus, I'll be good. I won't sneak out anymore." A warm wetness trickles down my legs.

"Eileeeeen?"

"Mommy? Oh God no, not Mommy. Mommy. Oh thank you, God. Ma, I'm coming."

6. Grandmother Jack

Grandmother Jack kept her money in a wad of kleenex between her breasts. She told stories about the olden days when she had a house of her own.

In Flowers of the Bay, Newfoundland, she kept a rope soaked in a washtub in her pantry. She used the rope to lace her boys.

One day, while Grandmother pickled cabbage for the winter, her six-year-old daughter, Molly, caught fire. Molly's apron strings caught aflame from the burning garbage. Two of Molly's brothers doused her with water. Grandmother Jack said it was the water that killed Molly.

She put Molly straight to bed. Then she laced her boys with the soaked rope. "They had to learn that if you threw water on someone afire you could kill them," she said.

Molly peeled the skin off her arms. She died before supper, before the priest made it across the bay.

7. Josephine (a skipping song)

> *Josephine*
> *Hated sex*
> *Hated kids*
> *Did her duty*
> *Had twelve*
> *Did it well*
> *She is proud*
> *None of them*
> *Went to jail*

8. Aunt Solange

Aunt Solange died young. I don't know why. At her wake, Uncle Ben forced my hand to her cracked lips. He said the touch would make me forget her yellow skin, sunken eyes and the stink.

When I tried to sleep, her corpse rolled toward me. Her eyes popped open like the ones on my doll.

After her funeral, her young children were put out among the older ones. Uncle Morey, her husband, moved from one to another. He gave his girls a hard time. He got a reputation for being a dirty old man. Between Aunt Solange and the wife before her, he fathered twenty-two kids. He always had a place to go.

9. The Merry Dancers

In Terre de Caïn, the northern lights are called Merry Dancers. They quiver rose into blue, yellow into green across the north sky above the hills. They dance rippling curves and surge from west to east, then reel back again.

A child learning to whistle is told that if she whistles while the Merry Dancers dance, they bellow down to her and swirl her aloft into their colours. She is consumed by them and is gone forever.

Ieva Martin

Where My World Began

Fragments of memory are all that is left of my early childhood. How much is real and what has been filled in by fantasy? There are more questions than answers.

I remember a bomb shelter. Did every farm in Germany have one during the war? As my mother wraps me in warm clothes and bundles my infant sister into a basket, I ask, "Why won't the Bobbies let little children sleep?" I am three.

The cement bomb shelter is some distance from the farmhouse. Four or five steps lead down to the inside. Were the thick bare walls and rounded roof really slimy? It had to be damp, or the frogs wouldn't have been there. Before we could sit down, we had to clear them off the wooden benches that ran along the length of the shelter on both sides.

I remember a horse trapped in a crater left by a bomb. It had to be rescued by firemen with ropes and pulleys. How had it gotten there?

Except for a walk with my mother along a pebbly beach, peaceful childhood memories begin in Sweden where we spent two years after the war before coming to Canada. The family was whole for the first time since my sister was born.

The town was Aspen. At the top of a hill, a long walk away from the train station where we disembarked, sat a tiny shepherd's cottage, red with white trim and set back from the main road. Birches stood beside the entrance.

Inside was only one room. On the right were the beds. On the left were a small wooden table, four chairs, a wood stove. I don't remember a pump, so there must have been running water, but there was no indoor bathroom. Did my sister's bladder problems stem from trips to the outhouse in cold weather?

Near the cottage, stood a large barn. Inside, in a pile of hay, was a depression where we thought a rabbit must sleep. One spring day, we left weeds we thought would work as paint brushes. We were excited when we found them gone the next day. On Easter morning, the depression was filled with coloured eggs.

Below the barn was a large field. For a while, a bull was kept there, a chain through the ring in his nose fastened to the ground. He pawed the dirt. We kept our distance. Another time (was it another summer?), the field was full of sheep. We loved the lambs.

One summer day, standing on a stone in that field, I proposed a game to my sister. The aim was to see who could smash her new doll's head first. I stood back and watched her ruin her doll. I don't remember being punished. I do remember the face of the doll she got as a replacement. The image of mine has faded.

Stephen Kamachi
The Swamp

My dad was in the Air Force. This meant moving every couple of years. We lived in Victoria, Chilliwack, and Marville, France, before my dad was transferred to North Bay, Ontario, in June 1967. I was six.

The houses on our street had just been built. Only one other family, the MacArthurs, had moved in before us. Tim

MacArthur was my age. Later that summer, Tom Ricci moved in down the street and the three of us became friends.

The forest beyond our street remained undeveloped. Behind Tim's backyard was a swamp full of tadpoles, frogs and small fish. We wore black gum boots and brought buckets and empty cement bags from nearby houses under construction. We caught tadpoles and polywogs in our hands. Sometimes we dragged cement bags along like nets. When I got home, Mom covered my mosquito bites with Surfadil, rubbery-smelling calamine lotion.

We kept the tadpoles in my garage in the pink plastic baby's bathtub I was once bathed in. Not one developed into a frog. Our tadpoles grew hindlegs, and their next stage was death. Victor Morin, who lived a couple of houses down, grew a frog, but he had a bigger tub.

Tom, Tim and I sometimes rode our bikes to Marshall Park, snake country. There were red racers, garter snakes and bull snakes. We found them under old mattresses or large boards. Tim always caught the most snakes.

Park's Creek was in Marshall Park. My mom did not like me to go there, but, since Tom and Tim were allowed to go, I went anyway. We laid a blanket across the creek and lifted it when we thought we had a fish. We used my dad's smelt net to catch minnows around the wooden bridge. We caught perch and shiners and the occasional stickleback.

When I started grade six in 1972, construction companies worked behind Tim's house. Trucks dumped gravel into the bog. Yellow bulldozers flattened the forest. Big pumps with long hoses drained water from the swamp. I sat with Tim at the edge of the ditch in front of his house and watched dead frogs spew out of the hose, float along the ditch and into the storm sewer.

Tieho Masinga

The Mirror, The Thing

Fani shouted, "Did you see it, Zanele?"

"What?" Zanele asked his friend.

"It came and disappeared," Fani replied.

"What? Where?"

Fani stood and picked up his stick. Zanele sat on the grass. He stared at Fani. Fani moved slowly in the direction of the river.

"I saw it," he said.

Zanele became angry. "Fani, this it you saw, does it have a name? Is it a he or a she?"

"It crawled toward me," Fani said. "Its eyes were green. I thought it would swallow me, but then it turned away and disappeared. My mother said it does not eat human beings. When I saw it, I knew it was what my mother had told me about. As it moved, the colour of its skin changed from black to green, and yellow spots shone on its skin. I was scared when I saw it. It could swallow a live goat or a sheep, you know."

"Fani, I can tell what you saw," Zanele said. "It has gone to the river to drink water. Let us go there and watch."

Zanele stood up, left his stick on the grass and moved slowly toward the river. He told Fani, "We do not need our sticks from the way you describe it. It is not dangerous. It must be full."

"What do you mean full?" Fani asked him.

"Because it has swallowed something," Zanele said.

"Swallowed what?"

Zanele smiled at his friend. "I said it swallowed something. It can be a goat, sheep or even a pig."

From a distance, they heard a rattling sound in the grass.

"I can hear it," Fani shouted. "It has moved away from the river into thick grass."

"I can see it. There, look, Fani! I knew it was a python," Zanele said. "Come closer."

Fani did not move. "I am scared," he said.

"It will not harm you," Zanele explained. "It looks pregnant." When Zanele moved closer the python opened its mouth. It spat some fluid. It tried to move its head but failed. Zanele sat by its side and caressed its skin.

"What are you doing, Zanele?"

"Come closer."

"I told you, Zanele, I am scared."

The python did not move anymore, or try to. It enjoyed the touch of Zanele.

"Come closer, Fani. I can feel there is movement inside. Come and feel it."

Fani went closer. He opened his mouth to say something, but no words came out. Zanele asked Fani to kneel down, then took his hand onto the python's skin.

"The reflection of the river and the hill! It is like a mirror," Fani said. "Let us take it home, Zanele."

"Who is going to carry it?"

"You." Fani pointed a finger at Zanele. "You know I am afraid of it. I like the mirror, but I am afraid of it."

"But who wants the mirror?" Zanele asked.

"I do not want to use the mirror, but I want my mom and dad to see it," Fani said.

"It is unfair to treat other creatures like that. Imagine someone doing that to you when you are tired and asleep."

"You are right, Zanele. I did not look at it that way. Let us leave it and go back to herding the cattle."

Zanele and Fani stood up and left the python asleep. Their shadows, reflected in the river, disappeared.

Steve Richards

My World

My world begins at 185 Pickering Street in the east end of Toronto. The roads are cracked and pot-holed. The abandoned distillery, Cherry Wines Co., and the old Shell Oil Refinery have smashed windows, boarded doors, missing bricks. We fear the haunted house on the corner of Pickering Street and Swanwyck Road. Someone was murdered there. Weeds hide the Whomsley *For Sale* sign.

Our house is ancient. It is a pink-bricked, two-storey detached building. We have crab apple and rock fights in the laneway next to our house. We play ball hockey and catch grasshoppers in the empty lot behind our house. The roof and veranda are newly repaired. We have a farmhouse kitchen.

My parents lower the floor of the basement six inches to make it into a rec room. There are gaps in the front bushes where the kids who jump over sometimes land. The backyard is lined with rose bushes to keep the neighbours out.

I am three. It takes three hours to reach the cottage from our house. Dad claims there is a short-cut. There is only one route to Lake Scugog. We travel in circles for hours. Not far from the cottage, the '57 Fairlane overheats. My parents wrap me in a blanket and walk to the cottage.

I am ten. My friends and I play hide-and-seek. Vladimir runs into a backyard behind a car. A Doberman Pinscher, trained for combat in Korea, jumps out and rips a golf-ball sized piece of flesh from his arm.

I am twelve. Lorne and Michael Castor, who are eighteen, chase me. They throw rocks and snowballs. I see this is fun for them.

I am thirteen. Robby Dickson comes over for Lipton's Chicken Noodle Soup. Robby doesn't blow his nose. He always has a green thing hanging. Robby hunches over his soup. He brings the spoon to his lips. He eyes his nose. Just before the thing dips into his soup, Robby inhales with a jerk. The thing double-loops and fires up his nostril. This is his last time for lunch.

I am fourteen. Dad comes home carrying a case of beer. He is drunk. Mom offers to put the beer in "cold storage." She throws the case out the door into the backyard. Dad is stunned. He sifts through them. Every bottle is broken.

Buddy from 191 Pickering Street has a fantastic butterfly collection. He pays us five cents for every container of grasshoppers we catch. He fries and eats the grasshoppers. He says they taste like chicken.

Lisa's all-time favourite sandwich contains sauerkraut, sardines and strawberry jam.

Fred Myers from 222 Whitby Street trains his German Shepherd to go shopping. Once a week Duke carries a basket, a shopping list, and money to the store. Duke returns with groceries.

A one-year-old Shepherd-Doberman is my pet. Whenever Dad tries to beat Mom or me, Ginger growls and poises to attack. Dad says, "Either the dog goes, or I go." The dog stays. So does Dad.

I am fifteen. We move to a bungalow in Weston, Ontario. It is between Eglinton and Lawrence near the Westway. There are tree-lined boulevards, newly paved roads, well-kept homes, good T.T.C. A hedge surrounds our home. There is a birch tree in the centre of the front yard. We renovate the kitchen and both bathrooms. The finished basement floods in winter. The parquet floor is lifting.

I am seventeen. I dream that my Uncle Walter dies. He is discovered dead the next morning.

Doug, a neighbour on our left, is in grade thirteen for the third time. His mother is principal of Valleyfield. His father owns a plumbing company. They own another home, which they rent, and a cottage. Lucy, his fifteen-year-old girlfriend, spends every lunch hour at his place.

Anthony hangs his pet rabbit.

I am eighteen. I dream about Aunt Ruth's death. She dies the next day.

Jim, a straight-A student in grade thirteen, lives to our right. His dog relieves itself on our lawn. Jim never cleans up the mess.

Ginger contracts distemper. Dad has her put away.

Mr. Gallo chews tobacco. He spits it out on the sidewalk. The kids nickname him Mr. Na-Na. Whenever they try selling him chocolate bars or raffle tickets for charity, he says, "Na-na-na-na." Mr. Gallo talks to himself.

I crack a joke while Lisa is eating Campbell's Chicken Noodle Soup. She laughs blowing noodles out of her nose.

I am nineteen. The front door lock is jammed. We try our keys. None work. Forcing the door also fails. Dad decides to break in through the family room window. I take a screwdriver out of my car. I remove the storm window. Dad forces the latch on the second window. As it gives, the glass breaks. Dad steps into the house. The Joneses watch us.

During March break, Dad and I go skiing. On the way to Georgian Peaks, he describes his younger days. He used rubber boots and homemade skis to jump barrels. We take the ski-lift to the Black Square slope, the most difficult. Dad curses me as he tumbles down the hill. At the bottom, he says, "Never again will I ski with you." We will go skiing this Christmas.

I dream that I am dead. It is dark, peaceful. My breathing is almost gone. I have only one sense—hearing. I want to turn over. I can't. Short breaths. My chest heaves. I want to sit up. I can't. Chilly sweat. I can't hear. I float.

I wake up and I write.

Paula Peters

My First Day at St. Patrick's Anglican

I looked forward to starting primary school in Grenada. I had visited St. Patrick's Anglican School on numerous occasions. It was the location of our annual church harvest. My sister was an upper class pupil and cousin Maggie was my teacher. All my classmates from Mrs. Redhead's Preparatory school were in my class.

I had a reputation for talking. I stopped only for breath. That day, by ten o'clock, I had spoken to Sally, Ann, Peter and Christopher and had been told to stop six times. I stopped talking to go to the bathroom. I went toward the door.

"Paula! Where are you going?" screamed teacher Maggie.

"To the outhouse," I replied.

"Did you ask for permission?" she asked sternly. I shook my head. "Sit back down, then ask."

Teacher went to help Margaret, the girl across the room. I was agitated. My bladder felt about to burst. "Teacher Maggie, can I go outside and pee?" I yelled. I prayed to God to let me live.

"That is the rudest thing I have ever heard. You will not go to the bathroom until breaktime." She turned and walked away. Beneath my breath I cursed (no one would believe I attended church every Sunday).

Crossing my legs didn't help. I couldn't take it anymore. I looked down. A big puddle formed beneath my chair.

"Teacher Maggie, Paula peed in her panty," screamed Jerry.

My classmates thought it funny. When I laughed, it was with relief. Teacher Maggie was not pleased. She made me mop it up. After my task, I stretched out my hand to Teacher Maggie to receive my punishment. She hit me with a ruler. It didn't hurt, but I cried to please her. I learned that trick from going to Sunday matinee.

At lunch time, Cousin Maggie and I walked to her mother's house for lunch. This we did for three years.

Sybil C. Horton
My India Rubber Ball

In the spring of 1941, we were losing the war in Europe, and I was losing my war as the new girl in grade three at Cordington Hills School, my third school in three years. I suffered from battle fatigue.

Although Saskatoon was recovering economically after the Depression and the drought, the recovery had not come down to my family. The war inflated the cost of housing. Our landlord sold our house. We moved again.

The only place Dad could find was a walk-up apartment that happened to be in Cordington Hills, an affluent area. We were poor like the people in my old school. We were out of place in Cordington Hills.

My old school, a victim of wartime shortages, was an old building without enough space for the students. Neither the plumbing nor the heating worked properly. There was no office, no auditorium, not even a staff room. For a playground, we had only open prairie. The teachers were recalled from retirement when the younger women went off to war. Mine, Miss Duncan, a kind old woman with blue hair was a terrible teacher. Discipline was no problem: we didn't have any.

It was a shock for me to move to the large and affluent Cordington Hills School. Gone was the freedom of the small school with few rules. Now I had sidewalks, fences, playing fields, and rules that no one explained. There were rules for everything. Boys and girls could not even play together.

The well-dressed, clean children came from nice houses. Our shabby clothes and home haircuts marked our poverty. The principal, Mr. Mortimer, was annoyed because Mom was sick and could not register us. Dad worked long hours and could not go to the school. Mr. Mortimer sent nasty notes home demanding Red Cross dues, gym clothes and other things we did not have.

All the girls owned India rubber balls. I owned a golf ball that my brother and I fished out of a slough. It squished when I bounced it and it leaked in my pocket. It smelled awful. I tried to clean it up with Dutch Cleanser. The other girls made fun of me.

Class time was bad but playground time was torture. A couple of loudmouthed kids made my life miserable. I bloodied their noses. Then I was in trouble with Mr. Mortimer again. To avoid my tormentors I slipped away to the front of the school on the girls' end. The fifteen cement steps were an ideal place to play alone with my golf ball.

One day, Mr. Mortimer saw me. He thundered, "Don't you know this is against the rules?" I told him that at my last school we didn't have any steps so I didn't know it was against the rules. He took my ball. I asked when I could get it back.

He thundered at me, "When I take a toy it is never returned!" He buttoned his light grey suit jacket over his round stomach and dropped my ball in the pocket. I tried to tell him it leaked. He sent me to the playground with threats of a strapping.

That afternoon, we marched to the auditorium for an important assembly. We sang patriotic songs, and a boy read a war poem. Then an important man talked about how we should buy War Savings Stamps. I thought if I had any money I would buy an India rubber ball and let the poor soldiers look after themselves.

Then Mr. Mortimer stood at the podium. The teachers sat on the stage behind him. There was a bulge in Mr. Mortimer's jacket pocket and a large dark spot, unmistakably wet. He couldn't see it for his round stomach, and the teachers behind him couldn't see it either. The rest of us looked up at him. Laughter rippled through the auditorium. He waved his arms and shouted, but that made him funnier. Everyone laughed but I was in a panic. Although the teachers on stage and the important man could not see what was happening, they no longer looked solemn.

The music teacher rescued the situation by banging out "God Save the King" on the piano. We stood at attention and sang with patriotic enthusiasm.

At home, I was afraid to admit I was in trouble again. Finally, my grief over the loss of the ball overcame me, and I told the story. My big brother giggled. He had guessed what was in Mr. Mortimer's pocket. He told Dad about the assembly. Dad snickered all evening.

The next night, Dad asked me to clean out his lunch pail. When I opened it, there was a new India rubber ball. He said I had earned it.

For me, this India rubber ball was the ultimate status symbol, better than store-bought clothes or barbershop haircuts. Mr. Mortimer didn't get the chance to take my India rubber ball. We moved again. I was thrown into a new war in grade four at Prince of Wales Public School.

Chapter Four

People

Use details of action, speech and setting to present a person you know.

Titus Cheong

Who Was Henry?

He sat four feet in front of the old black and white television, his legs propped on the coffee table with his cigarettes, a lighter, some empty beer bottles, a full ashtray and a can of lighter fluid he liked to use as a flamethrower. He had been there since 4:00 p.m. the day before.

"Good morning, Henry," I said.

"Yeah," he replied without moving.

Henry Martins, my housemate on Autumn Leaf Crescent in Erin Mills, was seventeen and believed the world was against him. He seldom washed his long, blonde hair or his clothes. He always wore faded jeans, faded T-shirts and his studded leather jacket. I knew little about his background except that he hated his parents who lived in Aylmer, his home town. I remember one heated phone conversation with his mother. Henry wanted to borrow money to buy a motorcycle and his mother wouldn't give it to him. He shouted into the phone and hung up on her. He never got the bike.

Henry was happy only with his beer-drinking friends from the plant where he worked as a lathe operator for a company that made parts for car seats. He seldom talked to me but when he did it was about his job or the music he liked. He worshipped Pink Floyd. He played the records full volume on the fourteen-hundred dollar stereo he saved for a year to buy.

Some nights, after he'd had a few drinks, Henry closed himself in his basement room, blasted his stereo, screamed along with the lyrics and banged the floor. I went down there only if I had to. The smell of pot made me sick. Other nights, Henry just watched television. Sometimes he fell asleep in front of the TV with a cigarette burning between his fingers.

"This fucking program is fucking helluva horse-piss," he said.

"Watch something else," I said.

"Fucking colour TV is what we fucking need! The fucking landlord is such a stingy son-of-a-bitch! I've had enough of this fucking shit." He pulled on his studded leather jacket over his

Iron Maiden T-shirt, took a half-full beer, picked up his cigarettes and walked out the door.

Henry was always going for walks. Even if there was a snowstorm, he'd still walk. I never knew where he went.

Once, he came back late—in a bad mood. Henry stomped upstairs. A minute later, he came down again holding a baseball bat in his right hand. "I'm gonna fucking kill that fucking asshole!" he screamed going out the door.

The next day, our neighbour told me someone at Erin Mills skating rink accused Henry of "messing around" with his girlfriend. Henry put things right with his bat. I never saw that bat again.

One Thursday, Henry came home early. I heard him banging on the front door. I cursed, thinking he had forgotten his keys again. I went down and opened the door. Henry, two large bandages covering his eyes, stood there and sobbed, "I'm blind, Titus, I'm blind!" He reached out, both arms shaking. "Accident at work. Didn't wear goggles. Chips in my eyes," he said between sobs.

I led him to his room and helped him onto his bed. He clung to me tightly. "Don't worry," I said. "It's probably temporary." I didn't really know. I was shaking too, but I tried to sound calm. I told him I would make him a coffee. He didn't want me to leave.

"It's so dark. I can't see nothin'." He gripped the mattress so tightly his knuckles turned white. I tried to relax him by making him talk. By 1:00 a.m., he was asleep.

That night I slept in his chair with my head on his desk. Early the next morning, the company van came to take him to the doctor for re-examination. I had to go to school. That was the last time I saw Henry Martins.

Two days later, my landlord told me Henry's brother had come to get his stuff while I was at school. Henry had moved to his brother's place in Toronto.

One month later, Henry called. "Thanks," he said. "I got my fucking eyesight back."

Alison Rasmussen

Dan The Man

"Don't forget your lunches on the counter and take your hats. It's going to be hot today."
"Yeah, okay, Mom," I yelled. I threw my ham sandwich, banana and chocolate chip cookies in my knapsack. "C'mon, Missy, Peter, we're going to miss the bus."

Andrea ran out the door behind me. Missy and Peter followed dragging their knapsacks on the ground. We ran to the bus stop, got on the waiting bus, said "Hi" to Barb, the counsellor, and jumped onto the seats. We screamed and laughed. Barb sighed, rolled her eyes. We were on our way to Chippewa Day Camp.

The driver pulled the bus into a large dusty parking lot and let us out. Barb told us to go and wait on the big hill with the rest of the kids. She joined a group of counsellors standing beside the hill.

"Yuck! I've been hit!" screamed a redheaded boy. He ran down the hill. A flock of seagulls followed him. He wiped his hair. "It smells awful!" A counsellor led him to the washroom. When they returned, the counsellors gathered at the bottom of the hill.

"Welcome to Chippewa Day Camp. Listen carefully. Your name will be called by your counsellor, so pay attention. We will begin with the seven- and eight-year-olds." Names were called out. Children stumbled, ran and jumped down the hill. They stood in long lines behind their counsellors.

"Karen Johnson, Beth Carlisle and Andrea and Alison Rasmussen." Andrea and I stood up and followed the other girls down the hill. "John Smith, Doug MacKenzie, Toby Chan and Jimmy Carhart." The four boys looked surprised. They got up and walked slowly down the hill.

Our counsellor, tall and thin with a mop of greasy blonde hair, told us to quit staring at each other and follow him. He led us down the beach, stood us in front of the large steel rack of canoes and told us to sit down.

"My name is Dan. You are in a co-ed group because there weren't enough twelve-year-olds signed up to make boys and girls groups. When you are with me, I want you to listen. I don't want to see anyone doing anything I didn't tell them to. I don't want anyone taking off. I want co-operation. Do you hear me? Co-operation. This is the oldest group and I want you to set an example. If you have any complaints, you can go home right now. C'mon, grab a life jacket. We're going canoeing."

Dan took the life jackets and tossed them at us.

"I want a boy and girl in each canoe. Let's go!"

We looked at each other. Nobody said a word. Nobody moved.

"Do I have to do everything?" Dan yelled. "You go with him, you there and you there." I moved beside Toby. Karen and Beth stood beside John and Doug. Andrea and Jimmy looked at each other. "Let's go now. I don't want to be canoeing all day!"

Dan dragged a canoe down to the dock. We shuffled around, got the canoes off the rack, put them in the water, pulled our life jackets on, paddled around the bay, rammed our canoes back into the dock, got out, took off our life jackets and pulled the canoes out.

"Now, wasn't that fun?" Dan said. Nobody answered.

On Tuesday, we hiked to Bruley Bay, five miles from camp. Dan yelled for us to quit talking, to quit walking so slowly, to cooperate. We missed the turnoff and were lost in the bush for two hours.

On Wednesday, we hiked to Squaw Bay, ten miles from camp. Dan yelled for us to quit talking, to quit walking so slowly, to cooperate. We missed the turnoff and were lost in the bush for four hours.

On Thursday, we went on an overnight camping trip to Sibly Park. "Now, I want to see some co-operation as a whole group. None of this boy-girl stuff. If this keeps up, you can all go home and stay there until you grow up!" Dan slammed his knapsack on the ground and marched away.

"If I ever have to listen to any more of Dan the Man and his stupid yelling, I'm gonna puke!" Toby said. Dan came back with his arms full of twine and rope.

"We are going to build lean-tos and I want everyone to cooperate. When you're finished, we'll be going on a hike." Dan threw the rope on the ground in front of us and walked away.

We built the lean-tos, started a fire and ate our lunches. Dan came back and told us to follow him.

Dan led us down a narrow path overgrown with grass, vines and bushes. "Is there poison ivy around here? I'm allergic to poison ivy." Jimmy scratched his arms. The path twisted and pine needles crunched under our feet.

"Where are we going?" asked John.

"We're going to the lookout!" yelled Dan from the front of the line. He pushed branches out of his way.

"How far is it?" asked Andrea. She slapped mosquitoes buzzing around her head.

"Never mind how far it is. Just keep walking." We walked for hours. It got dark and cold.

"Hey, Dan, I think we should go back. It's almost six o'clock." Beth looked at her glow-in-the-dark watch.

"Geez, you guys are lazy!" Dan turned around and stopped. "Uh . . . you guys, we're not on the path anymore."

"What! You mean we're lost again?" We stared at Dan.

"No, no. I know the way back." Dan led us into the bush. He pushed through the branches and stopped at the edge of the swamp. "Our campsite is on the other side of the swamp! We're going through!" Dan yelled.

"Can't we go around?" I asked, standing with the others at the edge of the swamp.

"No, it'll take too long." Dan waded into the middle of the swamp. "C'mon, you chickenshits. I want to get back to camp before it gets too dark." We walked in. The mud slithered into our shoes. It was cold and slimy. It smelled like horse manure. We waded through the swamp and stumbled up the bank.

"Let's go. We're almost there." Dan walked into the bush. We walked in circles for another hour.

"Dan, you don't know where you're going, do you?" I said. I ducked under a dead branch. "This is the third time I've crawled under this branch!"

"I'm not going any further." Beth sat down on the ground. Jimmy and Doug joined her.

"Okay. We'll stay here for the night." Dan walked around and gathered twigs and branches for a fire.

At 7:30 a.m., the search party crashed down the path two feet from where we had camped for the night. We followed

Dan and Jerry, the leader of the search party, back to the camp.

Police, reporters and parents rushed about, asking what happened and where we had been. A policeman with a pad and pencil walked over and talked to Dan. A reporter asked us our names. We stood in a group with Dan in the middle. We smiled. Cameras flashed. Saturday was the last day of camp. Our picture had been in the paper Friday. Toby brought a copy for Dan.

"I'm sorry about what happened yesterday," Dan said. He handed each of us a bag of salt and vinegar chips. "But if you would've cooperated, we could've made it back to camp."

Nobody said anything. The buses rolled into the parking lot. Dan walked toward the counsellors' cabin.

Sharon F. Yee

Marilyn

Marilyn and I gossip in front of an open gym locker in the Erindale changeroom. It's May 6, 1982, Marilyn's twentieth birthday. We met three years ago at the Chinese Gospel Church downtown. We're getting to know each other better because we're in the same psych class at Erindale. Marilyn reminds me of Marianne, the fake, ever-smiling, self-proclaimed cutie of the church. Marilyn has a more sparkling, giddy personality. It attracts the guys. Marilyn is beautiful. I want to be like her.

Marilyn giggles as she tears open the pink and yellow wrapping on her gift, pink stationery and a matching pen. I hope she likes it. Marilyn looks coyly at me and thanks me. She draws closer and kisses me. She fascinates me.

We talk about birthdays, Professor Krames and men. She asks, "Sharon, have you ever had a boyfriend?"

I say, "No." I think for a minute and get mad at myself for giving it away so easily. "How about you?"

She responds, "No. Now I'm an old maid. Heehee."

I tell her I'm interested in Peter Chu, who studies economics at York. She's never met him, so I invite her for dinner with us in Chinatown tonight. Marilyn accepts. She tells me Peter's last name means pig in Chinese.

The conversation changes to makeup. Marilyn says, "I never wear concealer or foundation."

I say, "I use it to cover the circles under my eyes." Marilyn moves closer to look at my face.

"Sharon, did you know you have a hump on your nose?"

"Yes, I know. I broke it playing basketball in grade eight. I caught a ball with my face. I didn't know it was broken until a doctor mentioned it to me during my grade nine physical." Marilyn examines my face.

"Really? Sharon, did you know your teeth are crooked?"

"What?" I say.

"Your bottom teeth."

I try to say "I know" with a closed mouth.

I look at her. Her foundation is flaking off. Why do I let her say this to me? I was excited about seeing Peter today, but now I feel like shit.

Marilyn and I sit at a table for four in the Golden Country Restaurant. She sits on my right. Peter walks in the front door. I wave to him. He sits down beside Marilyn. Why doesn't he sit beside me? He likes Marilyn's animated laughter. Marilyn giggles at his jokes. I think that if I say anything it will draw attention to my crooked teeth and humped nose.

I swallow lumps of food Peter spoons on my plate. He's playing the gentleman tonight. We drink tea and eat. I watch Marilyn eat gracefully with ivory chopsticks. I wish I could do that. I drop one of the sticks onto the red tablecloth. I listen to them talk. Peter's happy. Marilyn's happy. I'm miserable. Finally, dinner's over.

Peter picks up the bill and insists on treating Marilyn for her birthday, something I have never seen him do before. He is usually a tightwad. The bill is settled and we rise to leave. Peter helps Marilyn into her navy reefer coat. I shrug on my grey ski jacket. We're ready to go.

Marilyn smiles at Peter as he holds the door open. She makes eyes at him and asks if we'll walk her home. I don't want to, but Peter insists. We walk down Spadina to Queen.

Marilyn points to the Taste of China Restaurant her parents own. Peter waves a frantic goodbye as she walks to her front door. I'm glad she's gone.

Peter and I stamp our cold feet in the bus shelter. We wait for the Spadina 77 to take us to the subway station. The bus pulls up. I ask Peter if he'll escort me home on the subway.

"And go out to Mississauga? No thanks."

I'm hurt. I rub a clear spot on the foggy bus window. The bus rolls into the subway station.

Peter and I get off and walk with the crowd to the train entrance. He goes east and I go west. I turn to say goodbye, hoping he'll change his mind. He's absorbed. He's thinking of Marilyn. We part. I walk four steps and look back. I see Peter's head retreating into the sea of people.

Six months later, the news is out. Peter and Marilyn are engaged. I think about what happened. Maybe they deserve each other, I rationalize. Mr. and Mrs. Pig will live happily ever after.

Debra Antrobus Bruce

Angie

My mother's name is Angie. Originally, it was Agnes Michelle Kelly, then it became Angie Antram, then Angie Johnson, and now it is Angie Cole. I was my mother's first born, her first abandoned, her first abused. My mother is a beautiful woman, but hers is outer beauty. My mother comes into and goes out of my life—at her convenience.

I was raised by my Dad's mother. I heard that my mother called my Dad's mom on the phone and threatened to kill me if someone didn't come to get me. I was a year old. She lost custody because she was found to be an unfit mother. I had a sister, Barbara Lynn Antram, born less than a year after me. She died at two months from pneumonia. My mother put her out in the carriage during the winter months with nothing but a diaper on. My mother was not charged. I still don't understand why not.

In one sentence, I say how much I hate my mother for all the pain and hurt she has put me through. In the next sentence, I say I love her. She's still my mother.

I was thirteen when my grandmother died of cancer. Children's Aid put me back into my mother's care. My two half-brothers lived with her. They were five and six years younger. My mother worked as a cocktail waitress and left me to care for them. I had to cook supper. In the cupboards I found only booze and strawberry cake mix. I made the cake. We ate it with water on the side.

My mother worked nights. Days she either sunbathed or lay in bed with a man she picked up at work the night before. She lived common-law with several men and used them to get what she wanted.

She smacked me around. I ran away a lot. Mom hated me.

By the time I was fifteen, I had spent three months in the Children's Aid Receiving Centre on Huntley Street and four months in Whitby Psychiatric Hospital. Mom told the doctor she wanted me locked up for the rest of my life. She said I was mentally unbalanced.

Fortunately for me, the social worker on my case was replaced, and my mother lost custody again. A new social worker, Bruce Watson, removed me from the hospital and placed me in my Dad's sister's home with her five children.

Each time my mother married, she left her children and her responsibilities behind. I have two half-brothers, two step-brothers, and two step-sisters. Last I heard, my mother lives in Florida somewhere. I hear the marriage isn't doing well. She's forty-six now, and as much as she tries to hide those lines and wrinkles, they probably show.

Whenever she and I went out together, she told me to call her Angie. She didn't want people to know I was her daughter. She didn't want my son to call her Gramma because she would feel old. I'm glad she's not around now. I don't want her to hurt my son as she hurt me. I don't want to see the false fronts she uses to hide what she is.

She is the mother who never was.

Grace Abelarde
Papa

July 2, 1984. My father, my sister, Fay, and I travel on Highway 5 West in Alberta. It is the fourth day in a five-day journey from Bramalea, Ontario, to Surrey, B.C. The schedule taped to the dashboard shows that we are twenty-three minutes late for supper. My father's eyes meet mine in the rearview mirror. He booms out, "Okay, you guys. Plan B. You know what to do!"

Fay and I open the four side-windows and prop up the back one. I pick up the orange Nerf football, the Rubik's cube and the Sony Walkman and put them in the cardboard box in the corner. Fay places three bricks side by side, about eighteen inches from the hump over the right rear tire. She drags the Coleman cooler from its corner and takes out a long, green Tupperware breadbox. She wipes the icy water from its sides, and peels off the lid, leaving an inch or two open. We smell mother's special garlic, soy and vinegar marinade. At the front, Papa smacks his lips and Fay giggles. He pats his stomach.

"C'mon, ladies. We're behind schedule. I want dinner finished before we get to the hotel, so that we can shower before hitting the sack. We need the full eight hours, you know. Tomorrow's the big day," he announces.

I pull the Hibachi from its box and place it on top of the bricks. I take off the grills and pour Kingsford Matchlite charcoal into the Hibachi. Fay hands me a Bic lighter. I click the Bic and wait until the edges turn white on the black cubes before replacing the grills. Soon the van smells like an outdoor barbecue. Fay plugs the rice cooker into the cigarette lighter unit.

A yellow Volkswagen convertible tries to overtake the van. The girl in the passenger seat gestures wildly. My father slows the van, and the beetle cruises alongside us.

"HEY, MISTER. YOU'RE ON FIRE!"

"WE'RE NOT," my father screams. "MY GIRLS ARE COOKING DINNER." My father waves, turns up the cassette and lip syncs to Julio Iglesias. "Yep," he says, "Julio on the prairies. How's dinner, guys?" Steaks hiss on the grill. My father winks at Fay in the mirror.

At 8:08, thirty minutes after sunset, we pull into the parking lot of the Hotel Lake Louise, in Banff. My father works for CNR and he gets half off all CNCP hotels across Canada and some in the U.S.. We trail the barbecue smell across the hotel lobby. People around us sniff.

"Girls," my father says, "don't slouch. Hold your heads up. Be proud. What the hell!"

That night, my father places a person-to-person call to my mother who is vacationing in the Philippines. He speaks animatedly on the phone for the allotted three minutes. "The girls send their love. Goodnight, Sweets. Or should I say good morning? You're eleven hours ahead of us." He giggles.

He is still smiling when he comes in, through the adjoining bathroom, to kiss us goodnight. Lights out at 9:00. Right on schedule.

Brian Cartwright
Apt. 314

The kettle screams. Aggie hobbles into the kitchen and unplugs it. She makes a pot of tea and puts it on the stove. Cat food, furry with mould, sits on the counter by a bowl of milk. She scoops the cat food into the trashcan. She dumps the milk into the sink. It breaks into pieces. She pushes the pieces down the drain with a fork. She refills the dish and the saucer.

"Heeeere, Kitikitikitikitiiii! Here, Whiskers! Come and get your supper. There's a good kitty. Whiskers!"

But Whiskers doesn't come. Aggie pours two cups of tea and sets them on the kitchen table. She takes a deck of bent and frayed cards from the junk drawer. It says "Ft. Lauderdale, Fla." on the backs of the cards.

"Oh dear," Aggie says looking at the two cups of tea. She takes one and empties it back into the pot and puts the cup and saucer in the sink.

She sits down at the table and takes the rubber band off the cards. She plays solitaire, loses, plays again, and loses again. The alarm clock interrupts her third game. She hits it, gets up, collects the cards, and puts them back in the junk drawer. Aggie pours herself another cup of tea, gets a package of Snowballs from the cupboard and walks into the den.

She uses a pair of pliers to turn on the TV. Whiskers lies motionless on top of the set.

"Lazy," Aggie says.

She steps out of her fuzzy pink slippers, takes the quilt from the couch, unfolds it, sinks into the armchair and puts her feet on the ottoman. She wraps herself up to the chin in the quilt leaving one arm free. On the screen, Bob Barker grins in black and white at a row of contestants. They grin back at him.

Aggie watches and eats and drinks tea. Coconut shavings from the Snowballs fall in the folds of the quilt. She hits the TV with a yardstick when the picture rolls. She waves the yardstick in the air when she disagrees with the bids. She falls asleep after the first contestants' showdown.

She wakes to the test pattern. The cat lies on the TV. Aggie heaves herself free of the chair, picks up the pliers, switches off the TV, folds the quilt and puts it back on the couch.

Aggie yawns. She walks slowly to her bedroom.

She looks in the cracked mirror and sees herself in broken diagonal pieces. She turns away, takes off her housecoat, and drops it on the chair by the bed. She sets her glasses on the night table and puts her teeth in a bowl. She wraps herself in blankets. She switches the light off and falls asleep.

Lisa Oki

Gramma

I was nine when my grandmother came to Canada from Japan. My father, mother, brother and I waited two-and-a-half hours until she came out of customs. The automatic sliding doors opened, people pushed through, and out emerged a tiny woman, less than five feet tall, dressed in a Japanese kimono and traditional wooden shoes. She saw my mother. Tears filled their eyes.

"Reiko!" she cried, and she hugged my mom for a long time. I felt embarrassed. People stared at us. She let go of my mom and then hugged my dad, and then my brother who, only four, was scared of her. She smiled when she stood before me and looked into my eyes. I was already four inches taller.

"Risachan!" she said. Gramma had not seen me since I was born. Tears welled in her eyes and she hugged me tight. I remember my amazement at such a tiny woman having such a strong hug. I felt uncomfortable. She smelled like mothballs. She was a stranger to me. As we drove home from the airport, Gramma smiled at me and tears moved down her face.

Gramma stayed two years in Toronto before she returned to Japan. Years later I learned that Gramma had had stomach cancer. Most of her stomach was removed during her stay in Canada. Nobody told me anything about it.

I feel ashamed when I think how I treated her. She always had a smile for me and never showed her pain or grief.

Gramma wore a white apron that had two giant pockets. She wore that apron every day, and everywhere. Even gardening. Children from our neighbourhood talked to her and said, "Hi." She smiled, pointed to herself and said, "Gramma." She laughed as she patted them on the heads and gave out lollipops from Laura Secord. She always saved the green ones because she knew they were my favourites.

Everyone was nice to Gramma, except me. At times I almost hated her. I felt annoyed and embarrassed by Gramma's inability to speak English.

One day, I wrapped my delicate china doll in towels and left it in my schoolbag to take for Show and Tell. I arrived at school and the doll wasn't in my bag. I cried because I was the only person with nothing to show. When I got home, my mother explained that Gramma took the doll from my bag. She was afraid that I would break it. I screamed at Gramma.

"Say sorry! Say sorry! I didn't have anything for Show and Tell and everyone laughed. Say sorry! Say you're sorry!" She did not understand.

Many years after Gramma went back to Japan, I found notebooks filled with the alphabet, some words, and small phrases. Gramma had tried to learn English. I felt shame when I saw a page filled with, "I am sorry."

Two years later, I went to Japan with my family to visit her. Gramma is seventy, but she still works four hours a day in a pachinko parlour. She cleans the game machines and empties ashtrays. She takes me to the parlour and apologizes that she has to work while I am visiting. She says it again, "I am sorry."

I sit at one of the games and watch Gramma work. Businessmen sit at the games, flipping the knobs furiously, and smoking. Gramma tries to clean out the ashtrays and the men shout in Japanese.

"Stop it old woman! Don't bother me! Stupid, go away!" Their voices are cruel and harsh.

Gramma says sweetly in English, "I am sorry." The men laugh and ask one another what she said. They decide she is crazy and take pity. They shove 100 yen coins in her hand and pat her on the arm. In English, Gramma says, "Sankyou." They all laugh again.

The joke is on them. Gramma understands every word they say. Gramma sees me laugh and comes over to me.

She says, "I love you." I smile back and say, "I love you too, Gramma." She says I make her happy. I'm glad. Gramma's eyes shine in the dim smokiness of the crowded pachinko parlour.

Gordon Scott
You Never Visit

The drapes fluttered in the breeze. The chimes tinkled. I positioned the fan so that the air hit me. I closed my eyes. The sun bore down. I heard running water. I looked into the kitchen where Mrs. Santamera cooked furiously. She bent down with effort and opened the stove. She straightened up, clutched the counter and tossed her head.

"Set the table," she said almost singing.

I went inside. Roasting pork and boiling corn produced a wave of kitchen heat. I cringed.

I went to the hutch to get the dishes. There were three sets, one gold with little bluebirds, one white, one brown with yellow trim. I settled on the brown and set the table.

We sat down to eat.

"You never call me anymore," she said.

"I call you every night."

"Humpf."

Her gnarled hands raised a cob of corn to her lips. "Ugh," she spat. She dropped the corn on her plate. She picked up her napkin and wiped the pink lipstick from her lips.

"This lipstick tastes like cherry," she said as she bit into the corn again. "They don't make them like they used to. Everything now tastes like a fruit."

"Then why buy anymore? You have enough lipsticks to last you the next eighty-four years."

"Now why would you say that? What else may I ask, do I have to spend my money on if not a few lipsticks and some shoes?" She picked up a roll. The butter melted as soon as it touched the roll. "And I'm only eighty-one."

I mopped my forehead with a sleeve.

"Why don't you come over more?"

"I was here last week."

"When I was a girl, I was never alone, you know. I was always going here and there to a party. Oh. I was such a good dancer. The boys never left me alone. I was so pretty. You never want to dance with me."

"How can I dance with you when the doctor said for you to take it easy after that last fall? Your hip is still mending."

"Doctors, doctors, what do they know? I was the most popular nurse at Riverdale. Everyone wanted me to look after them. I always looked nice for the patients."

"I know, you told me."

"Did I ever tell you about Dr. Burns? He always wanted to take me home. He knew I was a widow—that man!" She clapped her hands.

"Yes, you told me."

She raised the knife and pointed it at me.

"You know he once grabbed me in the linen closet. . . ."

"I thought it was the operating room."

"Were you there? As I said, he grabbed me, but he did not get far. I grabbed his privates and hung on. I told him that I would scream if he did not let me go." She laughed and peered at me over her glasses. "Why aren't you eating?"

"It's too hot."

"What, the food?"

"No, not the food. It's ninety outside."

"Is it really?" She looked outside. "Look, look at my chimes. They are singing to me. How nice they are."

She got up from the table, picked up the broom and swatted the chimes.

I jumped from the table and took the broom from her as the chimes fell.

"What are you doing? Why did you do that?"

"Don't shout at me! I only wanted to hear them better. Why aren't they louder?"

"Because there's no wind. Please. Sit down and rest. I'll put them back up for you."

"Okay. But put them over there." She pointed to the opposite corner. "That way I can see them from my chair." She looked expectantly at me.

I went to the far corner of the porch to hang the chimes. When I returned she had combed her hair and applied fresh lipstick. I cleared the table.

"Never mind, never mind. Come. We'll talk. Let's sit by the pool. Where's my hat? I can't go anywhere without a hat."

I went to her room and brought out a hat.

"Not that one. That's for cocktail parties. Ugh? What do you know about cocktail parties? I need the big one. The one with the orange tie. You know that the sun is not good for my complexion." She caressed her cheek.

I went into the bedroom. Everything was in place: the white rug, the pale pink comforter, the ruffled curtains, the faded picture of her late husband, framed in silver, perched on the nightstand and the Bible on the other nightstand. A doll with blonde hair and a parasol was set between the pillows. Small bud roses sat in a vase on the vanity. I rummaged in the closet and found the hat.

She was sleeping when I returned to the kitchen. My shirt stuck to my back.

"Here is your hat."

She looked at me, then at the hat. She looked up at me again.

"Why are you wet?"

"Because it's hot in here."

"Is it really?" she said rolling her tongue over the top of her lips. "Cherry," she said.

"Would you like some lemonade?" I asked her.

"That would be fine. What are you doing with my hat? Are we going out?"

"We were going to sit by the pool." I poured out the lemonade.

She curled a strand of hair around her finger.

"Is it all right if we stay in here? I like the shadows on the walls when the sun is going down."

"All right."

She looked at me. "Why don't you ever visit me anymore?"

"I see you once a week. You know how work is."

She looked out at the empty pool. "I just don't understand."

Jennifer Sealy

Martha

Martha Allswell shuffled down the hall in her worn print dress. She carried a beat-up doll in her arms. The doll's hair stuck up at odd angles. Its plastic skin looked dull grey. Martha held the doll up for kisses when anybody passed. Other residents at Simcoe Manor did not kiss the doll, but we nurses gave it a small kiss on the forehead. Martha said it was her only child.

The second Sunday of each month, a stout dark-haired man came to visit. According to the guest book, he was Mark Allswell. During his visits, Martha said nothing. The baby disappeared until he left.

Martha's husband, Bert, lived in the lower east wing. I don't know why they didn't share a room; other married couples did. Bert was confined to a wheelchair, so Martha did the visiting. Every afternoon, Martha put on a prettier dress and walked to Bert's room. Every afternoon, Bert sat in his chair in the hallway while Martha slept in his bed, her freshly cleaned dress crumpled around her.

Two times were different.

Once, I walked into Bert's room and found Martha and Bert curled up together, his arm protectively around her. I left the room feeling I had invaded their privacy.

Another time, I was in the linen room. I heard a yell. This was not unusual, but I hurried toward the sound. It came from Bert's room, but it was not Bert's yell. Martha had crawled into the wrong bed and had cuddled up to Bill Bailey. Lynn and I took Martha back upstairs to find her baby.

Martha never took the baby on her visits to Bert. He may not have known about the child. Sharon, another nurse, said, "We can't tell Bert because it may not be his child."

Martha always smiled and said "Hello" when we went by her room—except on Wednesdays, Martha's bath day, a day she hated. After her bath, Martha sat in a chair at the end of the hall. She did not smile or speak. On these days, her baby lay unattended in her room. By supper, Martha forgot about her bath; she held her baby and smiled.

Tina Reyes
William

Winter air blows into the dingy, dark, creaky-floored community hall. Spidery-haired people in black walk in and out. Tarnished silver crucifixes dangle from their ears. Handcuffs stick out of army surplus pant pockets. Some people dance and jostle each other at the back of the room; others sit and look sullen in a haze of incense, cigarette smoke and hashish.

Onstage, William staggers on gangly legs in time to thrashing drums and guitars behind him. He hangs his head low, and in a sombre, throaty growl chants about burning flesh and melting skies.

William read these lyrics to our grade-twelve English class a few days earlier. Miss Marsden told him, "You are a gifted young man. You can be quite articulate when you choose to be." William's other teachers wonder how he pulls off 80s and 90s on his exams when he often skips school and never pays attention in class. Somehow he manages to discuss advanced Physics and Chemistry with Mr. Ivanovich and make sense.

He stood in the grey and white school uniform before Miss Marsden and the English class. His bony fingers twitched around the three-hole punched sheet of notebook paper he held in front of his pale face. His voice was hoarse and he cleared his throat as he read.

Now, on the community-hall stage, he spits the words out angrily. His sweaty, half-open white shirt clings to his heaving narrow chest. He grips the microphone. His knuckles turn white. Veins stick out on his skinny arms. His eyes, outlined in black, dart around beneath a mop of matted brown hair. He flings himself down to writhe and roll in epileptic acrobatics on the stage floor. Crouching behind a monitor, he draws a green plastic water pistol from his back pocket.

"Dance!" he snarls over screeching feedback, squirting water at the audience.

William sits cross-legged among scattered records on the floor in his friend's basement. He explodes balloons left over from the party for Richard's sister, Cathy, on her sixteenth birthday.

Cathy comes downstairs. She sees William and frowns. William has slept over three nights in a row. "How long is he staying here?" she asks Richard.

"Until Mum lets me back in the house," William says. He grins and shakes a finger at Cathy. "Once again, I say to you faith means not wanting to know the truth."

Richard hits him with a throw pillow. "Die, Heretic!"

"Wasted dickheads," Cathy mutters and goes back upstairs.

Richard's friends get stoned at Cathy's house because her parents are often away on business. After one of their dope sessions, William sneaks up to Cathy's room and tells her that he's never had an erection.

"That's your problem," she says. She doesn't share the awe other girls at school feel for Richard, William, their weird philosophies and "really cool band." William laughs and stumbles down the stairs.

"Underdeveloped wanker," she smirks. "I wouldn't be surprised if he's telling the truth."

William closes his tattered army jacket around his Batman T-shirt. He breathes puffs of mist, and his pointy nose turns red in the chilly night air. His unlaced, oversized Cougar boots crunch on the thick snow as he walks home alone from midnight mass.

Chapter Five

Jobs

*Write about a job you have held.
Choose one incident, a series of
incidents, or a period of time to present
your impression of the job.*

Gordon Scott

Trust Me

Miss Stanley glared at me. "Hit another client with that brush and you are out!" I glared back and combed out Mrs. Thompson. I had hit her because she complained too much.

Miss Stanley looked the other way. I yanked Mrs. Thompson's hair.

"Ouch!"

"Oh, I'm sorry."

This was the third comb-out this afternoon. I was tired. It was three o'clock, the air conditioner was broken, and a rash was developing on my hands again.

I left Mrs. Thompson to check on Mrs. White, whose perm fermented in the back room. Mrs. White reclined in a shampoo chair, her head hanging back into the bowl of the sink. She looked up at me and asked how the perm was taking. Three rods fell into the sink with her hair still wrapped around them.

"Fine, fine. It really looks good."

I hurried to Miss Stanley, the only instructor on the floor Saturday afternoons. She had the broadest shoulders of any woman I knew. She wore one-and-a-half-inch Perma Nails and a size-thirteen shoe. Talk had it she was once a ballplayer. I believed it. I explained the problem with Mrs. White's hair. She strode to the back of the salon.

"How are we today?" she asked Mrs. White, looking at the rods in the sink.

"He is such a nice boy," Mrs. White said smiling. "So good with the hair."

Miss Stanley took me aside and told me to neutralize the perm after rinsing off the perming solution. After Mrs. White neutralized, I rinsed again running my fingers through the stubble on the back of her head. I led her back to my station after drying my hands.

"So what are you going to do today?" Mrs. White asked.

"You just trust me," I said.

I cut off very little hair from the back of her head and styled the front. I set her under the dryer. I prayed that the rollers would stay put until I combed her out.

At the back another client, Mrs. Evans, gestured wildly and pulled at her blouse.

"Look what you've done to me!" she screamed.

Everyone stared. Someone had run for Miss Stanley.

"What the hell are you doing removing the cape?" I yelled. "I told you before not to move."

Some of the bleach had run down her back. An angry welt swelled up beneath the discolouration on her blouse.

She pointed and panted at Miss Stanley, who bore down on us.

Miss Stanley took me aside after calming Mrs. Evans. I craved the valium I had rejected from another student earlier that morning.

"Are you still doing Amyl, Gord? I don't understand what is happening with you today. You are one of our best students. Are you tired?"

"I have not done Amyl since the time I streaked Wanda and her hair went blue."

"Well, just comb out Mrs. White and go home. I'll see you Monday. Don't worry about anything. I know Mrs. Evans is a bitch. I'll look after her." She patted my arm.

I took Mrs. White out from under the dryer. I unwound the rollers. There was a bald spot in the back. I had left the hair on the crown longer. I pulled the longer hair over the baldness and backcombed the shit out of it. I lacquered it. I showed her the results. "It looks great. I knew I could trust you."

Patricia Muiser

Max

I work as the assistant to Dr. Wolfgang Zenker, a brilliant veterinarian specializing in small animals and exotics at the Burloak Animal Hospital in Oakville.

Sunday, June 28, the morning after the bash at Alyson's house, I got home and went to bed at 4:30 a.m. The phone rang. I rolled over to see the time: 5:15 a.m. I put the pillow over my head. The phone still rang. I got out of bed and answered, "Yes!" It was Dr. Zenker. There was an emergency at the hospital, and he needed my help. I splashed cold water on my face and drank two glasses of apple juice.

Nobody was at the clinic when I arrived. I played with Garfield, the clinic cat. I picked up Clyde, the land tortoise that wanders around the office. I fed Riki, the African Grey parrot, his favourite—raw spaghetti. Dr. Zenker arrived with Mr. Jackson and his dog Max.

Max, a twelve-year-old black Lab, had become sick Saturday evening. Max's stomach swelled at 3:30 a.m. He started convulsing at 4:30 a.m. It was now 5:45. Dr. Zenker and I lifted Max onto the examination table. I took Mr. Jackson, who is seventy-eight years old, to the waiting room. He said he had been up with Max all night. He shook. Tears dropped on his cheeks. "I don't care what you have to do, just save Max. He's the only thing I have left in the world." I told him to relax. He did not look well.

I went to help Dr. Zenker. He did not think the dog would live. Max's abdomen continued to swell. Dr. Zenker said the pressure from the internal fluid build-up had to be released.

I gave Max 4cc of Thiopental. His body relaxed. I put the oxygen mask over his nose. I talked to Max softly as I stroked his head. Dr. Zenker put the endotracheal tube down Max's throat. Two minutes later, Max breathed steadily, and we carried him into surgery. I shaved a square on Max's abdomen. I scrubbed it, alcoholed it, and iodined it. He was ready.

Dr. Zenker made a five-inch incision with his scalpel. Blood poured out of Max. Blood flowed over the table and poured onto the floor. Blood splashed on my legs and shoes. I didn't care. Gloves on, I pulled out some of Max's intestines.

"This much blood, must be the spleen," Dr. Zenker said. He reached in the incision with two fingers and pulled the spleen into view. "Just as I suspected. This dog has hemangrosarcoma." He handed me the spleen. "This tumour has eaten through the wall of the spleen, and blood drains through the hole into the abdomen. Take your gloves off and come with me."

I followed Dr. Zenker into the waiting room. He told Mr. Jackson that there was no hope for Max and that Max should be put to sleep now. Mr. Jackson cried. He held his head in his hands. "Thank you doctor. Please put him out of his misery."

I pulled 6cc of Euthanol into a syringe. Dr. Zenker gave Max the injection in his kidney. That's the fastest way. Max was dead.

I disconnected Max from the anaesthetic respirator. I went and got a large body bag. I put the body in the cooler where it would stay until the crematorium picked it up on Monday.

I washed my hands. I said goodbye to Garfield, Clyde and Riki. I went home and crawled into bed. It was 9:40 a.m. My last thought was to call Mr. Jackson on Monday and tell him about a Labrador breeder I knew.

Nic Disanto

Kodaklone

May 1985: "Kodak plant is hiring." I apply. One week later, the interview goes well. I take a physical: rubber gloves, coughing, blood tests and urine samples. I hate physicals.

May 30: second interview. "You have passed the physical. Your starting wage is $10.02 an hour. You are stationed in 'Emulsion.' Can you start Monday?"

Monday morning, June 3. I'm in the foreman's office at the world's largest film company. The office is small with thin, dull grey, portable walls.

"You'll be working in Dispersion until I get you a title job," says Ray, my foreman.

We walk through the cafeteria to get to the laundry room. The "cafe" is painted blue on three walls. The south wall is all windows. The employees in the cafe look alike. They have blank looks. They read the *Toronto Sun*. Ivan is the laundry man.

"Hello, Chief-ee! You need uniform? I fix you. What are you? Terty-two waist? I fix you."

Outfitted in Kodak whites, I join the Kodaklones. Twenty of us walk into the west elevator. The elevator has one dim green pan-light on the ceiling. All I see is the dim green square of light.

"Don't worry about the dark," says Ray. "By the time we reach the seventh floor you will have gotten your eyes."

The doors open on the north and south side of every floor. Some floors have only dim pan-lights. The sixth floor is not lit. The doors open. I lean into the darkness. I feel cold air. I can't see anything.

"Don't worry," says Ray. "You won't be working on that floor for a while. That's cold storage."

"People actually work in that? How can you work without any lights?" Two white figures appear in the doorway. The buzzer sounds. The door closes.

"It's easy," says one of the white figures, "just a matter of getting your eyes."

Dispersion, on the seventh floor, uses a chemical gel that comes in forty pound bags, six in a box. I file each bag on number-coded carts. An hour passes. Ray comes to see how I'm doing.

"What the hell are you doing?"

"What's wrong, Ray?"

"Take it easy. Break's coming and you're almost finished."

After break—10:30 a.m.—I work with full-timer Ricky Banz. "I've been working here for five years, Nic. I know everything about this place," says Ricky. "You've done more here in dispersion in a couple of hours than anyone else has done in a couple of days. Come on, I'll show you around. We'll go to cold storage. Full-timers call it the Kodak Hotel. I'll show you where the sleeping bags are. No one can see you down there, and if they need you, they'll page you. We can probably catch an hour nap before lunch."

For the next three months, I'll walk around in cold, dark hallways. I'll take a nap when I have nothing to do. I'll work slowly. I might even read the *Sun*. I'll make a lot of money. I'm going to be a Kodaklone.

Charles Helawa

The Job

Like many students in college, I was poor. Beer, Big Macs, and gas put holes in my pockets. To support my habits I worked in a detention home on weekends. Each twenty-four-hour shift earned me a hundred and fifty dollars.

The house on Burton Avenue sat between a Shell Station and Toni's Shoe Shop. There were no locks on the doors. This was not a prison but a holding place for kids ten to sixteen awaiting trial. They knew stepping out for a quick fag or other small deeds meant an early bedtime. They rarely caused problems. They didn't want to miss Starsky and Hutch.

Smelly walls, damp air, filthy floors, a bathtub grey from too many baths and not enough Comet, a seatless toilet surrounded by a large, sticky puddle were the special touches in our sleazy home.

I met Howard and Al on Friday night. Their wrists were red from handcuffs. Howard had done in his old lady's head with a baseball bat. Al was tamer. He looked innocent with his thick glasses and long bangs. He had thrown a brick through a store window and cleaned the tobacco shelf. Both boys were fifteen. They smiled a lot and used their middle fingers on me. The copper told them to wrap it up or else the even dingier cells downtown would be their home for the night.

I told them to hit the showers. I looked in the closet for clean sheets and found one gamy sweat sock.

I sent both boys to their temporary bedrooms. Howard took the small room beside the chimney. Al went to the big double room with the single three-legged bed.

The cop downstairs drifted into the office. His radio crackled about some 10-29. I offered a coffee, sat behind the desk and tried to look serious. I could tell by his noisy radio he had little time. The city was jammed with homicides, accidents, break and entries, and rapes. He took his notebook from his pocket, handed me papers to sign, then left. His coffee sat on the table, full.

After the hasty departure of my guest, I called it a night. I went upstairs. The hall was bleak and cold. My only comfort was a sleeping bag smelling faintly of perfume worn by the woman who worked there weekdays. I woke up cold and decided to get a blanket from the closet in Al's room. In keeping with the rest of that dump, the lights didn't work. I sensed something wrong. The window open, the bed unslept-in, Al's room was empty. I went downstairs and called the coppers.

I knew I had slept my last for that night. I sat and waited for my guest to return. Twenty minutes later two cops pulled into the driveway in an unmarked car. A third person sat in the back seat crying—Al.

The cops brought him inside. His glasses were missing. He wore a T-shirt and a pair of jeans. He had left his shoes behind when he went out the window. His face was white and his feet were blue. I handed him a blanket.

I knew better than to offer the cops a coffee. The last rejected cup sat on the desk. Their radios beckoned.

I sent Al back to his room without his clothes. If he tried to escape again, more than his feet would be blue. I shut the window and stood over his bed and watched him cry. He was practically blind without his glasses. He lost them running from the cops. I gave him a pair of my socks to warm his feet.

Al told me he was trying to escape his court date. He knew he would be sent back to training school. He had been there once and found it rough. The pals were huge and mean, and they beat him up every day. Al sat with me in the morning. He talked about how his father, a known screwball, took a belt to him almost every day. His mom was spending two years up the creek for assaulting a cop.

Al went to court on Monday. He was ordered to spend the next two years in a training school. I said goodbye and wished him well.

Brad Littleproud
The Jungle Line

Last summer, I was a student worker in the Oshawa G.M. plant. I worked on the Jungle Line. Every morning at 6:40, I arrived at the front lobby of "B body."

After I showed my identity card to the security guard, I walked down the factory aisles to section twenty-three. Cutting across lines, squeezing around cars and ducking overhanging frames, I came to column "O." This was my spot. There I put in ear plugs, put on gloves and an asbestos apron, and cleaned my safety glasses.

Our line was five hundred feet long. Our job was to weld car bodies so that they held together until they reached the arc welders. Around me, spot welders suspended on pulleys hung every six feet. The connected hydraulic hoses and electrical cables swayed from overhead troughs blocking our view of the lines around us. Fluorescent lights twenty feet above provided little light. Portable fans gave the only circulation in the factory's ninety degree heat.

At 7:00, the whistle blew, and the line started. I was on one side. My partner, Ron, was on the other. When a car reached us, I secured the sides with a cross-bar, spot-welded the side to the floor pan, then waited for the next. We had forty-five seconds before another car came along. At first, I needed the full forty-five seconds. By the end of six weeks, I needed only fifteen. A real professional, I had time to sit between jobs, read the *Toronto Sun* or just look at pictures of the Sunshine Girls taped to the support posts.

After a half hour, we switched sides. Now I put in a crossbar, ran to the front, welded the side, then ran to the back. Climbing into the trunk, I put in the speaker tray and a bar across the roof. Here I learned to be careful.

On my second day, I leaned against the bottom lip of the trunk as the line started up after repairs. Ron pointed to my leg. The metal had cut through the apron into me. I was taken to Oshawa General and given three stitches. I was back on the line in an hour.

The first five hours were the hardest. After a half hour, my shirt dripped with perspiration. When I looked down the line, I saw no end to the cars. Nothing changed. My actions became automatic. I didn't have to think. I daydreamed and became frustrated. Twelve dollars an hour kept me from quitting.

11:55. The lunch whistle blew. We had half an hour. Our crew went for six or seven beers at the Villa, a strip joint across the street. We returned mildly drunk before the line started again. After lunch, the car floors were littered with beer and liquor bottles, tea bags, sandwich wrappers and marijuana roaches. The air reeked of pot. White smoke rose from the change areas. Ron burned tea bags with his spot-welder. It smelled suspicious. Marc Diamond, our foreman, ran up and down the line trying to find the offenders.

From 1:00 on, the radios were tuned to Q107. We danced in the cars, played pieces of metal like instruments and sang crude versions of "Modern Love" and "Our House." Broom handles became microphones. Those on ten-minute breaks had water fights. People still working were targets. The G.M. tours avoided our area around this time.

When the 3:26 whistle blew, all activity stopped. No one sang. No water flew. We removed our glasses, took out our plugs, took off our gloves and threw our aprons into a laundry bin. In ten minutes, the plant was clear.

Sybil C. Horton
The First Day

We kneel for the Director of Nursing to pin on our newly-earned caps. We light our Florence Nightingale lamps, and recite. The candle light flickers as we "... pledge ourselves before God and in the presence of this assembly...."

In 1948, nursing is a prestigious profession for a woman. Fifty take the preliminary training; forty are capped. It is a gruelling six months. We are relieved we have made it this far.

We feel privileged to wear the student uniform of Saskatoon City Hospital, a pink dress covered by a starched apron and bib. The collar, cuffs and cap are starched as stiff as cardboard. Our goal is to earn the graduate black band for our caps. Our parents observe from the audience, our instructors from the stage. We have tea with them and return to the residence. The ceremony is a powerful initiation.

Our new uniforms and the ceremony increase our excitement about our first full day on the wards. Our training so far has been mainly in the classroom. My new cap bobs around because I have not yet mastered anchoring it. I am conscious of the swish of my starched uniform.

Miss Reesor on male surgery is my supervisor. She is kind but tough. I like and admire her. She was one of the top graduates in our school two years ago and now is assistant head nurse on the largest ward. She looks the ideal nurse from her immaculate white oxfords to the hairnet confining her golden curls. Her cap with the black band is firmly anchored.

She does break one nursing rule: the prohibition against the wearing of jewelry. She wears her diamond engagement ring. Her blue eyes dance as she speaks of her coming marriage to her childhood sweetheart. He is establishing a business in their home town. Once married, she will leave nursing and the city to become a traditional rural housewife.

The morning goes quickly. I am getting used to being called "nurse." After lunch, a burn patient is sent directly to our ward because Emergency is full. The ambulance attendants lift him gingerly. They tell me he tried to put out a fire in his gas station and was burned in the explosion. The city ambulance took an hour over bad roads to get him and another hour to get him to us. He has had no sedation or treatment.

Dr. Skelly is in charge. Miss Reesor hands me a blood pressure cuff and tells me to take vitals. I have done vitals only on fellow students.

The orderlies cut the remaining clothes off the young man. He is heavily muscled but looks helpless laid out on the bed. I have never seen a naked adult male before. I am appalled by his burns. Only his face and right arm are untouched. He fixes his blue eyes on me and struggles to speak. I lean closer, but he cannot form words.

"Vitals!" Dr. Skelly shouts. I call back numbers. The blue eyes again signal and again the patient cannot speak. "Pay attention to the vitals." Miss Reesor's voice is harsh.

A third time, the beseeching blue eyes distract me, so I stroke his face. I sense Miss Reesor's disapproval and withdraw my hand. This is not like the movies. There are no violins. There is controlled and noisy confusion as the patient is prepared for the OR.

The IV is established and Miss Reesor injects morphine into the tubing. She moves calmly and efficiently, anticipating needs and following orders. I marvel at her. "Vitals!" the doctor demands. I have problems. The pulse seems irregular and hard to count. The blood pressure is hard to hear. I feel I don't know what I am doing. I fudge some numbers and keep trying. The activity in the room is frantic.

"Vitals!" the doctor yells over the din.

"I'm sorry sir, I can't get them." I wait to be reprimanded. Dr. Skelly's eyes meet mine.

"Try once more, nurse." His tone is gentle.

I cannot get any count. I hear my voice, high, crackling, childlike. "I'm sorry sir, I can't get any count."

Everyone looks at me. All activity stops. The room is silent. The patient's blue eyes are still turned to me.

Dr. Skelly says, "Nothing could save him. Those are bad burns." I have never seen a dead person before.

He asks for the chart to inform the next of kin. His shoulders droop in defeat. Miss Reesor's voice is calm. "We don't have a chart yet. We don't know who he is."

For the first time, they look at the patient's face. Miss Reesor utters a low animal cry. She whispers, "It's Paul, my fiancé."

I am closest to her but stand paralyzed with horror. Dr. Skelly catches her crumbling body. He eases her into one of the old wooden wheelchairs and takes her from the ward, never to return.

I am left standing alone. The next shift reports for duty. My work is done. My legs carry me down the stairs, out into the sunshine, toward the residence.

The class motor-mouth catches up to me. "I had a great day. Did you?"

"Yeah."

"Want to go to first dinner?"

"No thanks, I'm going to second with Iris."

Her mouth motors on and I nod. At last, I reach my room. I place my one-day-old cap beside my Nightingale lamp. I fold my uniform carefully on the chair and ease into bed. My first day as a student nurse is over. I cry myself to sleep.

Pat Haramis

Jackson's Shell

"I don't know anything about cars Mr. Jackson, but I'm a hard worker."

"That's okay, Pat," he said. "I just need someone who is honest. You start tomorrow."

The alarm startled me. Six o'clock came fast. I pulled on my jeans and an old flannel shirt. I skipped breakfast. Mom made me a huge lunch.

The bells rang as my bike hit the black cord on the driveway of Jackson's Shell. The noise startled the attendant. He was inside—half asleep.

"Hi, I'm the new guy."

"You're late," he said. "Gus called. The asshole says he's sick. The son-of-a-bitch is probably going to the beach. You're on your own pal. Good luck. Saturday is a bastard."

He left. The bell sounded. My first car: a taxicab, a Pontiac Parisienne. I felt confident. My dad drove a Parisienne.

"Hi, what can I do for you?"

"Fill'er up—regular."

I put the nozzle into the gas tank at the rear of the car. The driver came out to talk. I put the nozzle on automatic.

"Looks like it's going to be another hot one, eh son?"

I placed my foot on his bumper.

"Yes, sir, I heard ninety degrees on the news."

My foot slipped and knocked the nozzle out of the tank. I rushed to grab it. Gas sprayed everywhere. I jumped on the nozzle and turned it off. The cabby's pants were soaked and he was furious. He jumped in his car and drove off. I paid for the gas.

The rest of the morning was free of problems but busy. At one o'clock there were no customers. I sat down for lunch. The bell sounded. I shouldn't have skipped breakfast. My stomach ached.

An elderly woman drove up to the unleaded pump and rolled down her window. "Check the oil please, but be careful, the engine's hot."

"Thanks," I said. I couldn't open her hood. She shouted out the window, "The latch is on the left under the grill!" I found it. I propped open the hood and searched for the dipstick. She pointed to the spot.

"Thanks again," I muttered. She needed a quart. I grabbed 10W30 and jammed the nozzle through the tin top. I held the can and poured the oil. Someone tooted. I looked up. My brother drove by waving. I waved back. The quart can slipped off the nozzle. Oil burned on the hot engine. The woman screamed, "What are you doing?"

"I'm sorry!", I shouted back, "I just spilled a bit." She wasn't visible through the smoke. I closed the hood. She paid and squealed away.

I filled cars, washed windshields, checked oil, collected money and hoped for a quiet spell. Quiet came at 3:00. I ran inside and grabbed a coke. I opened it. The bells rang. I slammed the coke on a shelf.

An old Buick Le Sabre pulled up to the garage doors. Smoke poured from under the hood. A small, greasy man jumped out.

"Thank God," he said. "I saw your sign, 24 Hour Mechanic. You don't see that much on Saturdays."

"I'm sorry, but I just pump gas," I said. "The mechanic called in sick."

"Shit-a-damn," he said. "Well I'm gonna need some water in the rad. Let it cool first or you'll crack the block."

I pretended to understand. "Yes sir, I'll get the water." I filled a pail with water and grabbed a long, plastic funnel. The funnel fit deep into the radiator. I waited. The man waited in his car. "It's been ten minutes," I said. "That should be long enough, eh?" He nodded.

I poured water into the plastic funnel. The water boiled before it reached the top. I took the funnel out of the rad. The bottom half was gone, melted inside the rad. I slammed the hood and shouted, "There ya go sir—no charge!" I threw the top half of the funnel in the garbage.

My replacement arrived at 6:30 pm. I quit at 6:31. I ate lunch on the way home.

Heather Mathys
The End Of The Road

It is a little past 11:00 on a hot July morning. I slide back the door of the dishwasher and steam rises into my face. I lift out the hot, wet dishes with a clean cloth.

Mrs. Rogers is strict about dirt. She warns me about bacteria. I have to keep myself clean so I won't contaminate anything. Mrs. Rogers told me the Health Inspector comes in and does a bacterial count twice a month. If the count is too high, the snack bar has to be closed. Such a thing has never happened in the thirty years she's been in business. I must always wear a clean uniform and apron and wash my hands before handling food or dishes. I must never touch my hair. There are rules for everything. They give me a headache.

Outside, I hear a car drive by. Through the screened window, I watch a shiny red convertible head down the gravel road. The car catches the sunlight. A teenager drives and the radio blares "Mother's Little Helper" by the Rolling Stones. It is 1966 and there are lots of good songs on the charts this summer. None of them, however, make me feel any better about this job, or myself, or being here. I fight tears. I feel helpless as a child many times. Isn't life ever going to get any easier?

Through the kitchen opening, I see two children and a woman waiting at the counter. My co-worker, Judy, is nowhere in sight. Mrs. Rogers insists customers come first, but Mrs. Rogers ordered me to get the dishes finished. Should I go and serve the customers? I never know what's right. Everything I do angers or disgusts Mrs. Rogers. This is my first job, a summer job. I am forty miles from Toronto, near a small town called Aurora. I live with the other snack bar girls in a sort of dorm just up the road. I am fifteen. All the other girls are older. They think I am stupid and laugh at me behind my back.

The snack bar is surrounded by acres of park and cottage territory. Mrs. Rogers and her husband own the building and the land. They rent out cottages and campsites. The snack bar is called "Vera's & Al's," the Rogers' first names. There is a beautiful beach close to Vera's & Al's. Someone named it Elm Beach. There are no elms near it. I have not seen an elm tree all summer.

My parents brought me to Elm Beach when I was small. To get to it, you have to walk down a steep stone stairway. I once burned the soles of my feet on the steps because I couldn't be bothered wearing shoes.

Vera's & Al's is one large room, divided into two parts: a dining room and a dance hall. A thick gold cord separates the diners from the dancers. Along one side of the dining room is the take-out counter where I work. A large, dirty fan whirls in a corner. In the dining room, people sit and stare out the window overlooking Elm Beach. They munch ice cream cones and hamburgers. The dance floor is shiny. Mrs. Rogers polishes it on her hands and knees every Sunday. A jukebox stands in the corner. There is a small stage on the other side of the room. Older people come here every Friday night to dance. Local bands play bad music.

All sorts of people come into Vera's & Al's. The hoody guys have long, dirty hair. In this hot weather, they wear leather jackets and black boots. They order "Swamp Water," a mixture of Coke, orange pop, ginger ale and 7-Up. Whenever I mix this drink for them, I feel their eyes on my back. Most of my customers are cottagers or people just up for a day of swimming, and they usually wear bathing suits when they come in. It was funny at first, serving half-naked people all the time, but I'm getting used to it.

Mrs. Rogers has a big, awkward body. She lurches forward when she walks as though a heavy wind pushes her from the back. She wears cotton ankle socks, oxfords and full, swirly skirts. Her calves bulge. Her hair is brown-grey, and when she walks her funny walk, the hair flies out on both sides of her head. She has buck teeth. Her loud voice sounds used to giving orders.

A crabby old lady, Lettie, does the short-order cooking. Lettie shoos me away. "My word, girl, you're one of the slowest I've ever seen. Go on out of here; you're no use to me in the kitchen."

I make terrible sundaes. Ice cream slops over the edge, and topping drizzles down the sides. People look as though they want to laugh, and they use lots of napkins. I drop hot dogs on the floor. My aprons stay soiled no matter how hard I scrub them. My long hair falls out of the bun.

I shut the dishwasher door and walk out to the counter. Judy is still not around. I reach into the glass cabinet to get a Malted Milk bar for a bratty-looking boy when I look up to see Mrs. Rogers stride towards me. Her glasses slide down her nose and her hair is wilder than ever. She shouts, "You come into the kitchen with me right now. Judy will look after these people."

I leave customers gaping at me as I follow Mrs. Rogers into the kitchen. She holds a piece of paper in her hand. She turns on me, shaking the paper under my nose. "This is a notice from the Health Inspector's office!" Trembling, I look more closely. There are numbers on it in the hundreds of thousands. "Those are the bacterial count figures for the first half of July. And look here!" Her finger stabs the page.

UNSATISFACTORY—

EXCEEDS ACCEPTABLE LEVELS

I look away. "I warned you about this! Never in all my years of running this place have I had a girl like you working for me!"

"I'm sorry," I whisper. My voice shakes. My mouth has gone dry. I feel like throwing myself at her feet, begging forgiveness.

"Sorry isn't going to help much, is it? You're finished here. Go to the house and get your things packed. I'll call your parents."

I turn and walk on shaky legs out of Vera's & Al's. I smell the wetness of beach sand in the warm air. I trudge up the road to the house. It is hard to breathe. I sweat. With trembling fingers, I free my hair from the bun. It must be getting close to noon. At the house, the girls on the 1-to-10 shift are probably getting ready. I will be facing them soon. I shut my eyes and pray this road goes on forever.

Marilyn Major

Room 601

Vacation was over. I pushed open the swinging doors to 6 west. A cabinet bulged with supplies outside of Room 601. There was a green sign: "Reverse isolation, burn case."

I was not surprised to see 601 printed beside my name. The undesirables were usually assigned to those returning from holidays, a nursing tradition. Dorothy, the night nurse, breezed around the corner. "It's an electrocution," she said.

I pulled Brian's chart from its slot and flipped to the blue pages. The intern's history wasn't as dramatic as the newspaper story. A twenty-one-year-old white male had driven his tractor over a fallen power line and had remained in a state of electrocution for six hours. He was now at the Misericordia Hospital emergency room. I reviewed the inventory of his injuries. I wondered what lay inside 601.

Only my eyes were visible when I entered his room. A paper mask concealed my expression. A cap hid my hair. The bed loomed at the end of the vestibule. The curtains were drawn. I pulled on the green surgical gown that hung on a hook by the door. A portable heater hummed as it worked to keep the room at ninety. "How are you today?" I said in my cheery nurse voice. The head turned toward me.

Brian's lack of hands was particularly noticeable at meal times. I thought of a sphinx as he chewed without expression. He seemed distant. I suspected he thought about his life: whether he wanted to live or not.

Phil Donahue wove his way through the studio audience on the TV as I exchanged Brian's old dressings for new ones. The bandages were like a suspense novel: the last chapter revealed all. Two hours later, the tale was told. I was exhausted.

My pep talk was well-rehearsed after seven days: "Wounds are healing nicely . . . you were lucky to survive . . . the rehab people work wonders." Testimonials about previous patients' successes were also part of my repertoire. Brian listened quietly to these offerings. Sometimes I wondered whether I was trying to convince Brian or myself. Brian dubbed himself the "Crispy Critter."

His care rotated among the 6 west nursing staff. Three months later he left for the Glenrose Rehabilitation Hospital. Eight of us watched the Smith's Ambulance drivers take him away on a stretcher.

The winter was mild that year. Many patients had come and gone from 601. One day, I removed Mrs. Lamont's thermometer from her mouth. "Thirty-seven five," I said before she could ask. "Pulse is fine, too." I jotted down her readings. It was two o'clock in the afternoon. I went to the desk to complete my charting.

Brian had been waiting. He looked different. He was dressed in jeans and a western jacket. He smiled. I knew he was there to thank me. He told me about his fiancée and his new job counselling amputees. He showed me his "bionic hands."

When he left, I stood and watched him walk down the long corridor.

Ann Porter

The Lawn Shop

The Lawn Shop operates out of a hundred-year-old house in a subdivision of new upper-middle-class suburban homes. Zumba, the puppy, runs out to meet me. The street is peaceful. As I walk closer to the house, I see the four white Lawn Shop trucks parked in the driveway.

After six hours sleep, I am back at work for another fourteen-hour day. It is 8:00. The phones ring, the kids scream, and Frieda, Zumba's mother, howls.

There is a porch off to one side of the house where the supplies, Diazanon and 2,4-D are stored. Eight teenage lawn sprayers wait to receive their routes for the day. Ken, the owner and boss, has gone out for breakfast. The boys grumble. "How come he makes us come so early when he's never ready?"

I go into the office. Hans, the three-year-old, hides under my desk. He wears no pants today. I hand him over to his mother and close the office door.

Now is the high point of the weed spraying season. There should be at least three full-time people working in the office. Instead there's just me, and the boss's wife, Margot. It is a full-time job for Margot to keep Hans and his two-year-old brother, Derek, entertained and away so I can work. She has little time to help in the office.

I have no official title. I am the Girl In The Office. I was hired to fill the office manager's job for two weeks while he was on vacation. He never came back. I am cheaper than he was. I am receptionist, typist, filing clerk, accounts receivable and payroll clerk. I am also the chauffeur and babysitter.

By 10:00, the kids are dressed and have finished breakfast. Margot takes them to the park. The phone has rung continuously since I got in. Now is my chance to get some work done.

Phones on hold.

Pink, yellow, blue. Pink, yellow, blue. The sorting is two days behind. The filing is four days behind. Without help I can accomplish the bare minimum of what has to be done.

Phones on again.

"Two days ago, I called, and you promised someone would be here yesterday. If no one comes today, I'm cancelling." I don't know why Ken wasted his money on the RUSH stamp. He never pays any attention to it.

Margot and the kids come back for lunch. Frieda is in heat. The beige poodle was after her in the park. Last time he got her, and Zumba was born. That poodle is not afraid to come in the house. I put Frieda in the office.

It's naptime. Finally Margot comes in and helps. She takes over the phones to deal with complaints. After an hour she can't take it anymore.

Phones on hold.

Margot spends the rest of nap time painting the bathroom. She has covered the bathroom tiles with aluminum foil. The toilet seat has zebra stripes. She paints Jamaicans and grass huts on the walls. A leopard-spotted floor is to follow.

After dinner, the children are not allowed outside. It is playtime in the office. They climb on an overstuffed armchair and jump off. When they fight over who jumps the highest, playtime is over. Over their objections, I lock them out of the office. Telephone soliciting fills the rest of the evening.

By 10:00, the kids are asleep and the house is quiet. Margot and I wait for the last trucks to return. At twenty after ten, I walk home through well-lit deserted suburban streets past houses with two-car garages and sprinklers sending fine spray over trim lawns.

Two months pass, and the office works differently. I have changed the system for handling orders, reorganized the files and replaced the accounting system. Customers don't complain anymore. The office works more like an office should.

One day, John, a seventeen-year-old driver for the Lawn Shop, comes to talk to me. "Ann," he says, "I can't figure my pay out, but I think that guy's ripping me off." John doesn't know tax law. John doesn't know labour law. I don't know either, but I do know where to call and find out.

"Ken," I say, "if I follow this formula you've given me, some of these kids aren't paid enough. And, you know, the law requires us to pay vacation pay." Ken says nothing. He does nothing.

I tell the workers they are not being properly paid. Things become uncomfortable. I decide to leave.

A few days after quitting, I stop by the office to ask Margot—we are friends—to join me for lunch. Julie, a young high school student I hired to help me in the office, does my old job. "Make sure he pays you what he owes you and watch the vacation pay," I say.

Margot and I leave for The Green Rooster restaurant two blocks away. In the middle of lunch, Ken comes—we have not invited him—and sits with us at our table on the patio.

Margot gets up to go to the washroom. Ken shifts in his seat.

"Ann," he says, "I don't ever want to see your face in that office again."

Margot returns and sits down. Ken says, "I've got to go now" and leaves.

Margot and I talk about the kids and the dogs as though nothing has happened. I wonder if she knows.

Bruce G. Tavender

The Arrest

I was in my favourite spot. The customers in the tape cassette aisle couldn't see me, but I could see them. Anyone under twenty years old was a suspect.

The unshaven one looked guilty. He wore a large black coat with big pockets. Big pockets and small cassettes went together. He held two tapes in his hand while he flipped through the others. He looked up and down the aisle. He continued flipping. This meant one of two things. Either he was looking for someone or he was checking to see if anyone was watching him. I suspected the latter.

He was on the move now. I nudged a customer and knocked over a display trying to keep up with him. He entered the stationery aisle. I followed behind him. He jumped when I entered the aisle. I walked up beside him, grabbed a pen off the shelf and left the aisle. I was careful not to look at him. I doubt he even noticed me. I did not look like a floorwalker.

I was sure he was going to lift the tapes. I gave him room but I followed him—far enough not to scare him, close enough to see his every move.

He headed toward the back of the store. I followed. He turned down the back aisle. I stuck my head around the corner just far enough for one eye to see him. In one motion, he cupped the tapes, opened his coat pocket and slipped them in. His eyes gave him away. They darted side to side as he moved to the front doors of the store. He looked guilty now.

He pounded through the front doors and headed in the direction of a red Volkswagen. I caught up with him. I touched him on his left shoulder.

"Towers security. You're under arrest," I said.

He panicked. He tried to run. I clutched his coat. He slipped out of it. I clutched his shirt. He slugged me. My glasses fell off my face. I fell to the ground. I couldn't catch him now. I couldn't even see him.

I picked up the coat he left behind. I pulled out of the pocket the two tapes, a package of Players' Light and a set of keys. The keys fit the red Volkswagen. I picked up my glasses and put them on. They sat crooked on my nose. One lens was broken. The other was cracked.

I phoned the police from the telephone booth in the parking lot. I told them they could find me by a red Volkswagen in the parking lot.

I returned to the Volkswagen and got inside. I opened the glove compartment and pulled out the insurance and ownership cards. I wrote down his name and address, turned on the stereo, leaned back and waited for the police.

Chapter Six

Women and Men

Write a piece about something you have observed or experienced involving relations between women and men. Use particular incidents to make your points.

Fook Ho

The Decision

I sensed the severity of the occasion when I came into the room. Father sat at the end of the big, ugly, black camphor-wood table. Mother and my two uncles sat on either side of him.

Uncle Tan and Uncle Bing, two village elders, were present on every occasion when important decisions were made. They were the most educated persons around. Uncle Tan, for example, had been to Canton, the nearest city. He stayed there for two years learning to be a teacher. He became the teacher of the only primary school in our village. He was the only one in our village who had ever met a foreigner. We respected his knowledge of the outside world.

I was twelve years old. Since I was asked to present myself at the family meeting, the decision must be about me. I was right: the meeting was to decide my future after I graduated from primary six.

In our family (and in most Chinese families then), everybody's business was a family business, and everybody had defined roles in the family. By tradition, as the second son of the family, I was supposed to enter the world outside our village and receive as much education as my family could afford. My elder brother, the first-born, was supposed to stay at home to take care of the family properties. As the third son, my younger brother was to be his deputy. Female members had no say in the family business. They were expected to marry and have babies, preferably male babies.

In the decision concerning my future, this tradition was challenged. My elder sister and I attended the same primary class. She was in every way more intelligent and more accomplished than I. She topped the class in every subject. Uncle Tan praised her as the best student he had ever taught. I barely passed most of my courses and sometimes failed one or two. I never reached the upper half of the class in overall academic standing.

Sister Ling was better equipped than I was to go outside the village and enter the Canton City High School. As a female member of the family, she was not supposed to receive that much education. She must stay at home. Uncle Tan objected strongly to this and argued with my father. Matters would have been less complicated if father could have afforded to send both of us. We were not that well-off. One of us had to stay.

After much discussion, my father made his decision. I was to go because I was a son. I do not remember the details of the argument. At the time, I was too young to make out who was right and who was wrong.

I do remember Mother weeping after my father made the decision.

Ingrid Babjak
The Dump

I lie on his bed. He looks at my chest and says, "Hey, not as small as I thought."

I blush, look away from his gaze and say, "Thanks."

"Hey, hear the one about the guy with the five dicks? Ya, well his underwear fit like a glove." He laughs and rolls on the bed. "Don't you get it?"

He reaches for my pants. I grab his hand. "John, don't even bother trying."

He looks at me and says, "Don't be a baby. You're seventeen, and we've been going out for seven months now. What the heck am I going to tell my friends?"

"Tell your friends?" I bolt up from the bed. "You talk to your friends about us? What do you do, make bets on when and where?"

He looks down at my feet. "The red nail polish is chipped on your baby toe."

I turn away. He puts a cigarette into his mouth and lights it. The cigarette reminds me of a pacifier. He is two years older than I am, but he is still a baby.

I put my blouse on. My back is turned to him, but I see him watching me in his dresser mirror.

"What are you doing? Don't go yet. Don't be angry. I'm sorry. It's just that Bob and Mary got it together after going out for only two months. Pete and Susie made it two weeks ago. Bob and Pete keep asking me questions about us, and I am embarrassed to report nothing."

"I know what you can tell them." I look at him in the dresser mirror.

"What?"

I comb my hair, put on lip gloss, and turn to face him. I look at his blue eyes and dark lashes, at the sprinkles of freckles on his nose. "Tell them we aren't going out anymore."

"That's no good. Let me tell them that we made it. We don't have to, but I'll just say we did."

I look at his mass of curly blond hair and his beautiful six-foot frame. I think, "You had to pick this guy. Colin, the average-looking, intelligent science student wasn't sexy enough. You went for John the Jock. An air-head. A space cadet. A doorknob. A gorgeous doorknob, but nevertheless, a doorknob."

I sit on the edge of his bed and talk to the solitary hair on his chest. "John, listen to me. We had some good times. The day we went to Ontario Place and rented the paddle boat was great." He grins and shakes his blond curls up and down like Big Bird. "Remember when you pushed me off the paddle boat and I fell on the duck?"

"I thought that duck was going to kill you," he says, clutching his stomach. "It was swimmin' and flippin' and honkin' at you. You were drenched and people were laughin'. That was good." He claps his hands.

"We did have good times, John, but I think it wouldn't be such a bad idea if we saw other people. Look, we're young, but not for long. Let's enjoy it. Let's go out and meet new people."

"You human bullshitter," I think to myself.

He gets off the bed and gently holds me by the shoulders. "Ingrid, are you trying to dump me?"

The next moment catches me by surprise. John the Jock cries. I have mixed emotions. On the one hand, I want to put my arms around him. On the other hand, I feel ashamed of my disgust with him. So a guy cries. I've cried in front of people before. Give Johnny a chance to cry too. I can't. I just can't face him. It's the old double standard. A man can't cry. I like my men tough, shockproof, and macho. I look at John sitting on the bed and dabbing his eyes with a Kleenex.

I kiss him on the forehead and say, "I'm going now. I'm sorry."

"What am I going to tell Bob and Pete?"

I turn towards the door. "Tell Bob and Pete you dumped me." He seems to smile.

I walk home alone with my purse flung over one shoulder. I dumped John the Jock.

Neveen Howard

Crilly

I went out with my first real boyfriend for a month. I had just turned sixteen when I met Andrew Crilly.

One night, I sat listening to Supertramp with Sally Gordon, my best friend, in her living room. Paul, Sally's boyfriend, called. He said he would come over around 8:30 and we'd all go out for pizza. A friend of his called Crilly wanted to meet me.

Sally and I had our coats on at 8:30. They came. They stood outside the door.

"This is Crilly," Paul said.

"Hi," Crilly said. He bent down and combed his hair in the glass of the door window. He had hair down to his shoulders and he wore a leather jacket. My mother will hate him, I thought.

Two friends of Crilly's waited in a truck on the other side of the road. Crilly parked his car in the driveway. We went to the Harbour Castle in Bronte. The guys decided to order beer. The waitress asked for identification. No one got served. The two guys from the truck left. They blamed Sally and me. We looked too young.

"I'm gonna kill those guys," Crilly said when we got in the car. Paul told him not to bother.

"No, I'm gonna kill them," he said. He drove the car over a curb and scraped the bottom.

"Bad shocks," he said and grinned. I laughed.

A week later I saw a slip of paper with my name and number on it in the back of Sally's car. Sally told me it was for Crilly. He wanted to ask me to a formal dance.

When he called me, he introduced himself as Andrew. I did not know who Andrew was. Andrew told me he met me at Sally's house last weekend.

"I thought your name was Crilly," I said. He laughed for a long time.

I went to the formal with him. Sally and Paul went too. My mom met Paul and Crilly when they came to pick me up before we went to Sally's. My mom talked to Paul for five minutes while Crilly stood by the door.

At the formal, Crilly told me we had to dance to "Rock Lobster."

"He'll do the worm," Sally said.

When "Rock Lobster" came on, Crilly took off his blazer and put it on the floor. When the B-52's sang, "Down, down, down," everyone had to slowly lie down. Crilly went on his back and moved in a circle around me. I lay still. Everyone clapped. I blushed.

When we went home, Crilly told me he had had a good time. I said I had too. He kissed me and left.

Crilly and I went bowling the next weekend with Sally and Paul. Crilly and I sat waiting our turn. Crilly turned to me.

"Do you want to go steady? I'll give you two minutes to decide." He got up to bowl. When he came back, I said, "Yes."

Near Christmas, Crilly gave a gold-coloured pin with a dog and two little puppies to Sally to give to me.

He called me three times a week. One night, he told me he had decided to get his ear pierced. We argued. I told him not to. He told me of his fights at school. He got suspended for a week.

My mother did not like him. She discovered the boy she had chatted with the night of the formal was Paul, not Andrew. One night after Christmas, Crilly came over to pick me up. He walked to the door in his T-shirt.

"I left my leather jacket in the car," he whispered. "I know your mother doesn't like it."

"Was Santa Claus good to you?" my mother asked him.

"He's always good to good boys," he said.

Crilly thought he had made a good impression on my mother. I assured him he hadn't.

One day, Lisa Warren walked up to me in the cafeteria at school. I didn't know her very well. She asked me if I was going out with Andrew Crilly. I told her I was. She said she knew him and told me he was definitely not my type.

Crilly stopped calling me in January. Sally told me to call him. Three weeks later, I decided to call. I took a piece of paper and a pen and wrote out a conversation. I contemplated his replies. I couldn't do it.

Two days later, I tried again. I revised my conversation paper. The questions included: Why haven't you called me? Do you still want to go out with me? Do you want to go to the dance on Friday night? I finally called. When I heard his voice, I forgot about the conversation paper.

"Sorry I haven't called in such a long time. A lot of things are going on," he said.

"Do you want to go to the dance tonight?" I said.

"I can't. I have to help my dad work on some stuff."

I didn't know what to say.

"Forget it. Just forget it," I said. I hung up. I cried. I put Supertramp on the stereo. I turned up the volume.

Two years later, Crilly walked into the variety store where I worked. He bought a large regular pack of Export A's. He had a beard. We smiled at each other. I said, "$2.07, please."

I still have the dog and puppy pin he gave to Sally to give to me.

Tim Kitagawa

Legs on the Bus

I got my first job when I was fourteen. I had always wanted a job. The Canada Life Assurance Company on University Avenue hired me as a filing clerk.

The adult world was closer to me. I rode with adults on the buses and subway. I worked with adults in a large company. I dealt with adults for the entire summer. By August, I considered myself an adult.

I read the business-oriented *Globe and Mail* on my way to work rather than the low-brow *Toronto Sun*. I wanted people to consider me a businessman on his way to the office.

I saw how people acted differently in different places. No one spoke to anyone else on the subway. Everyone said "Hi" to each other at the office. Men watched women on the street but not at work. Women never watched men.

On a crowded bus, a man would often offer his seat to a woman who stood. She'd smile and accept his seat. Sometimes they started a conversation. This seemed like a way to meet women.

I got my chance during the last week of work. I chose a chair next to the aisle on the bus. All of the seats were taken. Two men stood clutching the backs of two seats in front of me. The bus made a stop and a woman got on.

She put her fare in the metal box and walked to the rear of the bus. The two men let her pass. Each eyed her. She wore a white dress with red and blue flowers on the shoulders. She looked angelic. She stopped beside my chair and took hold of the back. I stood.

"Please take my seat," I said in a clear loud voice to the woman. I looked into her bright brown eyes. Two older women whispered to themselves, pointed at me and giggled. The two men looked back.

I felt everyone on the bus knew that I was not only a man, but a classy, articulate and valiant man. I knew Dad would be proud of me.

"There is nothing wrong with my legs. I can stand as well as you," she stated plainly and loudly. The two men snickered and turned to face the front. I got off at the next stop. I was a mile from the place I usually got off.

I didn't tell Dad.

Nigel McInnis
On the Way Home

On the way to the Appleton High Halloween dance, I tried to act cool, but she knew I was uncomfortable. She stared out the window.

"Sooo . . . how do you like my wheels tonight?" I asked, hoping this might start conversation.

"It's all right, I guess."

I turned the radio up.

When we got to the school gym where the dance was, I felt better. There, we could seek out our common friends and at least pretend we were having a good time. We didn't dance to anything but the slow songs. Fast stuff was only for the "discos" (the people who seemed to have fun at school dances).

Though she probably hated me by now, I wondered, as we danced, if I could possibly ask her out again. I almost phrased this question during the last song but chickened out.

At the end of the evening, after we went to Mother's for a pizza with Rick and Tina, we found ourselves in her driveway. Should I kiss her? Shake her hand? Tell her to go to hell? I didn't know. I stood stiff, silent, hands in my pockets when she said, "Uhhhh, my dad gave me two tickets to the Leaf game tomorrow—you want to go?" I hesitated for a moment, not really sure what had happened. "They're golds."

"Uhhh, sure, that sounds great," was all I could get out. The front porch light blinked off, then on again.

"Guess that means my parents waited up for me," Jeanie said. I put my right arm around her neck and drew her into what I thought was a passionate kiss. I tasted the pizza in her mouth, but I didn't care. Halfway through the kiss, I opened my eyes and saw hers were closed. "This is a good sign," I thought.

I watched her climb the steps of her porch, open the door, enter the house, close the door and turn the porch light off. I backed the car down the driveway.

Pulling away from the curb, I managed to get a little burn-out from my dad's Oldsmobile Diesel. I felt like kickin' some ass.

Pauline Stanley
Mick and I

Mick and I bicycled on stony back roads. We didn't say much going uphill. Downhill, we talked.

Mick's mom wanted him to go back to school. She said, "A sixteen-year-old boy should be learning a career, not working."

"What do I want university for?" said Mick. "They jerk you around so's you don't know whether you're a Liberal or a Nazi. They're all a bunch of shitheads." He drawled lazily, and I often found myself guessing his next word.

"Women latch onto a man, get pregnant, and they're made for life. It's the guy that's gotta earn the bread."

Mick had three older brothers and two sisters. One brother was in the Navy, and one sister was a single parent. Four out of five were on welfare.

Mick said all the kids had been mistakes. "They didn't have much in birth control for hicks in the country. Ma wouldn't have known who should put on the condom, or where. I tell you, she was the breedin' kind. She killed the old man havin' so many kids. He worked himself to death." I said I couldn't believe people were so ignorant and he said, "No. You see women were part of the stock. You had cattle, pigs, and chickens; and then you had women." His mother had beefy arms. Her stomach hung over her hips, and her cleavage spread down to her waist. Mick taunted her. "Good cow," he said.

He became an only child, like me, as his brothers and sisters moved away. His mother seemed to wither and weaken. She scrubbed floors and railed at Mick about school.

Living alone with her, Mick grew quiet, disturbed. He broke off riding with me. He picked fights at school, was expelled and took to waiting tables full-time. When I called on him, he was "out." He never phoned me back. He blocked me out, and snubbed me publicly, as he did everyone.

One day, I yelled at him, then cried as he cycled away. He clutched the handbrake violently, and the bike spun around. He threw the bike down and ran back at me. I fought, but he wrestled me to the ground, and dug his knee into my chest. He held my arms above my head, leaned against me, dropped his face down to just above mine, and snarled, "Women start cryin', and get whatever they want."

He let go of my wrists and fell on the gravel, panting. I sat up. When I had controlled my sobbing, he reached over and massaged the back of my neck until I looked up. "I'm sorry," he said.

We walked down to the creek. He told me how angry he was that his brothers and sisters had moved away. He couldn't explain why. He glared down at the dusty creek bed. He talked for hours. After that, everything was all right.

As we rode, I watched his hairy legs, watched the muscle pumping under the skin. His calves were tight and round with rippling veins.

He had a good body and liked to show it off, riding only in shorts on a hot day. I wore jogging pants, sleeves past my elbows and my dad's baseball cap—backwards so it wouldn't blow off. He'd say, "Christ, you look like you're goin' to the North Pole." But he didn't mind. If we passed women he liked, I could pass for his sister or cousin.

When we rode, Mick sometimes left me half-a-mile behind on hills. I yelled, "Hey, wait up!" and he shouted back, "Move your fat ass," and pedalled faster. I wobbled along, lungs pressing my throat.

Eventually, he pulled over and waited. He sunned himself as I cycled up. While I caught my breath, he told me what he'd done on the weekend or the night before. I laughed on cue at his boasts of seductions. I never dated while I knew him.

After these talks, I felt strange. I went home and gorged on peanut butter sandwiches and Coke.

One day when we pulled over on the roadside, he said, "You should have seen this chick Larry, Bill and me had last night. I swear, she would have turned you into a lesbian, unless you already are.

"She had the biggest tits I've ever seen on a thirteen year old. They were grapefruits. I think I'm in love. So she was wanderin' around on Jensen's drive by that pond. Real spaced-out. She didn't know where she was at all. She asked us how to get home. She described the place and we knew right away. Beckers' place, about two miles on down the road."

I'd heard these stories before. I waited to hear how she fell all over Mick, the best-looking of the trio. Mick talked fast.

"Well, she asks me what road she should take, and Bill looks at her and says, 'I can tell ya for a price.' Before you know it the stud's draggin' her off into the bushes tellin' her she'll like it. So she stops her screamin' and complainin' and before you know it we hear them gruntin' like pigs in heat. She's groanin' how late she is and he's bangin' her into the ground. We give them five minutes to clean up, then Larry and me sneak in. Perfect timin' too, cause just as Larry gets his pants down, Bill's rollin' off the chick. So there ain't much she can do if she's picky.

"I tell you, the girl was a virgin! It was her first, second and third time! She was lucky we came along, because that fruit was ripe for pickin'. After, she was wipin' her nose, and pullin' on her dress, drippin' with blood. She got washed up in the pond. We stuck around, and showed her the road she should take—gentlemen that we are. Man, I'm glad I got that address."

Mick punched me on the shoulder, got on his bike and pedalled down the hill.

When I got home, I started shaking. I took out a bottle of my father's Scotch, drank several burning mouthfuls, phoned Mick, and hung up when he answered. I wanted to tell him off. I wanted to cry and have him say we could ride again.

That night, I dreamt I followed him. He pedalled fast and I sneaked after him on foot. He ditched his bike and ran into the bushes. I lost him there. Larry came out of the forest beyond and ran towards me. Bill was behind him. One ran to the left, the other to the right. I heard Mick shout, "You can catch her, she's out of shape!"

The next day, I saw him at Mac's buying smokes. When he saw me, he started over, but I walked away. I felt guilty when I got home. I phoned his house. When he answered, I hung up.

Three weeks later, I met him at night, on one of the roads we used to ride on. He walked towards me on the other side of the road with a girl in a pink summer dress.

I looked down and walked past. Mick turned and drawled, "Fuck off and die, bitch." They laughed. He sang in falsetto, "Oh, Mickie . . . Mickie!"

I kept walking.

Irene M. Dutton
Miss Wood's Advice to Girls

When I was small, I often heard the phrase "because you're a girl." My father treated Ivor and me differently. I had to have long hair, wear pretty dresses, take dancing and elocution lessons—because I was a girl. My brother could roam freely. My parents expected him to be tough. Even when hurt, he was not to cry.

I never complained about being a girl when I was very young. I happily acted the way I was supposed to and never tried to change things. When I went to the grammar school, I realized that being female meant limitations.

Miss Wood, the headmistress of Canon Slade School, was fanatically protective of her "young ladies." We were never allowed to talk to boys. We had to wear hat and gloves when outdoors. We must never eat in the street. Miss Wood did not approve of interaction with the boys' school, but school orchestra was one activity we shared. Girls played flutes, clarinets and oboes, while boys played trumpets, trombones and tubas. Miss Wood felt that the brass instruments were "inappropriate for young ladies." They distorted feminine lips and faces.

When I joined the orchestra, I wanted to play the kettledrums. I loved the gleaming copper bowls and taut skin covers. Mr. Slater, our tall conductor, who spat when he talked, said "No." I could play the triangle, tambourine and bells, but there would be no drums for girls. He gave no explanation. Bunny Robinson got the kettledrums. I helped him with the rest of the percussion.

The kettledrums fascinated me. I wanted to play them and make the drumsticks beat out a long roll. Bunny could not do that too well himself, but he offered to show me how. It was not easy, and I was just rolling a little when in walked Mr. Slater. He was furious. He told me to follow him and stalked off to Miss Wood. I didn't know what I had done wrong. I was frightened. When Mr. Slater came out of Miss Wood's office, I went in. The headmistress told me that I must never touch the drums again. Only boys were allowed to play them.

"You see, Irene," she said, her face with its orange-peel skin only inches from mine, "Girls have . . . appendages that make playing the drums quite out of the question. There is an embarrassing amount of movement that onlookers don't like to see."

I was twelve. I didn't know about breasts. Good thing Judith Brown hadn't tried to play the drums. And wasn't Bunny Robinson lucky? His appendage didn't show when he beat out a drum-roll.

Mary Alilovic

Okay

I worked behind the cheese counter the Saturday afternoon Terry asked me out.

"Are you serious?" I ran to Lisa for a pen. I wrote my phone number and directions to my home on deli paper. "He asked me out!"

I acted like a fool. UNCOOL—forgot all the rules.

At 3:00, I punched my card and ran to my station wagon.

3:05. I was home. He'd be here at 7:30. That's only four-and-a-half hours.

7:35. I was ready. I had on my tightest jeans and prettiest sweater. No Jontue though, this was a Chanel No. 5 night.

7:45. Still waiting. I curled and recurled my hair. Maybe something terrible had happened. Had I been stood up?

The phone rang. The first ring wasn't complete when I picked up the receiver.

"Mary? Hi, this is Terry."

Great. He'll know I was sitting by the phone. "Hi."

"I think I'm lost. I'm at Kipling and Evans."

I hadn't been stood up. I explained again how to get to my house.

8:16. There's a knock at the door. I check my makeup in the hall mirror and open the door.

"Hi."

"Hi."

"Sorry I'm late."

"That's okay."

"Are you ready?"

"Yes."

"Let's go."

"Yeah, um . . . bye Mom!"

We walked out to his black Toyota. He got in the driver's seat and reached over to unlock my side. He shifted into drive and we drove off. I saw my mother standing at the front door. She waved.

"Well, what do you want to do?"

"I don't know."

"Wanna go downtown?"

"Okay."

"Do you like work?"

Knob Hill Farms dominated our conversation. Along the Gardiner and up Yonge Street, we spoke only of work. He parked in a city lot, paid two dollars, and we began our date.

"What do you want to do?"

"I don't know. How about walking on Yonge?"

We walked North, then turned around and walked South. Both of us had our hands in our pockets. It drizzled. While looking at Marilyn Monroe in a poster shop, we touched shoulders. Both of us jumped back. We pretended we didn't notice.

"She's beautiful," I said.

"She's okay. Are you hungry?"

"No." I was, but girls don't eat in front of guys. "Are you?"

"Yeah, a little bit. McDonald's okay?"

"Okay."

We walked into McDonald's. I looked into a mirror. Oh God! I was tempted to run to the bathroom, but I didn't. If he doesn't like me at my worst, it'll never work out.

He ordered a Filet O'Fish, a Quarter Pounder with Cheese, large fries, and a Vanilla Milk Shake. "I'm glad you were only a little bit hungry."

He smiled.

Dumb joke. I watched him eat.

"Want some?"

"No thanks."

"You sure?"

"Yes." I looked into the mirror behind him. Oh shit! I was starving.

"C'mon, have one fry."

"Oh, all right." He finished in fifteen minutes.

"You ready to go now?"

"Yeah."

We walked out of McDonald's and back to the car. He didn't open my door. He started the car, and we were on our way home. Terry talked about back massage. He told me he had heard about my skilled hands. He asked me to give him a massage.

"Sure. No, not here in front of my house! No, not here in Hedgestone Court, my aunt lives here! Oh, okay, this is all right."

He parked in Taviton Court. After massaging his shoulders for a while, I asked, "What time is it?"

"Twelve-thirty."

"I think it's time to go."

"But I didn't give you a massage."

"That's all right. This one's free." I was going to say, "Maybe next time," but I didn't know if there would be a next time. He stopped in front of my house. My hand was on the car door handle.

"Well, thanks for the most boring evening of my life. Bye." I jumped out and slammed the door. That was a stupid thing to say. It was supposed to be a joke. I screwed up.

He drove away. I hated myself.

Sunday was empty. I dreaded seeing him at work the next day.

Monday at work, the door behind my cheese counter opened. It was Terry.

He said, "Hi."

I said, "Hi."

He said, "You know about Berik's party Friday night?"

"Yeah," I said.

"You wanna go?"

"Okay," I said, "okay."

Lynn MacKenzie

My Story About Men and Women

"Arnie, I have to write a story about male/female relations."

"What's this for, Lynn?"

"My writing class!"

"Oh."

"Can you remember the time, before we were married, when I had been running all over the place? I'd started right after work and didn't get home 'til quarter after ten. Then as soon as I got in the door you said, 'Where the hell have you been?'"

"What's that got to do with anything?"

"Well, I'm trying to think of a time when we weren't communicating. That time, I had run about five errands after work and hadn't even had time for supper. I was frustrated and tired, and as soon as I walked in the door, you started on me."

"Why do you have to write about an argument that we had?"

"Because it's interesting. It's something everyone has experienced, and it was funny."

"Sure. Why do you have to make me look bad?"

"I'm not going to make you look bad. I'm just going to present what happened."

"Look, Lynn, why can't you write about the time I was out, and you demanded to know where I was?"

"Because that wasn't really funny or interesting."

"Lynn, I don't want you writing about our problems. You'll make it look like we have a bad relationship."

"Don't be silly; everyone has arguments. You're always worried about what other people will think."

"No I'm not. But why don't you write about something nice that's happened?"

"Like what in particular?"

"Like our engagement, or when I asked you to marry me."

"But Arnie, that's not something about male/female relations. It has to be something that typically happens in a relationship."

"Well, I don't know. Why don't you write about our wedding day, and everything that happened then?"

"Arnie, that would be boring. You still don't understand. I have to make this interesting."

"What was boring about it? I think it was interesting."

"No. I want to write about the lack of communication that happens in relationships."

"What do you mean? We always communicate."

"Not always. Look at right now. You're telling me what you want, and you're not listing to what I want."

"That's baloney. Why do you need this course anyway? Is it something that you are required to take?"

"No, but I do need a half credit. Besides, it's an interesting course, and writing is important in business."

"So you won't be able to graduate without it?"

"I told you, that's not true. But I enjoy it. It gives me a break from my business classes."

"I don't understand why you can't write something nice."

"I already told you what I want to show. Never mind, I've got it! Thanks for your help, Love!"

M. Nakamura
Dreamer

59-63-24 Hup, hup!"
"One steamboat, two steamboat, three steamboat...."
She sat on a tree stump and watched them play. It was the first spring-like day in March. The setting sun made her squint.

"It's up! it's up!"

The football spiralled through the air. Gary caught it.

Touchdown.

She wanted to stand up and clap, but Peter might not like it. She wrapped her arms around her knees. Her hands were cold and the ring slid off her finger. She thought about asking Peter to get it tightened, but she didn't want to complain.

The wind picked up.

She stood up. She was cold. A walk back to the South Building would take at least ten minutes, she thought. She looked out onto the field. Peter, Scott, Alan and Steve were in a huddle. Gary and his team waited.

Gary called out to her, "Are you cold?"

She nodded. "Go into our townhouse and get warmed up."

"Thanks."

She turned and walked up the slope. She wondered how he knew. He always noticed her.

It took two minutes to walk to their house. She opened the screen door. It banged as it fell shut. She left her mittens and coat on the couch beside the door.

A half-full coffee cup and a cereal bowl, milk hardened on the edges, sat on the coffee table. Books littered the table: a frayed Psychology study guide, a Mississauga bus schedule and a book of Snoopy cartoons. A potted spider plant sat on a table in the corner of the room.

She walked into the kitchen. An empty box of Mini Wheats sat on the crusty, sticky counter. The cupboard doors above the sink were open wide, no-name peanut butter, corn syrup, honey and Kraft Dinner inside. Dirty plates filled the sink.

On the kitchen table was a Bell Canada phone bill. She leaned forward to look more closely. She noticed several calls made to Brantford, Peterborough and Kingston. The longest call of thirty-four minutes to Kingston cost eighteen dollars. Steve had probably made that call; Gary came from Brantford.

At the end of the table, on top of a computer printout, lay a wallet. She thought it might be Gary's. Maybe there would be pictures of a girlfriend. She hoped not. She opened the wallet. The first thing she saw was a Bookstore credit card. The name on it was Scott Paterson. She carefully replaced the wallet on the table the way she had found it.

She walked back into the living room and sat down. Sun came through the window. It was warm on her back. She tried to imagine what Brantford looked like. She pictured Gary playing tennis. He probably looked great in shorts. She saw herself with him. They walked in a park where flowers grew, and they held hands. He looked down at her. She looked up into his eyes. They were green. She saw that last week in the study room when he caught her staring at him.

She smiled to herself.

A half hour had gone by. They were probably wondering what she was doing. She picked up her coat and mitts, ran out the door and into the cold air.

Peter stood beside the tree stump. The other guys were still on the field. She walked toward him.

Peter said, "Let's go."

Jennifer Brown

In Morning

Tammy Taylor lies in bed. Early morning sun beams through the open corners of the curtains. Dust floats to the floor. Darcy, her husband, lies next to her and mutters. Tammy looks at him, his closed eyes, his open mouth, his unshaven face. She touches his curly hair. She cries silently. Mascara smears her cheeks.

She feels for her slippers, her housecoat. She walks through the quiet house and opens the door of the room where their nine-month-old baby still sleeps. Blankets lie on the floor. Sweat-matted hair frames Melissa's face.

Tammy takes Melissa into the kitchen, makes coffee and puts her slippered feet on the high chair. Her housecoat falls on either side of her legs, revealing her torn nightgown. Steam rises from the cup to her face. She blows ripples in the cup. Her head pounds. Hot coffee burns her tongue. The clock ticks. She rests her head in the palm of her hands.

Melissa reaches and pulls Tammy's housecoat. Tammy covers her face. She breathes through her fingers. She shuts her eyes. Melissa cries. Tammy fastens the straps behind the high chair and around Melissa's stomach.

Tammy stands at the sink. Melissa screams. Water runs over Tammy's fingers. Darcy, now up, steps behind her and touches her shoulder. She stares through the window. The kettle whistles. Melissa screams and pounds the table. Tammy turns and watches Darcy look outside.

Darcy says, "Looks like another beautiful day out there. What's for breakfast?" He turns and she follows.

Ieva Martin

Manville

I became discouraged after I realized that the male establishment, which had the power to give me a chance, wouldn't do so because I was a woman. The first rude shock came just before the end of high school.

We lived in Asbestos, Quebec, a company mining town. Every year Canadian Johns-Manville Co. Ltd. gave at least one scholarship to a student graduating from Asbestos-Danville-Shipton High School.

In the previous two years, there were three recipients. The year before there had been two.

Mr. Gaw, the high school principal, warned me that filling out an application was probably a "waste of time." I was surprised since Sandra Olney and I alternated in getting top marks on term tests.

"Why?" I asked.

"Because," he answered, "Johns-Manville has never awarded a scholarship to a girl."

I did not get the scholarship. Neither did Sandra. At graduation she got the general proficiency medal. I received the science medal. Barry Gibson was the sole recipient of the CJ-M scholarship that year. His average was at least ten percentage points lower than Sandra's or mine.

I'm not sure when I approached Mr. Morrison, General Manager of the CJ-M manufacturing plant and chairman of the scholarship selection committee. I must have run into him during the summer I worked in the plant. Mr. Morrison rationalized the committee's policy by explaining that boys were more likely to return and work for the company. In other words, I suppose, they were a better investment. Barry never worked for CJ-M. Nor did any of the other boys who have previously received scholarships. I did, for two summers and one whole year, for much lower wages than those paid to male university students recruited from outside the province.

University brought more disillusionment. I wasn't prepared for the assumption that women went to university in order to get their MRS degree. In my family a university education was taken for granted as it is in most Latvian families (I have heard that eighty percent of all Latvians have university degrees).

I still try to analyze why I flunked out of McGill. The easy answer is: I goofed off. I studied bridge instead of physics. But why? Partly it was immaturity. I was sixteen years old when I started and away from parental supervision for the first time in my life.

I arrived at university with no study skills. But why didn't I develop these when I knew I would have to? Was my problem what is referred to as "women's fear of success"?

I now believe there are two indirect reasons for my failure. Sitting around the dinner table in the women's residence, I heard the seniors complain that they couldn't find jobs unless they had typing skills. Meanwhile, graduating young men were being hired by large corporations and placed into management training programs. These corporations would not hire women except as secretaries. I had already worked as a secretary.

There was another reason. I knew that I did not want to live my life alone. But I was also aware that in a marriage the husband had to be superior in every way—he had to be taller, he had to be more intelligent, he had to be better educated. . . . At five feet eight inches, I was already taller than the average man. By the time I put on spikes I was close to six feet tall. On a badly done IQ test I scored 140. That made me more intelligent than most men. If I continued my education, I would narrow the field of available men even more.

In my third year of a B.Sc., I knew I had flunked out. I looked for a permanent job. It was only now that I became conscientious. Two months after I joined Pitney-Bowes, I was left in charge of the office when Miss Martin, the office manager, went on holidays. I supervised three more senior women. But I still could see no future in that firm. The next step up was office manager, but Miss Martin had nowhere to go in that company and having worked for them for twenty-five years, was unlikely to leave. I left Pitney-Bowes.

I joined H.V. Chapman and Associates, management consultants who dealt only with executives. The Toronto-based firm had recently opened an office in Montreal. There were three male consultants and me. As the workload expanded and another typist was hired, the consultants tried to get head office to agree to let me do some of the consultants' work which they felt I could do. Head office refused. I decided there was no future with this firm either.

I applied for a job at Xerox through another placement agency. The job involved training office staff in the use of newly acquired Xerox copiers. I thought it might be a foot in the door. I scored highly on some tests. Xerox didn't hire me. They couldn't understand why a person with so much intelligence wanted this job. At that time, all sales personnel were white-shirted, conservatively-suited men.

And so it went on for a while longer. In May 1966, I married Bob. Andrea was born nine months and six days later.

Jeff Robins

Real Soon

I decided I had to call her. I dialed the first six digits of her number, lit a cigarette and dialed the last one. The phone rang five times.

"Hello?" It was her mother. She was out of breath.

"Hi, Mrs. H. Could I speak to Ann Marie, please?"

"Just a minute, Jeff. I'll call her."

I heard a muted, "Ann Marie. Phone."

Ann Marie picked up the extension and yelled, "Got it!" There was a click as the other phone disconnected. "Hello?" she said.

"Hi," I said, "Watcha doing?"

"Oh, not much."

"How do you feel about going out and getting something to eat?"

"Sure, where?"

"How about Vetere's?"

"I hate pizza, let's go to Sheridan Gardens."

"I hate Chinese food," I said. I don't really, but I wanted pizza.

"Get a hamburger, then," she said.

"Yeah ... okay."

"Oh!" I said, as if I had just thought of it, "Do you think you can get the car?" I hated asking that.

"Yes," she said, "But I wish you would hurry up and get your licence."

"Real soon!" I said, "See you in about ... twenty minutes?"

"All right. Bye." She hung up.

"Rag!" I yelled.

I slammed the phone down as my sister came down the stairs.

"Ann Marie?" she said.

"Cassie, I gotta break up with her. I can't take her anymore."

"Yeah, you do, but you won't," she said.

"No, really," I said, "We're going over to Sheridan Gardens and I'm going to tell her there."

"Sure, Jeff," she said, "Like you did last week and the week before and...."

"Shut up! I know! But this time I really have to."

"Sure, Jeff."

"Listen, jerkface," I said, "I don't care what you think."

I went upstairs to change.

I was brushing my teeth when the doorbell rang.

"Jeff," Cassie said, "Ann Marie's here!"

"Just a minute," I said, spraying toothpaste on the mirror. I finished up and walked down the stairs.

"Hi," I said.

"Let's go. The car's running," she said. I looked over to Cassie sitting at the dining room table.

"Sure, Jeff," she said.

"Seriously, Cass. I'm not kidding anymore. I'm going to have to pound the crap out of you if you say it again. See you later."

"Sure, Jeff," she said into her book.

I tossed a shoe at her. She laughed as we walked out to the car.

Our conversation in the car consisted mostly of, "Will you please get your licence?" and "Why don't you quit smoking?"

I answered both: "Real soon."

This upset her. She quit talking. I didn't mind.

When the waitress finally got to us, we both ordered burgers and fries.

"This might sound pretty stupid," I said, "but was there any special reason we came here for burgers?"

"Because I didn't want pizza," she snapped.

"You can get friggin' hamburgers at Frank Vetere's," I said. A lot of people turned to look.

Ann Marie didn't say anything. Our food came. We ate without talking. I finished and read the "Daily Special" card. When Ann Marie finished I lit a cigarette.

"When are you going to quit smoking?" she said.

"Never," I said, "I love smoking. It is my one true joy in life. When are you going to quit bitching?" She looked hurt. I felt good.

"Sorry," she said, "I guess I have been ragging a lot lately. I'm sorry."

I didn't feel good anymore. I wanted to apologize to her. I wanted to hold her. I had to say something before I changed my mind. I cleared my throat.

"I think we should stop seeing each other," she said.

Wait. "What?" I said.

"I said . . . I think, maybe we should break up."

"Oh, well . . . yeah we should . . . maybe."

We sat for a few minutes looking around the restaurant.

"Now what happens?" I said.

"Should I take you home or what?" she said.

"Yeah, okay," I said.

The cheque came. She wanted to pay half.

We didn't talk much in the car. I stared out the window. I could just see the top of the sun. Shades of red and purple coloured the sky.

I looked up as Ann Marie pulled into my driveway. She put the car in "park" and turned to face me.

"Call me sometime . . . if you want to," she said.

"I will," I said.

I leaned over and kissed her. It was a good kiss. I wanted to kiss her again. I got out of the car and said, "Thank you." She said, "Bye, Jeff."

The lights were off when I let myself into the house. I curled up in a corner of the couch and watched the pattern the remaining sunlight made on the wall.

I didn't feel anything.

Saudade Gaspar
The Day After

I shook the L'Oreal STUDIO line sculpting mousse. I pressed the nozzle and sizzling foam squirted into my hand.

It stopped. All that absorption, firmness, support without greasiness or flaking. Thanks, L'Oreal, for styling my hair just right. Eaton Centre, Applewood Lanes, King Sullivan's Mines, *American Ninja*, Mr. Greenjeans. You were remarkable.

Exhausted water reserves, depleted manganese oars, extinct *Tyrannosaurus rexes*, depreciated word processors, consumed Habitant Instant Pea Soups with Ham. Degradation, drainage, destruction—these go with me, and Tony has left.

Memories, fatigue, loneliness; the tingling loss sensation, the moisture dripping down the Inglis frost-free fridge. I cried because I lacked control.

Control—the power to not fuck up: I didn't have it. Had Mother taught me how to react to a confused, neurotic boy? Neither had Henry Wisewood Fecundary School.

> *Sleep, sleep . . . to forget*
> *The asshole you once met.*

Rain, the natural depressant, depressed me.

My insides collapsed. The centrifugal force within me broke down.

I never loved him.

I toss the L'Oreal into the wicker wastepaper basket.

Next time, I'll try Alberto.

Jane Anthony

The Steak

I woke up ill at 10:30 that Saturday morning. I was in the first trimester of my second pregnancy. Morning sickness was a part of it.

I washed and went to the kitchen for breakfast. I saw a steak in a bowl. I wondered why it was there. I did not expect company for dinner. Even if I had, one steak was not enough. One steak put to thaw in the morning would not feed six that night.

I tried to eat, but my morning nausea did not permit much of a breakfast. I vomited. I asked my husband, "What would you like for lunch?"

"I took some meat out of the freezer. We can have a stew."

The only meat I saw was the steak. I went to the kitchen to look again for stew beef.

"What meat? Where?"

"The meat in the bowl on the counter."

"You got to be kidding. You expect me to cook a steak for lunch? We are moving up in the world."

"What do you mean by that?"

"Well, I will explain it to you. Something I observed with people here is that they do not have steak for lunch."

"Oh. I did not mean to cook it as a steak. I want you to cut it up and boil it in a stew."

"What? That is utterly ridiculous."

"The best way to cook food is to boil it."

"Really? What about baking, frying, broiling? Some cultures seldom if ever boil food. Boiled is one way. Some foods are better fried or baked than boiled."

"The best way to cook food is to boil it."

"Well. If you want that steak boiled, you boil it. You can cut it up into a million pieces and boil it if you want. I am not going to."

"You were born in Trinidad."

"What does that have to do with anything? I know where I was born, where my parents were born, where my brothers and sisters were born. I even know where you were born. What does my birthplace have to do with anything?"

"Trinidadians boil their food. You should too. Women in Trinidad always boil meat to make stew. Since you were born in Trinidad, you should do the same."

"That is the most idiotic thing I ever heard. Firstly, I was not a woman in Trinidad. I was a child in my mother's house. I did what she wanted in the line of cooking. Secondly, I left Trinidad thirteen years ago. I accept some of the ways around me now. Cooking is one."

"Well, if you were in Trinidad, you would boil it."

"Maybe so, but I am not in Trinidad and I am not going to."

I don't know what happened to that steak, but I know I did not boil it.

Hugh Bancroft
The Happy Wanderer

There is a smurf on my desk. He has a pole over his shoulder with a handkerchief looped over the end behind his back. He's The Happy Wanderer. Cora gave him to me on September 9, 1981, two hours before I left Deep River, the small town in northeastern Ontario where I grew up, to work in Banff.

I didn't want to leave. I told Cora that two days before I left as we lay on her living room floor. I cried in her lap while I told her.

I wanted to leave Deep River at the end of grade thirteen. I had played euchre at the youth program in Mackenzie High School for six summers. There wasn't enough wind at Deep River to keep me interested in windsurfing. John worked at the Petawawa Forestry. Donald worked for the Ministry of Natural Resources at Achray. Ben worked at the Chalk River Nuclear Laboratories. I worked weekends at the A&P. I was ready to leave Deep River as soon as I graduated.

My high school graduation dinner and dance was on Saturday, May 29th. I decided on Wednesday, the 19th, to ask Cora Blair to be my date. On Wednesday, the 26th, at the beginning of second period, I sat down in the study carrel beside her. Cora was the referee who chased Neil, Peter, me and our two-litre bottles of Manor St. David's Sauternes off the field hockey pitch during the Ottawa Valley final.

I nodded hello. She nodded back. I asked her what she was studying. Math. I asked her how she was doing at synchro. Fine. I asked her if she enjoyed refereeing field hockey. Too many drunks on the field. I turned back and read how water acts as a solvent. I looked over and asked her if she was going to any parties that weekend. No. I asked her if she'd go to the grad with me. Yes. I told her I'd pick her up at 6:30.

My mother told me to phone Cora to ask what colour her dress would be. Pink. I ordered the corsage at Pinecrest Florists. At 6:25 on Saturday, my parents and I drove to Cora's house. I got out and rang the bell. When Cora answered the door, I handed her the box with the corsage in it. My mother told me from the back seat of the car to pin the corsage on Cora's dress. I held the corsage to Cora's waist. My mother told me that nobody would be able to see the corsage on Cora's waist. Cora took off her shawl. She wore a strapless dress. I held the corsage up to her chest and tried to pin it to the dress. Cora laughed and said she'd carry it.

After the dinner, the speeches, and the dance, Cora and I sat on the sand beach at Bradley's Point. We drank white San Pietro wine, frozen after seven hours in the freezer and watched the sun rise.

I waited for Cora as she wrote her math final. I had two bottles of French white wine, corn-on-the-cob, and hot dogs with me.

We paddled fifteen minutes across the Ottawa River before I remembered I had left my dog tied up outside the exam hall. We paddled back and got the dog. It rained when we reached the Quebec shore. We sat in an abandoned Indian hut and swatted blackflies, mosquitoes and deerflies for two hours until the rain stopped. We didn't drink the wine because I forgot the corkscrew. When the rain stopped, we paddled back through the fog and ate pizza at the Grecian Villa.

Cora asked me to help her with her synchronized swimming. I stood at the side of the pool and watched her faded blue Speedo swimsuit: it was cut high over her hips and low between her breasts. I told her she'd please more spectators if she just sat on the side of the pool.

Cora read one of my stories. It was about my conversations with a maple tree that turned colours in the first week of September. She liked the story. She told me to keep writing. Miss Philips, my English teacher, marked that one "schizophrenic" and suggested I see a psychiatrist.

Cora worked at the Deep River Tourist Information booth on Highway 17. When the weather was rainy and cold, I took her a thermos of hot tea. When it was hot, I took her a chocolate milk shake from the Laurentian View Dairy.

We raced the hundred yards of water to buoy two from the end of the municipal pier. She practised her synchronized swimming on the way and beat me by thirty yards.

One Wednesday afternoon after work, we paddled across the river and made love on the sand beach. We wouldn't have noticed if anybody had walked by; we were counting on the dog to scare away beachcombers. The dog—half German Shepherd, half Golden Lab—nudged us with her cold nose as we lay on the beach.

I drank two litres of Manor St. David's Sauternes before Cora and I arrived at the Blackfly Ball. During the polkas, we demolition-danced against John Selkirk and his partner. I bet Cora that Led Zeppelin played "All of My Love." She led me home and left me on my side porch after the dance.

We played backgammon on her living room floor and listened to Neil Young sing "After the Goldrush." We turned off the lights and listened to Rory Gallagher play "Shadowplay."

My parents told me I could live with them during the next school year if I enrolled in grade thirteen again or worked full-time at the A&P. I told Cora. She asked me if I wanted to stay in Deep River. No. She told me to leave for Banff on September 9th. She would stay and attend grade thirteen at Mackenzie.

When Cora gave me The Happy Wanderer, she asked me not to say goodbye. I told her I wouldn't. She kept my Led Zeppelin records to make sure she'd see me again.

Jennifer Brown

Those Grey Eyes

Mother drew back the lacy curtains and peered through the window. She gazed down the driveway through the snowbanks. Her grey eyes, lined with deep wrinkles, looked transparent. She stared out the window.

"I wonder where Father is," she said, not to me but to herself. The fire cracked. She turned from the window.

"I guess I could get more wood for this fire. It burns fast when it's dry."

She pushed back her auburn hair that fell into her face. "Give me a hand, will you?"

Mother's fingers turned purple as she pushed away snow settled on the logs. Her wedding rings sat loose and twisted around her finger as she placed the logs into my arms.

I felt tiny in my father's chair. My eyes dried as I watched blue flames sizzle snow from the logs. I turned to feel the heat on the side of my face. Mother sat in her rocking chair, one hand folded over the other. Her eyes narrowed. She said, "Father is working with that woman producer. I don't really find her attractive. Do you?"

She rocked faster. "He is working with her a lot lately." She stood up, brushed her skirt over her knees and walked over to the window. Her lips were tight. A scar from a childhood fall blended into her tight wrinkles. She crossed her arms and wrapped them around herself. She pressed her hands against her small frame. She got up and walked into the kitchen.

"I wish we didn't live so far out in the country," she said as she returned with a dust cloth. "We get a lot of dust from the road here." She hummed nervously as she dusted frames of pictures. Before she dusted the clocks, she showed me the stained cloth.

When she opened the curtains to dust the window sill, she smiled. "There is your father now, Jennifer. Set the table. It's time for supper."

My father walked in.

"I really wish you would use the train more often, Father. I don't trust the roads. I thought you were in some accident," she said.

Mother kissed and hugged my father. Over his shoulder, I saw her face. The corners of her thin lips turned up and her grey eyes, grey like cold steel, stared into nothing.

Rosamund Elwin

The Wedding Dress

The dress hangs in her closet, bloody and dirty. Delia bought the dress, a plain bridal dress that fit her small body perfectly, from Syd Silver on Yonge Street. Her younger sister helped her choose it.

Delia met Tony one year before they were married. To Delia, Tony—tall, slim and handsome in a tough way—was the perfect man. He was kind, considerate and spontaneous. One Friday, he picked her up unannounced and took her to the Sheraton Centre downtown for the weekend. He bought her flowers and champagne and spent over three hundred dollars.

Delia had ended her relationship with another man a month before she met Tony. She did not know what to do with herself. She had never been on her own, without a boyfriend.

When Delia met Tony, she was flattered by his attentions. He helped her cook dinner and do the laundry.

He did tell her that he was not a landed immigrant. He lived with his mother and sisters after coming from the West Indies six months before. One of the reasons Tony wanted to marry Delia was to get his immigration papers.

Delia was frightened of Tony's temper. She was frightened of his family. She believed if she refused to marry him his family would do something evil. Tony's future, and that of his mother and sisters, depended on their marriage because Tony needed his immigration papers.

Delia believed they could make the marriage work. They were in love.

The wedding was at three in the afternoon. There were one hundred guests. Delia had her hair curled. She had a facial, and she had her make-up applied by a professional. The ceremony started on time. Tony looked handsome in his tuxedo.

Their reception was in a rented hall. Tony thought a guy dancing with Delia held her too close.

"I will fix you when we get home," he said.

After everyone had partied to exhaustion, Delia and Tony got into their car and drove home. Delia's heart pounded. Her palms were sweaty. She did not know what to expect, but she knew he was angry. She wished Tony would say something. She lifted the hem of her wedding dress and followed him into the elevator. She followed him down the hall to their apartment.

"That was one of your men you were dancing with. I know you are seeing one of them. Why did he hold you so tight? I don't want any man dancing with my wife."

Delia was shocked. "Those are my friends. Those are your friends," she said.

Tony called her a liar. Delia denied having an affair with any of them. Tony punched her in the mouth and knocked out her front tooth. Blood ran down her chin. Delia ran to the bathroom and looked in the mirror. Her face swelled. Her tooth hung by a piece of flesh. She pulled it out and threw it in the toilet.

Tony came into the bathroom. His anger was gone.

"Sorry, sorry, I don't know what came over me." He helped her undress. She threw her blood-stained, white wedding dress over a chair.

He made love to her.

Tony believed one of the husband's duties was to discipline his wife. He beat her again when she was late home from her job as a shipping clerk at Sears. He yelled at her and beat her if his dinner wasn't on time.

Delia was tempted to go to the Immigration Department and report his illegal status in Canada. After he beat her, Tony said he was sorry, and she felt for him.

"He is not really a bad man," she told me. "He is a good father. He loves his kid. He is a damn good lover too," she said.

Two years after the wedding, the bloodied dress hangs in the closet. One day, she will take it to the cleaners.

Chapter Seven

The Family

Present a picture of life in the family by detailing an event or chain of events you have experienced or observed.

Jill Watson
Best of Friends

"Janet," I yelled to my younger sister. "Where the hell is my turquoise eyeliner?"

"What?"

I walked up the stairs and pushed her door open. She sprawled on her bed and flipped through *Vogue*.

I said, "Where is my turquoise eyeliner?"

"How should I know? I didn't touch it." She glared at me over the magazine.

"Yeah, just like you didn't touch my green sweater or my black patent belt!"

"Screw off."

"You don't have to be a bitch. Just tell me where it is."

"I told you, I didn't touch it. I wouldn't use that piece of shit anyway." She turned back to the magazine.

I slammed the door and went back to the kitchen. Her purse hung on the back of one of the chairs. I unzipped the middle section and rummaged through it. The eyeliner wasn't there. A pack of DuMaurier Lights was. I took the cigarettes out of her purse and headed back up to her room. I stood in the doorway.

"Janet," I said. "When did you start smoking?"

"I don't smoke," she said.

"No? Then how do you explain these?" I dropped the cigarettes on top of a Calvin Klein underwear ad. She brushed them aside and flipped the page.

"Do you think it's cool?"

She looked up at me. "Yes, Jennifer, I think it's the coolest thing in the world." She rolled her eyes and looked down at the magazine. I snatched the cigarettes up and waved them in the air.

"Do you think Mom and Dad will think it's cool?"

"You would do that, wouldn't you?"

"Depends. Is my eyeliner going to show up in the next ten seconds?"

"I don't know," she said. "I think I might have seen it in my top drawer." I opened the drawer. My turquoise eyeliner peeked out from under a pair of pink undies. I took it out and threw the cigarettes back onto her bed.

"Okay, you're off the hook this time, but I'd find a better place to keep my cigarettes if I were you."

Two weeks later, I watched TV in the den with my mother. She told me she found a pack of cigarettes in Janet's underwear drawer.

"Do you know anything about them?"

"Yeah," I said. "She told me she's hanging onto them for a friend."

"Do you believe her?"

"Sure, why would she lie to me?"

Mother shrugged.

I ran upstairs to tell Janet she owed me one.

Charmaine Browne

Parental Guidance

"Why me? Why always me?" Vanessa sat on her bed and cried. Her father came home from work and found a glass in the kitchen sink. He wasn't too upset at first. Then he found out it was Vanessa's.

"Didn't I tell you to wash your dishes? Come here. NOW!" He took the cowhide belt from around his waist and hit her. With every lash came a warning. "Listen when I talk, girl, listen!"

She listened last week in his church, Keele Street Baptist. He gave his sermon on parental guidance. "Parents, show your children God's way. Show them you love them. Handle them firmly; they'll respect you more." That same afternoon, he beat her because she talked during the service.

Vanessa Jefferson was small for her thirteen years. When her family first moved to Delmonte Crescent in Malton, Vanessa hoped the beatings would stop. She started out as a good student at Greenbriar Public School. But these past three years she did badly. She fell asleep in class. She wouldn't talk to anyone. She wouldn't play at lunch.

Her mother worked at North Borough Hospital as a registered nurse. She had different shifts, so she worked either days or nights. When her mother worked days, Vanessa ran home from school to start the cooking. Then she cleaned all the rooms in the house, washed the dishes, and set the table. All this had to be done before her father got home.

If not, he beat her. Vanessa had suffered dislocated joints, broken bones, and bruises that took weeks to heal. Her most recent injury was a dislocated elbow. She hadn't come "right away" when her father called her. He took hold of her arm and pulled her elbow out of its joint.

Vanessa's mother knew what was going on, but if she said anything he beat her too.

One day, her father took Vanessa to the backyard. He pointed out two spots on the ground and said, "That's where I'm going to bury you and your mother." He laughed and walked back into the house.

Vanessa sat on her bed and thought. He hated her, but why? Her younger brothers and sisters never got a lick. Why not? Maybe it was her face. She went to the mirror. "I'm not that ugly. Even if I am, it's his fault. So what is it?"

One night, Vanessa's mother was working. It was 6:00, time to give Byron and Bernadette their baths. Vanessa ran the bath and called Byron. As she stooped to test the water, Byron came up behind her and pushed her in. Byron laughed hard. Vanessa knew that if her father saw her wet clothes he would be mad. She hit Byron and told him to shut-up. Byron screamed. She tried to calm him down. Too late. Her father came up the stairs. In one look, he took in everything. Without a word, he took Byron downstairs. Vanessa shook. He came up again.

"I'm sorry, I'm sorry Daddy. I didn't mean to, really I didn't."

"Get into the bathtub."

"With my clothes on?"

"Get into the bathtub."

"Please don't beat me Daddy, I won't do it again."

"I said get into the bathtub, NOW!" She stepped into the tub.

"Sit down, close the curtain and don't move until I tell you to, and not a word, y'hear?" For four hours Vanessa sat in the tub. Finally, Daddy came, told her to get out and go to bed.

The next day, Vanessa was sick, but Daddy said, "Go to school." Vanessa spent most of the day in the nurse's office. The nurse said she was going to phone Vanessa's parents. Vanessa lied and said no one was home. Her mother was sleeping. She had to work that night. When Vanessa got home, she threw her boots behind the back door. She felt cold and tired. She couldn't cook the curried chicken and rice. She went to bed. Ten minutes passed before she heard her father's voice. "Vanessa, VANESSA! Come down here right now." Vanessa made her way downstairs. She walked over to her father and looked up. Quietly he asked, "What were you doing?"

"I was lying down, Daddy."

"Why?" he asked.

"Because I wasn't feeling well."

"You didn't do your work, and there's one other thing."

"What, Daddy?"

"Haven't I always told you to put away your boots in the basement?"

"Yes."

"This afternoon when I opened the back door it bounced back in my face. I looked behind the door and saw your boots."

"I'm sorry," she said, "I didn't mean to. I'm sick."

"Sick or not, I'm going to teach you a lesson. Who won't hear will feel." Vanessa's father didn't have on a belt this time. He picked up the hammer on the kitchen counter and came toward her.

Vanessa screamed.

Mary Beth Shickluna
You'll Have To Ask Your Father

"Hi, Mom, how are ya?"
"I'm fine. What is it you want?"
"Nothing. Why?"
"Mary Beth, whenever you start with that line, I know you're after something."
"Thanks a lot."
"Well, it's true, isn't it?"
"No, I just called to see how everyone was."
"Mary Beth, I just talked to you yesterday. What are you up to?"
"Nothing . . . a couple of friends want to go skiing for a weekend—I don't think I want to go, though."
"Good."
"Good? Why? Why couldn't I go?"
"Well, for one thing, it isn't very safe for young girls to go off by themselves like that."
"Oh, c'mon Ma, there'd be lots of people around."
"I know. That's exactly what I mean. Who wants to go, anyhow?"
"Kim, Theresa and Anne. Just those guys."
"Where are they planning to go?"
"Holiday Valley—you know where Crossley has her chalet."
"Forget it!"
"Why? I can take care of myself."
"Do they drink?"
"I don't know. Yeah, I guess so."
"Well it's not safe to drink and drive."
"Who said anything about drinking? Besides, we'd be staying there."
"You mean they want to stay overnight?"
"Yeah. I already told you that."
"You did not."
"Mom, I did so."
"Your father got the phone bill today."

"Say I can go and I'll get off the phone."
"I thought you didn't want to go."
"I said I didn't think I wanted to go, but now I think I do."
"Well, you're not going."
"Why not?"
"Because I said so. Mary Beth, we've been through this."
"C'mon Mom, they're nice girls. I've never gone anywhere by myself before."
"Who's going?"
"Mom, I told you. Kim, Theresa and Anne."
"Who's Kim?"
"A girl from school."
"That tells me a lot. Have I met her?"
"No. Wait. Yes you did, at graduation."
"What does she look like?"
"Mom, c'mon! I have to let them know."
"Mary Beth, you don't know the first thing about skiing."
"So, I can learn."
"How can you afford to go, anyhow?"
"I've got money. C'mon Ma, what do you say?"
"Where did you get the money?"
"I saved it from the summer."
"I thought you put that toward your tuition."
"I did. There was some left over."
"How much?"
"I don't know. Can I go?"
"I don't know."
"Well, when will you?"
"Watch it or you won't be going anywhere!"
"Sorry . . . but Mom, listen. It's only for two days and it's during reading week. I need a holiday."
"Don't give me that—you need a holiday like I need two heads. Do I get to go too?"
"So I can go then—great! Thanks, Mom."
"I didn't say you could go. You'll have to ask your father."

Bonnie-Jayne Errett
The Weekend Mom Came To Town

It was a Saturday in November. I rode the Yonge subway from York Mills to Bloor. I had spent the day with a friend at her house in North York. I planned to meet my mother who was in Toronto for the weekend. My father had stayed behind in Edmonton. I was to meet Mom at the Bond Place Hotel a block east of the Eaton Centre and the Dundas subway station.

Mom told me her friend Emmanuel, from Montreal, would be in Toronto that same weekend. Emmanuel came from Peru where he took dance and bodybuilding. Mom was a dance instructor in Edmonton and met him last summer at a dance seminar in San Francisco. Mom wrote in her letter that Emmanuel was competing in a body-building competition that weekend and would be staying in the same hotel. She wanted me to meet him. He was twenty-six.

I looked forward to seeing Mom. I had not seen her for two-and-a-half months. We arranged to meet at the hotel at 7:00 that evening.

At 6:30, I knocked on door 1019. The door opened. Mom looked surprised to see me.

"Oh, hi. Come in," she said as she chewed on a blueberry croissant. I walked in. I sat on the double bed. A cot leaned against the wall.

Mom introduced me to Emmanuel. He sat beside the television. "Hi." I sounded cold.

We walked west on Dundas to Chinatown. We ordered the "dinner-for-three" at the Golden Dragon. Dad had taken me there in September when he came to town for a conference. The Golden Dragon was his favourite restaurant.

After dinner we walked to Cineplex Nine. *Octopussy*, starring James Bond, started at 9:45. In the theatre Mom saw to it that Emmanuel sat between us.

After the show, we walked back to the hotel. The big record stores, Sam's and A&A's, were closing. It was midnight.

Emmanuel watched the sports highlights on the television.

"Well, I'm going to bed. I'm tired," I said. Nothing happened.

I pulled Mom into the washroom. "Is he staying with us, here, tonight?"

"Well, yes."

"Why is he staying in the same room?"

"Because . . . he is a student and . . . he couldn't afford to pay for his own."

Mom and Emmanuel set up the cot. I shared the double bed with Mom and Emmanuel slept on the cot. I could not sleep. Emmanuel snored, rustled, and grunted. I cried silently.

Emmanuel's alarm-watch beeped at 8:30. Emmanuel got up and took a shower.

"Is he spending the day with us?"

"Well, yes, he wouldn't have anything else to do."

"What did he come to Toronto for?"

"Well, he is here for a body-building competition."

"Then why isn't he going to it?"

She paused. "He was not actually competing. He was just going to watch . . . but then it was cancelled."

Get the story straight, I thought.

"Then why did he come to Toronto?"

"Because he had already made plans to come."

"Oh sure, Mom."

I turned and went out the door. Mom followed yelling explanations. "Forget it Mom, I don't want to hear it. I don't care."

I ran up the hallway, out the fire exit and down many flights of stairs.

I got off the stairway on the fourth floor. I ran to the elevators and pushed the button. The doors slid open. Mom stood in the elevator. She tried to catch me, but I ran to the fire stairs at the end of the hall. I lost her. I got to the main floor and went to the telephone.

"Operator."

"I'd like to make a collect call to Edmonton."

Dad answered. "Dad, what is wrong with Mom?" I shook as I spoke.

"Why, what happened?"

"That guy 'Manuel stayed in the same room with us. It was awful." I cried.

Mom walked off the elevator. She looked around. She did not see me because a tour group of senior citizens stood in the lobby. I turned round to face the telephone.

"Did this upset you honey?"

"Yes, I didn't know what to do. I didn't want to stay there last night. I wanted to leave."

"Listen, honey, go back to the room and get Mom to call me."

"All right, bye."

I hung up the receiver and dried my tears. I went back to the room. Mom was not there. The shower was still running. I stuffed my things in my knapsack and ran out leaving the door open. I ran down the stairs to the eighth floor. I took the elevator the rest of the way. I left the hotel.

Dundas Station was a block away. I took a train north to Bloor and another west to Islington. From there, I transferred to the Route #1 bus to go back to residence.

It was Sunday and the buses ran slow. I had time to think.

Saudade Gaspar
Papa

171 Leslie Street, 1974. Reflections rushing, bombarding me. 10986 St. Clair Avenue West—Arlington Hardware, 1087 Gerrard Street, 453 Manning, 85 Oxford. . . . It's sad—I never knew anyone for long.

Never settle down. Never. Something inside the man compelling, pulling, nagging, urging, driving, possessing, goading him. Father said it was money. Buying three- or four-storey houses: renting, repairing, renovating. To increase real estate values? Ha. He was a carpenter.

His fantasies—my reality.

Father wanted us to excel in school since he never did. Passing grade four at Escuela Primaria de Oviedo was tough—he bribed Sr. Juan Fernandes with five hundred pesos. Yet, he threatened us constantly. And sometimes he'd hit. Until crying. To hit was to reduce suffering in the long run. We'd forgive him. He was sorry.

Maybe I never understood. Father yelled when lights were left on, or water was running, or something was in the way, or when he felt like it. He told us we were stupid and ignorant. Sometimes I wasn't sure if I loved him.

But I did. In April 1974, he took a two-month trip to Valencia. Embarrassed with tears, I dared not look at him. He cried more than I did.

I was his favourite.

Ieva Martin
The Motherhood Myth and Me

Betty Rollin in "Motherhood: Who Needs It?" attacks the Motherhood Myth—"the notion that the maternal wish and the activity of mothering are instinctive or biologically predestined."

Rollin quotes a psychiatrist, a psychoanalyst and motherhood-researcher, a sociologist, an anthropologist and a demographer to prove that mothering activity is learned, not instinctive. The Motherhood Myth was created. It worked—at least from society's point of view—and was reinforced through "Madonna propaganda." "Madonna propaganda" romanticizes motherhood and hides the "less than idyllic child-rearing part of motherhood," Rollin writes.

Amen!

I had not wanted to get pregnant. I cried when the gynecologist told me he suspected it. Bob was secretly happy but outwardly calm.

I did not have to wait long to encounter Madonna propaganda. An acquaintance, upon learning I was pregnant, gushed about the wonderfully creative process I was involved in. I didn't understand what she was talking about. To create requires conscious effort. I never had such control. I did not choose to conceive nor did I select my child's combination of genes. It was strictly random process. Once the fertilized egg implanted itself in my uterus, I was its victim. Like a malignant growth, it fed off my body and increased in size. Within two months, I could no longer fasten the buttons on my waistbands.

My brother-in-law told me I had a special glow. I dismissed this as a male line calculated to appease a pregnant woman. I was often nauseous. I could no longer tolerate cigarettes or alcohol. Even one glass of wine made me vomit. At night, I had two dinners. After I brought up the first, I ate a second.

Being pregnant meant being aware of the nearest bathroom because I had to go every hour or so.

Being pregnant also meant waddling instead of walking. It meant having a hard time getting comfortable in a prone position. It meant jumping out of bed in the middle of the night because of leg cramps. The only way to relieve the pain was to lift my heels and shift the weight of my body to my toes. Pregnancy was also having a leg give way as the child inside me kicked a vulnerable spot.

I was well aware that giving birth was painful, but I didn't know I wouldn't be able to sit down afterwards. The pain of breast-feeding a child the first two weeks was passed over too quickly in the books I read to prepare for this experience. I dreaded feeding time but missing a feeding was also painful. My breasts leaked at inopportune times.

The question I ask myself is: Why do so many women suffer from post-partum blues if becoming a mother is such a joy? I know why I cried the first week home. Because of an inflammation of the breast, I had a temperature of 103 F. Bob was out on the road somewhere. I was left alone in our high-rise apartment with a crying newborn. I knew no one else in the building who might be there during the day. I was bleeding profusely and had exhausted my supply of sanitary napkins. I felt utterly helpless.

Before my first child was born, I fantasized how I would spend my spare time at home. My boss, who had five, warned me there would be little spare time, but I had to experience it to believe it. I don't know how I survived before we got a second car. Regular visits to a pediatrician had to be planned well in advance. Grocery shopping during the day was impossible. Going anywhere had to be fitted in between naps. A small baby naps twice a day but absolutely refuses to do so if you need a nap yourself. My hands developed a rash from rinsing cloth diapers in the cold water of the toilet. This rash flares up every winter.

For me, one of the biggest disappointments of childbirth was not regaining my waist immediately. When I woke up in the recovery room, my stomach felt almost as big as when I went into the hospital. I wasn't sure it was all over. When it was time to go home, I could barely squeeze into a loosely-fitted dress.

Bob took time to adjust to being a father. Initially, he saw no reason why both of us had to stay home with Andrea on weekends when the skiing was good.

I felt trapped. I didn't realize how much until later. I was engrossed and overwhelmed by the responsibility. I read books on child development and nutrition. To stay sane, I needed intelligent conversation. I tuned in Bruno Gerussi on CBC radio and Dick Cavett on TV.

When Bob came home, he was content to stay there. I needed to get out. Bob did not understand this need. I cried easily. One day, I heard cabin fever discussed on the radio. The symptoms matched mine.

I had to regain an identity that was separate from my husband and my child. I joined the gardening club in Burlington. I took flower arranging and sewing courses. I read. Confidence started to come back when I taught night school sewing for the Halton Board of Education. I thought about returning to university. The need became more acute. I applied to Guelph University and the University of Toronto. Both refused me. I was hurt. I reapplied to U of T the following year. They refused me again.

I decided to fight. Now that I am almost finished my four-year B.A. at the U of T, the Faculty of Arts and Science feels vindicated for giving me a chance. For me, the rest of my life is just beginning.

Linda Tompkins

The New Kid in School

After I turned fourteen, my mother and I fought more often and more intensely. I resented having to launder everyone's clothing, clean the house, babysit my sisters on weekends and tell my mother where I was going whenever I left the house. Minden is a small town, and my mother always had one ear to the grapevine. Her information was thorough.

I had just finished my grade nine mid-term exams at Deer Ridge Secondary School. DRSS was a small school with about 350 students from Minden and surrounding country farms. I wanted to celebrate the end of exams with my friends.

I pleaded for a week and was allowed to see *Jaws* at the Metro Theatre. My curfew was 11:00. I loved the movie and as the house lights came up, I saw it was already eleven.

I ran out of the theatre and all the way home. It snowed as I ran down Oakview Drive in the darkness. I pushed myself to move faster.

My mother waited at the foot of the stairs with my stepfather's leather belt. Between breaths, I tried to tell her that I was sorry I was late.

"When I tell you to be home by eleven, I mean eleven, not one minute later. Pull down your pants," she said.

"I'm only ten minutes late, Mom. Please don't."

"Don't make me angry, Linda. Turn around!"

"No. You can ground me if you want, but you're not going to beat me."

She slapped my face, then brought the belt back to hit me. I grabbed her wrist before she could swing and held the belt away from me.

I said, "I'm not going to let you touch me. Forget it!"

She tried to hit me with her other hand. I grabbed her arm. I said, "I'm serious. You won't touch me." She struggled, so I squeezed her wrists with all my strength. She relaxed her arms and I let go.

She yelled, "You little fucking bitch. Pack your goddamn bags! In the morning you're out!"

As I walked into my bedroom, I saw my diary on my bed. The lock had been torn off. All thoughts of apologies disappeared. I felt violated and angry. I wanted to leave. I packed my bags.

I stood in the London bus stop with five pieces of unmatched luggage at my feet. I was going to my father, a stranger to me. I hadn't seen him in ten years. He spotted me with help from a school photograph I had sent my grandmother. He introduced himself and told me to call him "Dad."

He took me to Mother's Pizza, and over lunch, I told him what had happened.

He said, "Your mother called me at midnight last night, told me to expect you on the bus and hung up. You and I have one thing in common: neither of us can get along with Julie." He told me I could stay in the basement of his townhouse. He told me that I would have to enrol in school by myself because he had to spend the next three days in Kitchener selling hydraulic equipment to a factory.

I moved into the basement with the washer, dryer, sink and water heater. I spent two days lying in bed.

On Monday morning, I waited by the front door, ready to follow this girl who lived across the street. She would lead me to North London Collegiate Institute, wherever that was. I followed her to the bus stop and boarded behind her. The bus was full and I lost sight of her. I panicked and glanced between people's heads to make sure she was still there and I hadn't missed the transfer. I was afraid to be lost somewhere in London. I tailed her right to the front entrance of the school. The main doors were ten feet high and six feet wide, and there were three connected red brick buildings, each the size of Deer Ridge.

I stood before the front door for a few minutes. I was frightened when I entered the foyer. I chose the corridor on the left and looked for the office. I walked past all of the open classroom doors. I felt hundreds of eyes watch me. Time went into a twilight-zone dream-crawl. I tried to move faster, but my legs water-walked.

I turned a corner, and a scary looking hall monitor jumped out at me, grabbed my sweater, and demanded to see my hall pass. "Whaddyamean you don't have one?" he said. "We're talking a trip to the office and a detention for sure!" I shook as I tried to explain that I was new and lost. He gave me directions to the office and I found it.

I was ignored for twenty minutes before a nurse-type secretary asked why I had been sent down. I told her I was there to register. She hmpphed and asked where my parents were. I explained that I had just moved in with my father and that he was away on business. She hmpphed again and said, "You realize he will have to sign all of these papers?" She pushed a stack of them at me.

I sat down to fill them out and looked at the first page in the pile. I wanted to cry. I didn't know my name. Until then, I had used my stepfather's name. At school and at home, I had been Linda Philip. But that wasn't what was on my birth certificate. When I had completed the forms, it hit me. My name was Linda Tompkins and everything I had known was changed.

When I gave her the forms, the nurse gave me a map and a schedule of my classes. She pointed me at the door, and as I was leaving said, "You couldn't have chosen a worse time to enrol. Second term exams start the week after next, and you will have to write them."

I bit my lower lip and once in the hallway, lost my sense of direction. I wandered up and down identical corridors. The end of class foghorn stunned me. I came out of a daze to find myself swept down the hall by a sea of students.

I managed to stop this guy and ask him where room 353A was. He laughed and told me I was in the wrong building. He pointed to an identical building across a walkway. He said the room was on the third floor. Another horn sounded.

I was late, and as I crossed the walkway, my stomach gurgled and I felt nauseated. When I found the third floor, I was ten minutes late for physics class. I checked every door for room 353A. Dread washed over me. I found the class. I looked through its window to see the bearded teacher gesturing wildly with a pointer at the blackboard. Thirty kids, with their heads down, wrote furiously.

I was about to knock on the door when gorge came rising to the back of my throat. I tried to swallow, couldn't, and realized I was going to be sick. I had passed a washroom looking for the class, and ran for it. I prayed. "Please don't let me puke on the floor; let me make it to the can!"

I burst through the washroom doors and lunged for the nearest stall. I was sick all over the toilet seat. The sight of toast and eggs floating in the bowl made me sick again. I convulsed until everything was out and then I dry heaved.

I put the seat up and rested my forehead against the cool porcelain. I wiped up the seat and floor with toilet paper. When I had finished, I washed my face at the row of sinks and rinsed out my mouth. I looked at myself in the mirror and cried.

The foghorn sounded again. I rushed into the farthest stall. I locked the door, sat on the seat and pulled my feet up so nobody could see me.

Jordin Neumann

My Father, Football and Me

I hate playing football. It hurts. Touch is fun. I enjoy watching football on Sunday television. That is enough. But I play full-contact for the Erindale College team, and the playoffs start tomorrow.

Earlier in the season, I liked playing. A new school. A different team. Another position—from quarterback to receiver. Practices were tough. I made new friends. We got through it together. We were a team. Still, I had to prove myself. If the ball came to me or was near me, it was mine. If the ball carrier came in my direction, he was mine. I made the hit. I got hit. It hurt. Then I did it again. I ran with confidence. Nobody could beat me. No damn way! I proved myself.

Now I'm scared. It happened last game against St. Michael's. Two interceptions sounds like a good game. I think the coach saw it. My teammates didn't notice. I played scared. I tried to concentrate, but I wasn't there. If my father had seen the game, he would have said, "You were just going through the motions." He knows me well. I hate that.

Dad played ball. He went to Western Michigan on a scholarship. He was also a receiver. Uncle Pete went pro after high school. Almost nobody does that. Uncle Pete is in the hall of fame now. Uncle Joe told me once that Dad was better than Uncle Pete until Dad broke his leg. That ended his career. Uncle Pete has arthritis and back problems from his days with the pros. Everyone in the family says he still lives in his football glory days, the late fifties and early sixties, when he played for the Hamilton Tiger-Cats. My father hates him. Sometimes my father, like Uncle Pete, dwells in the past.

Scarborough has not lost a game in two years. We play them tomorrow. In our first game, they beat us 24-0. It could have been worse. The coach played me the entire game. On defence, I got burned for the first time all season. I lost confidence. I got hit more. I hurt more. I don't want to play them again. Our only hope is a muddy field. It should keep the score down.

I weigh 151 pounds. I rely on speed and agility. Mud steals this advantage from me. It helps the slow and strong beat up the weak. I'm weak.

The game is at 3:15 tomorrow. Dad's still working then. He wanted to come. I don't want him to. It would spoil his memory. The last game he saw was my best: three touchdowns and two interceptions against Victoria. Dad said nothing after it. He just shook my hand. His eyes glowed with pride. He took me out to dinner. We discussed how I could have played better. We got drunk. I loved the attention, and Dad loved the football.

Tomorrow should be my last game, but the coaches voted me to the All-Star team. I don't want to play in the game, but I have to. I am the star.

Roger Pires

Visiting Home

It's getting late, I thought. He should be home. Cookie, the cat, lay on his back beside me, legs curled over his white belly. His head hung over the edge of the sofa, his fangs exposed.

I read another line of Jane Austin's *Emma*.

> Emma Woodhouse cultivated a subtle manner to outwit her innocent friend Harriet Smith for the hand in marriage of Mr. Knightly.

I reread the line. I reread it again and slammed *Emma* shut. Cookie stuck his face in his paws, sighed and went to sleep. I stood up and vaulted over the living-room table. Cookie followed me down to the kitchen. Potatoes boiled on the stove. Steam covered the windows.

"What time did your father say he was coming home?" Mother pushed toothpicks into the browned breasts of the chickens. She stuck a green olive on each toothpick. Beautiful.

"Well?"

"Ma, it looks great. I'm really starving." She laughed and kissed me on the cheek. I reached for a wing.

She tapped my wrist and pouted. "You better wait 'til your father gets home."

"He should be home already. Holy jeeze, we're going to miss most of the first period."

My dad had to get permission from the foreman to leave work early. He had to give up eighty dollars worth of work time to go to the game with me.

I wasn't in Windsor often—once a month maybe. I knew my dad wanted to spend as much time as he could with me. My mother put her arms around me. She looked at her only son, the son she rarely sees. She was enjoying my presence. She didn't want me nervous or upset.

"Yeah, but I sure wish he'd get home." I snorted a laugh. My temper was down.

"He's doing his best," she said. "You better get a head start on your father. I know how much you eat."

"Nobody eats as much as that guy," I said. I pointed at Cookie. He crouched at his bowl and chomped. "He's a stomach with legs." We laughed and stared at our fat cat. He jerked his head up. Boots clopped at the doorstep. My father's key went into the lock and the door opened.

"Hallo d'ere." We met my father at the door. My mother hugged him, and I gave him five across the palm. Cookie rubbed his legs.

"So how was your day?" I asked.

"Oh, pretty short."

"Gee, your face is all dirty," said my mother.

"Yeah, I had to work in the foundry today. What time is it?"

"Five after seven."

"What time does the bus leave for Detroit?"

"Seven-twenty and every twenty minutes after that."

"Sorry about that."

"It's all right," I said.

"Those guys are a bunch of turkeys. I've been asking them since Monday to leave early today and they forget. This time I told Ron, the other foreman, and he said, 'No problem, have a nice time.'"

He asked my mother, in Portuguese, if dinner was ready and went to wash up. Mother put dinner on the table. When my father had washed his hands and face, we sat down to eat. We finished in five minutes.

"We'll miss half of the first period," I said.

"Well, what can I do?"

"No, no, it's okay. There's no rush. Let's have a good time." He put his hand on my back and smiled.

"Sure," he said, "let's just enjoy the evening. It's okay if we miss ten minutes."

The Leafs, our team, lost to the Red Wings 9-2.

Rick Alexander

Goodbye

It was the Bone annual weekend. Every June the boys got together at Bone's parents' cottage. We drank beer, smoked cigarettes and hustled women. I told my parents I was going on the annual fishing trip. I had to beg to go every year. My parents were concerned about my missing church.

"You'll have to ask your father," Mom said.

"I'll have to talk to your mother about it," Dad said.

When Mom and Dad were on speaking terms, they discussed it.

"Your mother says you can go, but only if you're back for church on Sunday night."

I didn't complain. It was the best deal I could strike.

I packed Friday afternoon. First on the list were the cigarettes and cigars under the mattress. Second was the fake identification in the corner under the carpet. Last were the condoms behind the books in the closet. I rolled them all up in my sleeping bag.

Mom drove me to Tim's house where we were meeting.

"How come there are no fishing rods?" she asked. Tim stood motionless.

"Bone has a bunch up at his cottage," I said.

I kissed Mom goodbye and she drove away.

I unrolled my sleeping bag, pulled out the cigarettes.

"You told her you were going fishing? I told my parents I was going to get drunk, and if I was lucky, I was going to get laid," Tim said.

Tim was taunting me, but he was right. At eighteen, I shouldn't have to ask to go away for a weekend. I shouldn't have to sneak out of the house for a smoke. I shouldn't have to chew a box of Clorets before I came home after a night of drinking.

All weekend, I ate, smoked, drank and swore. I thought about returning home, returning to the excuses, returning to the lies, returning to the game. Saturday night, I thought out loud. I told the guys about the rules in my home: church on Sundays, no smoking, eleven o'clock curfew.

"I wouldn't last three hours there," Tim said.

"Why don't you leave?" Derek said.

"The thought never crossed my mind."

"Why don't you move out and move in with me for the summer? My parents leave tomorrow for ten weeks in Holland," Pierce said.

It was easy to say yes. I was drunk.

I arrived home Sunday just before church.

"You'd better hurry or you'll be late, son," Dad said.

I paused, swallowed and went downstairs.

"I'm not going. I don't like going. I'm leaving tonight." I sat on the edge of my bed and stared into nowhere.

Dad hurried down the stairs.

"What did you say?" he asked.

"I'm leaving you and Mom for a while." I looked up. His eyes were watery, his face pale. I had never seen him like that before. I felt like shit.

"Why?"

I didn't expect that question. I thought he would get pissed off, pack my bags and show me the door.

"I'm tired of the rules, Dad. I'm eighteen now and I'd like to make some of my own decisions."

"I'll always have rules in my house, Son."

"Yeah, I know that, Dad. I just want to try living by myself for a while. Just for a few months."

"I'm late for church. We'll talk about it tomorrow."

"Yeah. We'll talk about it tomorrow, Dad."

The steps creaked as he climbed the stairs. I heard the front door close. They were gone.

I packed everything and phoned Pierce. He said he'd pick me up in fifteen minutes.

I sat at the kitchen table and wrote.

> *Dear Mom and Dad.*
>
> *I left tonight. I couldn't stay any longer. I'll be at Pierce Dooley's. His number is in the book. Please phone soon. I'll miss you.*
>
> *Love,*
>
> *Rick*

Laura D. Rubino
Cindy

Cindy's bedroom smelled of strawberry bubble-gum, CHANEL No.5 and Lysol spray. At the bottom of the oak toy chest, inside the Malibu Barbie camper, next to Ken and Barbie, Cindy hid the sealed jar of water and cigarette butts. Underneath the pink bedspread, in between the mattress and the box-spring, next to the matches, Cindy hid a pack of Players Lights.

Three empty Diet Coke cans stood on the white, French Provincial, night table. At the foot of the night table, a digital bathroom scale covered the burn hole in the bedroom rug. Sammy, her Siamese cat, sat in his usual place next to the bathroom scale and purred. Sammy kept Cindy company at night.

Four old *Teen* mags, opened to different pictures of Bruce Springsteen, covered the wicker, glass-topped desk. Big sister Cathy gave Cindy her old *Teens* after she bought the new issues. "You know, Cindy, I shouldn't be giving you my *Teens*," Cathy said. "You have to be a teenager to read 'em, you know." Cathy was thirteen, Cindy ten.

That Saturday night, Cathy went to her friend Elicia's sleepover. Cindy stayed home. All the little sisters stayed home. Cindy stole her sister's new *Teen* and took it back to her bedroom.

Behind her ears and on the back of her neck, Cindy poured CHANEL No.5 her mother didn't want anymore. Cindy tried on her big sister's training bra. The fat on Cindy's chest filled the tight bra. Cindy smiled as she admired herself. Secured to the frame of the dresser mirror, Bruce Springsteen smiled back. With the bra still on, Cindy went to bed.

At 4:37 in the morning, Cindy awoke—hungry. Cindy rarely slept past five. She got out of bed and turned on her Mickey Mouse night-light. She groped under the mattress for the matches and cigarettes.

She thought about her mother. "Yes, you're right. What's worse, *I know* you're right. It's a filthy habit—it's awful—but it's the only way I can ever hope to lose this weight," Cindy's mother explained to guests.

Cindy opened the oak toy chest and searched for the jar. She needed more light. Cindy removed Mickey's head from the night-light. The naked light reflected off the glass of two framed photographs on the wall over her bed.

In the first photograph, Cindy's mother, a slender woman, stands with her eleven- and eight-year-old daughters on her left and Cindy's father on her right. In the second photograph, Cindy's mother, now stocky, stands with her thirteen- and ten-year-old daughters. Cindy's father is not in this picture.

Cindy lit a cigarette and sucked in the smoke until it filled her. She stared at the wall. She replayed in her mind the scene of her father's leaving six months before. As she exhaled, Cindy thought, "One day, I'll be as thin as my shadow."

She finished the cigarette, added the butt to the collection in the jar, sprayed the room with Lysol and went back to bed.

Emilio Sinopoli

Wrong Room

September 4, 1981. My aunt Connie Sinopoli died of cancer. Hers was a different kind of funeral because she expected to die. She made a point of seeing each of her relatives alone in the months before her death. This gave us a chance to say goodbye. When she died, her body lay in a funeral home way out in the western suburbs.

I waited with my sister Mary and my common-law wife Darlene in front of A&A Burgers at College and Ossington for our ride.

When Frank, Mary's future husband, arrived, she told him we had to pick up my father's cousin, Grace, and give her a ride to the funeral home. This upset Frank because he believed that his new 1981 Cougar could carry only 800 pounds, or four people. More would ruin the car.

When we got to Grace's, Frank blew the horn. Grace came out and told us that she would be ready in a minute. Five minutes later, Grace approached the car with another woman.

"Where do you want to sit?" Grace asked the woman.

Frank's face turned white when he saw the two of them. Together they weighed 600 pounds or more.

Frank said, "Mary, whose funeral are we going to, your aunt's or my car's?"

Mary, Darlene and I knew Frank was upset, so we didn't say anything on our way over. We listened to the conversation, in Italian, between Grace and her visitor from Argentina.

The visitor said, "Grace, I don't believe that it snows in this country."

"What do you mean, you don't believe me!" Grace said.

"Look, you're probably trying to make me look like a fool because I stole your boyfriend forty years ago."

"Look, rattle brain, it does snow in this country."

"How come it's always in the high 80s or 90s when I come to visit you?"

"Look, make sure that this is your last trip, and don't write any more letters either," said Grace.

"Why, you old hag, I haven't written you a letter in forty years. I have never written you—period! Besides, I can't write."

"Who the hell has been writing all these years?" said Grace.

"My daughter writes all my letters to you."

"Now, you are trying to insult my intelligence. Well, when we get back home you can take the first plane out of here and I will pay for it myself."

"Ladies, we are here!" shouted Frank.

"What the hell did he say?" asked the visitor.

"How the hell should I know? I don't understand English," snapped Grace.

"Well, he sounded very upset at you. You should ask him what he wants."

"Why don't you drop dead?" said Grace.

They argued, and we got out. I told them we were waiting.

They couldn't get out of the backseat. They were stuck. Frank jumped up and down. Mary looked at me and signalled for us to start walking. When we reached the building, we turned and saw Frank trying to pull them out.

Darlene, Mary and I laughed until we sobbed. A gentleman in a black suit walked up to us and gave us some kleenex and said, "Children, he or she is with God, so don't worry."

Frank finally got the ladies out. When they got to the door, Frank said, "Mary, you tell them to take a cab because I am not driving them home."

Mary told the two old women to go on ahead. After we got inside, we stopped for a few seconds. Grace and her visitor kept on walking. They wore black 'kerchiefs and hung their heads, looking sad.

They walked into the first room off the lobby. Mary and I looked at the name on the sign above the door: "Mr. Chan Lee." Grace and her friend walked up to the casket and got down on their knees and prayed. When Grace finished, she stood up and looked in the casket. She screamed.

We waited outside the door.

Anne Markey
Laura

The kitchen door bangs shut, cuts at the phone cord. Low rumbles of conversation seep through. I knock twice, walk in. "Hold on," she says into the phone. She glares at me.

"What do you want?"

"It's ten o'clock. Our deal is you go to bed now."

"I'm going. See you tomorrow Dee." Halfway up the stairs, she whirls around. "Get off my back, you bitch! Quit bugging me!" We scream accusations and curses at each other.

I was eighteen when I had Laura. Great Aunt Marge said I was lucky. When Laura was a teenager, I'd be young enough to understand her. I don't. For fourteen years, I fed her, kissed her better when she fell. I cried with her over fights with her friends. I love this child. Now her life is a secret. Laura won't let me touch her. Laura wants to be free.

Laura gets up at six a.m. to wash and blow dry her hair. At eight a.m., she misses the school bus. Make-up is all over her dresser. She paints her cheeks bright red, her lashes dark black, her eyelids mauve. Where did she get the money for all that make-up? At fourteen, she wears a girl's size ten pants and worries about being too fat. She once made herself vomit after eating. I worry about anorexia.

Her father and I talk to her teachers. They say "she has the ability to do much better." Religion, math and geography are failures. School is a social occasion. Laura talks too much in class. Mrs. Walsh tells her to sit in a different seat. Laura refuses to move. Mrs. Walsh pushes her out of the room and into the office. A girl at school threatens to punch her out at lunch time tomorrow. Tonight she cries, afraid of the next day.

Clothes, dirty and clean, cover her bedroom floor. Most of them aren't hers. Laura takes my nylons and Carol's make-up. She demands her grandfather put a lock on her door so "no one can touch my things." Her bed has no sheets. Laura uses an old comforter to cover herself and the dog. Every night, Tim is shut in her room. The dog gets all the love Laura doesn't give me. Sometimes I insist Tim stay downstairs. I feel small when I hurt her that way.

Laura marches through the house with her hands clenched. The little kids stay out of her way. Music from Rush, Iron Maiden, Ozzy Osborne push at the windows. Piercing guitars and angry lyrics suit her now. Yesterday, she came home with a roach clip and was surprised when I knew what it was.

Cheryl and Denise pick her up for a party. For the first time, I get to meet these friends. Cheryl wears a tiny button on her jacket that says, "What the fuck are you looking at?" A button on her purse advertises, "I'll try anything twice." Denise's earrings are red and pink feathers and hang down to her shoulders.

To Laura, going to Harbourfront is a drag. So is the Saint Lawrence Market, High Park or any place we go as a family. She refused tickets to watch Karen Kain dance Swan Lake. Laura saves her allowance for Def Leopard tickets.

I find it hard to punish Laura. If I send her to her room, the radio blasts through three floors. She'll deafen herself. "No phone calls." I have to stay in and watch the phone. Desperate, I threaten to send her to boarding school. Switzerland should be far enough. "You want me to be a lesbian?" Laura asks.

She spends every other weekend with her father. I couldn't cope without that break. All I remember from last week is anger. Times I lost control and how we hurt each other. Monday Laura comes home. "I hate that bastard. I'm not staying there again." Her father doesn't deserve that. I send her upstairs for a half an hour to calm down.

Fifteen minutes later, I knock on her door and go in. She's lying across her bed, her face in the pillows. "Laura?" She won't look up. I lie down beside her. Her whole body goes rigid.

"Get out of here. I want to be alone."

I rub the back of her neck. I talk about when she was little. The time we visited Aunt Nelly's farm and how Laura was amazed to see potatoes growing in the dirt. She kept pulling them up. Her favourite book was *Hop on Pop*. We read it every night.

I tell her how much I love her. Her body relaxes a little. I rub her back and talk about her sisters. Laura's calmer. We laugh about Carol's new boyfriend. He's so skinny. Laura rolls over and faces me. I put both arms around her and pull her close.

Laura cries. "I'm so sorry. I take everything out on you. I don't know why. I don't know what's happening to me." I cradle her head on my chest. We rock back and forth.

Chapter Eight

Wild Cards

Write about anything you want. Match your style to the thought and feeling you want to express.

M. Nakamura

M.M.N.

My name is Margaret Miyuki Nakamura. My mother was going to call me June, after the month I was born. Margaret was her favourite name as a little girl. Mom says Margaret has substance.

Margaret is not like those modern names: Lisa, Stacey and Sandra. I think Margaret is an intelligent, established and refined name. It certainly isn't glamorous. Famous Margarets include: Margaret Thatcher, Margaret Atwood and Margaret Laurence.

I know three Margarets. Two of them belong to my mother's Guild at the Metropolitan United Church. They have failing eyesight and false teeth. The other was my grade-nine music teacher. Sixty-five-year-old Margaret Snider taught me the viola. She shopped at D'Allairds, the polyester palace.

In grade three I wanted to be called Michelle. Then I met Michelle Johnston. She had cooties. I didn't like the name after that. In grade six I wanted my name changed to Mike. I think it had something to do with Mike Kovak. He was two years my senior and my heart-throb. He never noticed me. My classmates called me Maggot-Pie. Mark LeBourdais found that nickname in the library dictionary. Maggot-Pie stuck for three years.

My middle name, Miyuki, is pronounced me-you-key. It is a combination of my father's name, Mikio, and mother's name, Yukiko. It is Japanese and means "as beautiful as the fresh fallen snow." I ask people their middle names just so they ask me mine.

Nakamura means "centre of the village." Dad explained to me that *mura* is Japanese for village and *naka* means centre.

Five years in a row I stood in line to receive an honours certificate from our principal. I never worried that my name would be mispronounced. I am sure Joseph Quattrociocchi took a deep breath before his name was called.

Nakamura is a good name because N is neither at the beginning nor end of the alphabet. This is a good place to be on a class list. If my French teacher, Mrs. Gordon, decided to give a surprise oral test and began with the A's, I was safe. If she tried to get crafty and start with the Z's, I was covered.

There are sixteen letters in Margaret Nakamura. Each name has eight letters. MARGARET NAKAMURA

My initials M.M.N. look nice together. It flows when you recite them. In grade thirteen I captained a co-ed intramural volleyball team with Dan McDonald. We called ourselves the M & M's. We won every game except the last. I had a girl's intramural team later that year. "Get the Nak" managed one win out of fourteen games: that was by default.

I like my name. I don't think I want to marry.

Jennifer Sealy
The Boyfriend and the Albatross

Terry and I had been going out together for a year. Terry was twenty-two when I met him. I was eighteen. We both lived at home and we both went to school. Terry studied music at Humber College. I was in my last year of high school. Everyone told me it was time to decide what to do with my life.

I wanted to write. I had no confidence though. I didn't know if I could do it. I told Terry I wanted to write. I told my father I didn't know what I wanted to do.

Terry asked me to write a story for him, my first real story. I tried to write something he would like. I wrote about camping and dreaming and driving down the highway. I called it "Dreamtime." Every night after supper, I worked on it. I sat at my desk and wrote and rewrote that story. My parents were pleased; they thought I was doing homework. The story was in its fourth draft by the time I was finished with it. I read it over three times.

I gave the story to Terry one year from the day we met. I rolled it up and tied it with a red ribbon. We sat in his car, parked in the lot in front of Mr. Grocer's. I sat in the passenger seat while he began to read. I was nervous. I watched people going into the grocery store. I tried not to care.

Terry read silently for about half a minute, then he read one sentence aloud. That sentence went, "I sat in the passenger seat, eyes riveted on the window. . . ." He laughed. "That sounds stupid," he said. "Eyes riveted on the window." He laughed again.

I tried to smile but I wanted the story back. I didn't want him to read it. It was his story though so I stared out the window and said nothing. Terry continued to read. A few minutes later, he laughed again. It was not a funny story. There was nothing funny about it. I reached out and tried to grab it away from him, but he pulled it away still reading.

"I don't want you to read it now," I said. "You can read it later." I reached for it again and got hold of one corner of the title page. I pulled and he pulled and the page came off in my hand. I grabbed again. We both pulled. He gave up trying to read. He let go when he heard the paper rip.

"It's my story," he said. He leaned over and reached for it. I opened the car door and saw the large brown puddle on the ground. Terry reached again. I held the story over the puddle. He reached again. He lost his balance and fell in my lap. I let the papers fall. They landed in the puddle and floated. Brown ooze seeped over the edges. I put my foot down on top of them and they disappeared. I got out of the car and jumped in the puddle standing on the story. Terry moved over to the driver's seat and stared out the window. Saying nothing, he turned the key in the ignition.

I reached in the puddle for the papers. I felt the dirt under my nails as I scraped the paper from the pavement. The pages were intact. I laid them on the pavement in front of me. I folded them, put them in my pocket, and got back in the car. I did not look at Terry. He backed out of the parking lot and drove me back to school. Terry never did finish the story, and he never asked to.

I wrote my second story in English class. Miss Braden read *The Rime of the Ancient Mariner*. She read in a loud, high voice:

> *Alone, alone, all, all alone*
> *Alone on a wide wide sea!*
> *And never a saint took pity on*
> *My soul in agony.*

I blocked her voice from my mind and wrote my own story. I wrote about my Saturday job at Hillsview Manor.

> *I began my day by cleaning the nurses' station. I wheeled my cart down the hall. I passed by the lounge where five of the residents, three on the couch and two in wheelchairs, watched Ed Allen on television. More than half the residents in our wing were in wheelchairs. Every morning the nurses wheeled the ladies to the lounge and put the television on for them.*
>
> *"Okay, ladies, on the floor." Ed did a series of leg lifts. Vida leaned over and spat on the floor. Ruth's head nodded, and she slumped lower on the couch. "I'm so glad to see so many newcomers this morning," Ed said.*
>
> *I moved on down the hall. Eva, one of the residents, stopped by my cart.*
>
> *"Would you like a headache?" she said.*
>
> *"No thanks," I answered.*
>
> *"I have one you could have," she said and wheeled off toward the dining room.*
>
> *I had almost finished cleaning the nurses' station when I heard a commotion down the hall. I recognized Mrs. Dunley's voice. I walked down the hall and saw Mrs. Dunley hit Vida over the head with her slipper. "I won't have it in my house," Mrs. Dunley said. Vida had spit on the floor. Debbie, one of the nurses' aids, wheeled Mrs. Dunley back to her room.*
>
> *"Why do you take me away? I have done nothing wrong," said Mrs. Dunley.*
>
> *When she was gone, Vida leaned over and spat on the floor again.*

"Jennifer," Miss Braden said. I stopped writing and looked up. "Jennifer, what is the significance of the albatross falling off the mariner's neck?"

I looked at her. I tried to think of something to say. Behind me, Margaret spoke. "It means that he has been forgiven," Margaret said.

I put my story away.

Pauline Stanley
So Many Things

We lie in bed in the late morning light. He swings his legs across to the floor and moves off toward the coffee table.

"You are empty. You are of no use to me," he says. He smiles and looks up. "Not you. The cigarette pack." He throws it in the garbage.

Then comes a time he says, "But I don't love you. I'm just not infatuated with you." And I see the split. This time we are in a park. There is a chill. I can tell he is looking at me, but I stare down at my knees, down my orange pantlegs, into the yellow tree blossoms I crush with my feet. They fall from the tree in spring. They are all around us. I have never noticed them before.

I cry. It all seems senseless. I feel drained and full of hateful rebuttals, but I say, "I know you don't love me. You've told me a million times." I feel in my pocket for another Kleenex and blow.

We should be moving on. There are many things to do on a Saturday. I stare down at my broken pink shoes.

Suzanne Ponikowski

LTD

All summer, Buzz talked about getting a bike and by August we actually had the money saved up. I didn't think this would become reality—I'm no good at saving. We did it though. Buzz had five hundred dollars and I had three hundred. (Since my share wasn't full, I said my part was a contribution for his birthday next month and the bike was all his.)

Buzz was working, so he left it up to me to go and buy the bike. I took Fritz because he had owned many bikes and did his own work on them.

Fritz's first bike was an Indian. Those bikes are priceless now. He bought his for about thirty dollars in the early sixties. This bike was a basket case, but he and his friend got it on the road in no time. They were about fifteen then.

One time, Fritz dumped a Harley when a truck cut in front of him. The bike slid down the pavement. Fritz slid behind the bike. The bike smashed into the truck and bounced back into Fritz. Fritz survived, but the fender of the Harley had Fritz's ass print in it and the keys in Fritz's back pocket had been filed down by the pavement into metal toothpicks. Fritz pulled himself off the street, struggled onto a streetcar, and took himself to St. Joseph's hospital. The doctors told him he was okay and he hobbled home. His back was never the same.

Twenty years later, a doctor told Fritz he had two tale bones because his backbone had been split in half. Because of this injury, he walks in his cowboy boots with his back totally stiff and straight; Fritz intimidates people—they think he's on a power trip—with this very definite, very proud walk. Fritz walked with a bounce in his step that day. We were going to check out a bike.

I was torn between buying a nice bike which needed work or a so-called (by Buzz and me) "slab" bike which was certified—slab because that's usually what the seat is shaped like. It's an embarrassment to get caught riding a slab bike.

Fritz and I were going to see a dude who had a nice Yamaha Special 650 for sale. We looked at the bike, parked on the street, before knocking on the guy's door.

"Looks pretty good. See the back tire? How wide it is? Dis thing's equipped for touring."

"Why? For better road contact?"

"Yep. No leaks on da road or anything. Knock on his door an we'll take it for a spin."

I knocked. No answer. I looked through the front mail slot. I saw stairs straight ahead and two nice helmets on them. The ad said helmets came with the bike. Come on, Come on. Answer the door. There was no answer.

We went home and phoned about an uncertified Kawasaki LTD 750—my very favourite bike in the whole world, besides Harley. They wanted nine hundred for it, but we couldn't look at it until tomorrow which was Saturday. Well, at least Buzz could come too.

The next day on the streetcar, we kept checking out the picture of it in the bike trader. The photo was underexposed, and all we could see was the dark outline of the bike: it looked mysterious and powerful. It had a backrest too.

The house was on a street off Lakeshore Boulevard. We got off about five stops too soon. The Exhibition air show was on, and it was a nice walk. I alternated between asking Buzz what kind of plane that was and asking Fritz what kind of bike that was. Buzz and I gawked at every bike that passed. I kept worrying that by the time we got there, our bike would be sold.

The house was a shabby, run-down bungalow with peeling paint. A fat woman with a big mouth, a beer in her hand and dirty kids hanging on her side came to the fence. The yard was sunburned, hard packed ground with dry, brown tufts here and there.

"Youze must be here fer da bike," she said.

"Yep," Fritz said.

"Do you have a dog?" I asked.

"Nope. Jus a stupid cat. Cummon in."

At this point, a younger skinnier version of our hostess appeared in the doorway with a baby resting on her hip. She was maybe twenty years old.

"Dey here fer da bike?"

"Yeah. Go show'em where it is, dere."

We walked around to the back. The bike—it went well with this place—had cobwebs on the instruments and weeds all through the spokes. The chain looked as though it was crumbling to dust. The oil was pitch black. The fat woman waddled over.

"It was my son's bike. He only had it a little while an' he wiped out. Den he left it sittin' and he owed me money so I'll sell it. He'll be out in a minute."

"Ya talk too much, Ma," the young one put in.

"Great," I moaned. "This is our first bike too." (Really, I couldn't wait to ride it. I loved it.)

"Oh, shit. You're in fer a ride," the fat one warned.

Fritz, Buzz and I (in this order) circled the bike in a surveying ritual. Five major dents stood out on the exhaust and gas tank. Scrapes were everywhere, especially on the left side where the engine was chipped and the rear shock and tail light were bent. Still, the bike had a majestic air to it. I loved it. I looked at Buzz, expecting to see disappointment, but no, he shared my feelings. We must have been nuts.

A big, grubby, biker-like dude came out of the house. Fritz interrogated him.

The dude shook his head slowly and dramatically. "Nope. She's a two stroke, all right."

Fritz said, "You sure? What about da overhead cams?"

"So it's really a four stroke? Waddya know?" We even put oil in with da gas cauze we thought it was a two-stroke. Why doncha start 'er up?"

Yeah, right. As if this thing would start. Fritz had the honours (of trying at least). He jumped down on the kick start over and over until he got tired. The biker dude took over and after a few tries, succeeded. It sounded like a Harley, maybe because it needed new mufflers. I loved this bike. I looked at Buzz—he loved it too.

"Tach's not workin," Fritz said.

"Neither does the speedometer. But you can get dem downda road at TO Cycle fer twenty bucks."

"Wanna take 'er fer a spin?" the dude asked Fritz.

Without replying, Fritz turned the monster around and took off. He'll get either killed or busted, I thought. Fritz rode well and I smiled. I looked at Buzz. He was beaming.

When Fritz came back, he saw our smiling faces and knew to proceed with the bargaining. We talked that dude down to seven hundred and fifty dollars.

We pushed the bike toward home. "A buck a cc," Buzz announced.

Emilio Sinopoli
Animal Lovers

Linda and Nancy have been friends for thirty years. They met in their late teens on a hunting trip with their boyfriends in Northern Ontario. They have two things in common: they both love animals and they both love shopping at the most exclusive shops in Toronto: Holt Renfrew, Creeds, Birks, and a few others in the Bloor and Bay area.

One Saturday morning, Linda and Nancy walked out of Holt Renfrew carrying bags with the store's name on them. They walked along Bloor Street, past the street vendors, and up Bay Street to Cumberland Avenue. They were going to Linda's car to put away their parcels when they came across a dead cat in the street. The cat, torn in half, had been struck down by a car. This grotesque scene spoiled their day.

Nancy said, "God shouldn't let the person responsible for this heathen act go to Heaven."

Linda replied, "If I had a gun, I would shoot the man who killed this poor innocent cat."

"How do you know it was a man that ran the cat over?"

"Because a woman would never hit a cat and leave it on the street. Only a man would do something stupid like this."

"What are we going to do now?"

"Maybe we should go and put our bags in the car."

As Linda and Nancy put their bags in the back seat, Linda said, "Why don't we empty one of the bags and put the cat in it, then go to a cemetery and bury it?"

"That is a marvellous idea," said Nancy.

The two women went back to the cat. Linda wore her husband's golf gloves. Nancy carried a pair of pliers from the trunk and a Holt Renfrew shopping bag. When they got to the cat, Nancy passed the bag to Linda. They both got down on one knee. Linda opened the bag. Nancy picked up the first half of the cat with the pliers and dumped it into the bag. Then she put the other half in the bag. They decided to put the dead cat in the trunk and then go and have a coffee at the 4-D Diner. As they walked toward the diner Linda asked, "Do you think that the bag might leak in the car?"

"Oh my God! Steve will kill you if it does."

"You're right. My husband would never forgive me if I ruined his golf clubs."

"Why don't we go back and put the bag on the roof of the car until we finish our coffee?"

"Yeah, okay, let's do that. You know, I feel so bad about the poor creature with its guts squashed and its body split in two."

The two women went back. They put the bag on the roof of the car and walked to the restaurant.

They sat at a table closest to the window to keep an eye on the car. As they drank their coffee, they stared at the car in deep thought about the cat.

Suddenly a woman with long brown hair wearing designer jeans and a green Roots sweat shirt came up to the car. She looked around. She grabbed the Holt Renfrew bag and ran toward the restaurant.

The woman walked in with the bag and sat at a table next to Nancy and Linda. Nancy and Linda looked at each other and didn't say anything. The woman set her purse on top of the table and the bag under the table on the floor between her legs. The waiter came, and the woman ordered a coffee. As the waiter walked away, she leaned back in her chair, opened the bag and looked in. She fainted and fell on the floor.

The waiter rushed to help her. He tried to revive her and couldn't. Another waiter phoned for an ambulance. When the ambulance arrived, the attendants picked her up and laid her on the stretcher. They put her purse on her stomach, placed the Holt Renfrew bag on her chest, rolled her outside and lifted her into the ambulance. Red lights flashing, siren wailing, the ambulance pulled into the Saturday traffic.

Linda Tompkins
Spring Rolls and Beer

Johanna walks through the alley with me and we see the right-to-life protesters barring the back entrance but we ignore them and walk past them and I shut my ears to their rantings because I've made my decision and the security guard unlocks the door for us and we walk in and he locks the door behind us and I am nervous but I don't go back and we go upstairs and we sit in the waiting room and we look at the other patients and I wonder which people are having abortions and which people are there for support and I fill out a form and I go into the office and pay my $275 and I give the receptionist my OHIP number and she gives me a muscle relaxant but I'm not relaxing and I go back to the waiting area and I pretend to leaf through magazines and I can't stop thinking what will happen and will it hurt and will Ted still love me and will my life be different and what's taking so long and then I'm called into another office and the woman doctor describes the procedure and informs me about possible complications and gives me a glass of water and I drink it and I sign the release form and I go back to the waiting room and Johanna tries to keep my mind off what will happen and I'm glad she's there even if it isn't working and my name is called so I go upstairs and they tell me to take off my clothes and put on a hospital gown but to leave on my underwear and I come out and I see three girls sitting in recliners with blankets and drinking hot chocolate and eating arrowroot cookies and I'm hungry and no one seems to be talking and I'm frightened and a doctor takes me into an examination room and I see Dr. Morgentaler and he smiles at me and he says not to worry but I do and then I lie down and another doctor puts salve on my lower abdomen and then runs this long cold instrument like a rolling pin over my uterus pushing hard and I try not to cry and the ultrasound is over and I really am seven weeks pregnant and I have to go through with the abortion and I'm scared and I want Ted but it's time to take me in so I follow the doctor into the room and Dr. Morgentaler is going to perform my abortion and I look around and I see a long table

207

covered with paper and the stirrups at the end and they tell me to take off my underwear and I do and I get up on the table and lie down and put my legs in the stirrups and a counsellor is there and she holds my hand and shows me how to use the gas if I feel any pain and she asks me questions and I try to answer but someone's stabbed me and it hurts and I inhale some gas and she tells me to tell her about my dentist and I try to but the pain takes my voice away and she holds my hand tighter and I close my eyes and one more stab of a saw cuts into my side but I don't cry out and I keep my eyes closed and I think about Ted and I want it to be over and the counsellor says my name so I look up and she smiles and tells me it's over and she puts a pad between my legs and helps me with my underwear and I thank Dr. Morgentaler and I sit in a recliner with a wool blanket over me and I eat arrowroot cookies and I ask the other two girls how theirs went and one says it really hurt and they are both having post-operative cramps and I close my eyes and drink hot chocolate and I want to leave so they make sure I am okay and I get dressed and I go downstairs and Johanna is there and she asks me where I want to go and I tell her the Rivoli for spring rolls and beer and she takes me.

Right then, one life was gone so two could begin again. I cried.

Laura D. Rubino

Change

Change. I rush from the bathroom with a towel around me. I open the closet door in my bedroom. The muted greys, faded blues and washed-out blacks now act as backdrop to the bright reds, electric blues and soft pinks. It's time these colours came out of the closet.

I dress.

In the dresser mirror, I see a little more colour, a little less weight and not enough skin. Undo one more button on the soft pink shirt—now, that's two from the top. The hair—I'll fix that after exams. The nails: not polished, not pretty, just clean. The hands: take off that gold band, dammit! That's over. Yeah, I think it's finally over for me, and I survived.

Turn away from the mirror and run your fingers down the six strings beside the bed. Turn away from the mirror and look at yourself. Mr. Guitar, no more sad songs. Mr. Guitar, listen to the singer and not the song; it's not the pretty words but that the feeling is strong!

Dammit, when I put my mind to it, I can do anything. That's not being conceited; that's the truth. Yah, I can do anything, but that doesn't mean that I have to do everything. You tried that once—more than just once—and you failed.

God, I hate failure. If I don't finish writing Professor Allen's assignment, I'll know failure again.

At school, they're not quite as scared of me as they used to be; I'm not as harsh. I've softened some of the hard lines. I wear yellow too.

Some still wonder what I am. I think that I know, now: I'm different—thank God; I'm loving—the gold band; I'm alive—thank myself.

The gold band:

> *Heaven gives its glimpses only to those,*
> *Not in position to look too close.*

Next month I get my glasses; I'm nearsighted.

Take off the band, but don't throw away the gold. Gold is a precious metal.

I hope that he doesn't actually read this assignment. Don't read this, Allen.

What does he think about me? I wish that I knew. Hey, Allen, what do you think about me? Besides the fact that I'm crazy, warped, *loca en la cabeza*? That last one is Spanish, Allen.

Shit, I took a lot of languages in high school: French, Spanish, Latin, Italian, English. I took a lot of everything in high school—jack of all trades, master of none. Yeah, I can do anything; but I've stopped trying to do everything.

Professor Allen will hate this. That's okay, I hate it too. It's not my style. Neither are the muted greys, faded blues and washed-out blacks. If you're still reading this, Allen, I've got a few things to say to you.

You taught me to trust myself and to trust my reader. I didn't believe that anyone understood my themes. I had to spell them out and show the readers how to react. You taught me subtlety and suggestion—muted greys, faded blues and washed-out blacks. You taught me to suggest brighter colours and let readers paint them in their minds.

Change: write in muted greys, faded blues and washed-out blacks; live in colour. I finally got it right, dammit!

Chapter Nine

Interviews

Interview someone about something that interests you, and produce a piece using material collected in the interview.

Nancy Nieuweboer
Growing Up in Beirut

Nadia Odeh was born in a small house in Beirut, Lebanon, in 1967. As a young child, she attended a private Catholic school while her three older brothers went to public school.

"I attended a Catholic school in Beirut where nuns taught me French and Arabic. But, after grade three, it was too dangerous to go to school. The bus that picked me up was in risk of getting bombed. So my mother taught me at home in Hadas. Dad worked in some kind of factory while Mom stayed home taking care of us and cooking and cleaning.

"Our home was part of a villa. We lived above a butcher's shop. The butcher brought live cows to his shop and slaughtered them on the street in front of our place. I watched while he placed the cow's head on a platter and cut its neck with a long knife.

"He skinned it as flies gathered. Blood gushed into the sewer. One time, a cow escaped and ran up the stairs to our apartment. What a mess she made—all over the floor, the fridge, everywhere.

"Another time, we had a flood. An old water tank in the attic leaked, leaving a foot of water. Everything was ruined. My dad drilled a hole in the floor to let the water run out.

"I loved that place. From the balcony, I could see the Mediterranean. The country was beautiful then.

"I had two friends who lived just around the corner. Together we searched for big black bugs in white flowers that grew in the field behind our house. We strung them and collected them in matchboxes. For adventure, we ran across the field to an abandoned castle with huge stone walls, broken windows, overgrown courtyards. We climbed a wall to get in. Inside, we found rooms to hide in. I sprained my ankle once jumping from the wall to get out. I tried to keep it secret. The hospitals were not nearby, and most were occupied by injured soldiers.

"The fighting became worse, and soon it was not safe to play outside. Villas around us were blown up. Our balcony had many bullet holes. The sound of falling bombs was familiar. The kitchen provided the best shelter. Sometimes, we stayed there for days. After Dad's death, things got worse. Often, we hurried to underground bomb shelters. I hated those. People everywhere. Scared people everywhere.

"A close friend of the family was blown up in his own backyard. Women and children stood and stared as army jeeps dragged people on ropes down the street. Mom received harassing phone calls, threats to kill us all.

"It was time to leave. It wasn't easy, but Mom pulled it off. We left almost everything behind. Rugs, chandeliers, furniture, and our home country."

Nadia was eight when her family arrived in Toronto. "I was frightened but curious. The city was all so new and strange. I felt like a baby exploring its world. I wish I could have that feeling again.

"You know, I really miss Lebanon, my grandmother, my town, my people. Grandmother visits Canada sometimes. She always returns to our homeland. I will never go back."

Alison Rasmussen

Personality and Goodwill

Jane walked beside me. "I'll be glad to get home. I'm bushed." Jane moved her red knapsack from her left shoulder to her right. She wore light blue sweat pants, a baggy yellow sweat shirt and white Nike running shoes. Her blonde hair was tied in a short ponytail. No one would think Jane once suffered from anorexia nervosa.

We went to Jane's apartment. We sat among pillows on the living room floor.

"So you want me to tell you what it was like to be anorexic," Jane said. I listened.

"I was always pretty sensitive. I was also a perfectionist and I never wanted any problems. I just wanted everything to be nice and happy.

"My problem with anorexia began in high school. I was seventeen. I hung around with a popular crowd—ones who dated a lot, wore nice clothes and went to parties all the time. Sometimes they made me feel like I didn't belong, like I wasn't good enough. I was pretty, I knew that. I had nice blonde hair and a clear complexion. Boys were friendly to me and I liked that. I admit that I was a bit chubby at the time, but I was nowhere near obese. My friends would say, 'Jane is so pretty, but she's fat,' or 'Jane would have lots of boyfriends but she is a little bit too fat,' or 'Jane has got such a nice personality. Too bad she's fat.' I heard these things over and over.

"At seventeen, you can be pretty sensitive about how you look to other people. I began to feel disgusted with myself. Being fat bothered me.

"One day, my sister and I had a huge fight. We were screaming at each other. She didn't want me to borrow her clothes. She told me I was too fat to fit into any of them. When she said that, I just looked at her. She looked like she wished she hadn't said anything. I left her standing there and went to the basement. I sat in the dark for a long time. Nobody knew where I was. I heard Mom call me for supper. I didn't go. I didn't want to see or talk to anybody. I skipped dinner.

"Later, I came back upstairs. Mom had saved me something to eat. I took it and threw it in the garbage. The next morning, I went on a diet. I would skip breakfast and bring some cheese and fruit to school for lunch. I played basketball and volleyball after school, so I always came home after everyone had eaten. If I didn't have sports I stayed and did my homework in the library. It was easy not to eat. I was losing weight. I always threw out dinners Mom saved for me. I made my own dinners; lettuce and cucumber sandwiches, celery, cheese or yogurt. I did this every day.

"Soon, my dieting efforts began to show. I received many comments about my appearance. 'Oh, you look really nice,' or 'You've lost a lot of weight.' By that time I had lost fifty pounds. I weighed one hundred.

"I still felt fat. Each time I looked in the mirror, I saw a fat, ugly person. I didn't feel skinny enough so I kept on dieting and losing weight.

"Mom asked me why I stayed so late at school. I told her I had sports or that I needed the privacy to work. She knew something was wrong, but she didn't know what to do. I wish she had said something to me. I think she thought I would grow out of it.

"I joined a synchronized swimming club and the track team when basketball and volleyball seasons were over. I read somewhere that exercise helped you to lose weight. I exercised a lot. I would run five miles, do a hundred sit-ups and ballet exercises before school every morning. I became a chronic exerciser. I had to keep moving.

"One day, the school counsellor, Mrs. Zalukey called me into her office. It was right after track practice. I was suspicious. Why did she want to talk to me? I hadn't done anything wrong.

"Mrs. Zalukey asked me how things were going in school and at home. I said, fine. She asked me if I was eating properly. I remember saying yes. I was scared. Everybody wanted me to be fat again. She gave me some pamphlets that said what I should eat and how much. I looked at all the foods listed that I would have to eat. They wanted me fat. I threw the pamphlets out. I didn't eat.

"My period stopped. I was always cold, always hurting. I was always tired, too. I had bruises on my knees from them being together. They were so bony. If someone bumped into me, it hurt. I weighed eighty-five pounds.

"I went to visit my sister in Ottawa. When I got there, she just stared at me. What's your problem, I thought. Now you can't say I'm fat! All her friends stared, too. I didn't feel very comfortable. I overheard one of them asking my sister if I had some kind of cancer. My sister tried to talk to me, but I wouldn't listen. I went home to my dieting and exercising.

"I came to my senses the morning I couldn't get out of bed. I was so weak. I stumbled down the stairs and went into the bathroom. I looked in the mirror. I finally saw what I had become. I looked ugly, so skinny and pathetic. My hair was just sitting there like straw. My eyes had black circles underneath them. My cheekbones stuck out from my face. I slipped my pyjamas off. I could see every one of my ribs. It was gross. My hips and backbone stuck out. I had no stomach. I could fit two fists between my legs when they were together. I looked like a skinny old woman. I was only seventeen!

~~Account payable~~
- Vacation pay ✓
- record of employment ✓
- inter company matter
- EDT sept 89 ✓

~~PPRR bank book~~

Calculate
~~Calculate~~ Calculate
~~Cat.~~
Calculate

中秋加華青年節
MID-AUTUMN CHINESE CANADIAN YOUTH FESTIVAL

主辦：全加華人協進會（平權會）
多倫多分會

日期：一九八五年八月三十一日
（星期六）
時間：下午六時至九時
地點：多倫多市大會堂

Presented by
Chinese Canadian National Council, Toronto Chapter

Date: August 31, 1985
Time: 6:00 p.m. to 9:00 p.m.
Place: Toronto City Hall

文娛匯演 — VARIETY SHOW

民歌比賽決賽 — FOLK SONG COMPETITION FINALS

攝影展 — PHOTO EXHIBITION

畫展 — ART EXHIBITION

花燈遊行 — LANTERN PARADE
（免費派發燈籠給兒童）(Free Lanterns for Children)

協辦：
加園華語中文節目
加拿大華人舞蹈協會
加拿大華人教育基金
安省華人社團聯席會議
全加華人專業人仕聯會
多倫多華人合唱團
多倫多華商總會
加拿大中國民族樂團演奏隊
星島日報
安省公民及文化部
全加華人協進會（平權會）

Sponsors:
Chifu Radio (Chinese Voice)
Chinese Canadian National Council (National)
Chinese Canadian National Education Fund
Council of Chinese Canadians in Ontario
Federation of Chinese Canadian Professionals
Chinese Canadian Choir of Toronto
Chinarts Dance Association
Toronto Chinese Chamber Orchestra
Sing Tao Newspaper (Canada) Ltd
Ontario Ministry of Citizenship and Culture
Chinese Instrumental Music Group of Toronto
Chinese Fortuna

"I didn't know what to do. I was so scared. I went to the kitchen. I never realized how hungry I was. I stuffed food into my face. Pickles, bread, cookies, peanut butter, bologna, anything. I got sick and threw everything up. I was so scared. I didn't know what to do.

"The next day, it hurt to get up. I went to school anyway. I did the most courageous thing that morning. I went to see Mrs. Zalukey. She just sat there and listened. I really appreciated that. I admitted I had a problem, a serious problem. She told me I had Anorexia Nervosa. I had heard a little about it. She explained that it was a psychological fear of getting fat, fear of growing up or a need to feel in control of your life. She tried to make me understand that what I was doing was very destructive. I was so scared.

"I refused to see a doctor or go to the hospital. We planned to meet each day. I knew I wanted to be pretty and healthy again. I was so skinny and ugly, you wouldn't believe it. I never wanted to look like that again.

"I met with Mrs. Zalukey each day during my last year at high school. We talked about school, my friends, what I wanted to do after high school, who I identified with, and what I did in my spare time. I began to gain weight. It took me four months to gain eight pounds. I began to look better and feel better. I got my weight back to 110 pounds.

"I found out a lot about myself and other people. I'm glad I realized what I was doing to myself before I got into using laxatives or vomiting to make myself lose weight. I've read about others who weren't so lucky, like Karen Carpenter.

"When I think back about it, I sort of understand why I became anorexic. It was peer pressure. I felt like I had to be like those other girls, to have boyfriends and be invited to parties, to be popular.

"High school was a hard time. Not academically but emotionally. There was always pressure to look good, to be the best. I learned that appearances don't really count for much. What counts is personality and goodwill. If a person doesn't have personality, then all they have is a body.

"I still keep myself in good shape and I watch what I eat, but not like I was doing fifteen years ago. I focus on good things in my life today, rather than the negative things that happened in the past. I realize that when I was anorexic, I was not only hurting myself, but also my family and close friends. They thought I was going to die.

"Getting caught up in society's idea of what a person should be is stupid. Wherever you go, you see someone or something telling you to lose weight, that you're not skinny enough, that you're fat if you don't look like a toothpick.

"I overheard a woman say that she wished she could have anorexia for a month or two to lose some weight. Hearing that made me mad. Nobody should wish for that."

Scott McDonald
Bill Bates

Bill Bates puts the coffee on the counter in front of me. He leans against the Coke dispenser and tells me about his work as dog catcher for Berwick Township.

"Caught one 'bout two weeks back, had no collar, no tags. Seen 'im down by the second concession, you know, the Huff road. Well, sir, I got that dog into the back of the Ford, took it back to the farm and put a hole through its head with my .22. Just when I get finished burying the damn thing, I see the goddamn O.P.P. cruiser pull up."

Bill's Tastee Burger restaurant sits in a slight depression in the roadside of Highway Two near Berwick. It has six tables and one counter with five swivel stools. The illuminated menu board, yellow with age, lists burgers, fries and Tastee-Dogs. Flies buzz at the corners of the windows looking out onto the highway. An old retired farmer sits in one of the booths and smokes quietly.

Bill continues. "The cop gets out of his car and says, 'Bates, you caught that dog, didn't you?'

"I said, 'Yessir.'

"'And I bet you just finished burying it too, right?'

"Again, I said, 'Yessir.'

"The cop told me I was in for a shit load of trouble. Half an hour after he left, I get this phone call from some guy off of

Highway Two, wants to know where his dog is. I tell him it's under half a foot of ground behind my tool shed. Now this guy says it's worth fifteen hundred bucks! Said he had the papers to prove it. Told me he was phoning the cops. I just told that son-of-a-bitch the cops just left, and I was sending him a bill for thirty-five cents, price of a bullet, then I hung up. Never heard from him since."

Bill pulls a fresh, green pack of Export A from the display case. After lighting up, he explains, "Township only pays me five thousand a year. What the hell do they expect me to do? Book the friggin' things in at the goddamn Holiday Inn? Christ no. A bullet costs a lot less than a can of dog food."

I finish my coffee and tell Bill my dad figures he needs a face cord of split wood for the cottage. "Great," he says, "I got that in the back of my truck now. You come with me. I don't want to unload it all." We make our way to the door.

As we head out onto Highway Two, Bill tells me about his truck. "Bought it for sixty bucks, cost me another sixty for my buddy who owns a garage to certify it."

"Price of three two-fours?" I ask. He laughs. Maybe he thinks I'm okay, even for someone in university.

"Thirty goes to the government, an' ya don't ask where the other thirty goes," he says.

Bill's truck is a beat-up 1975 black Ford Ranger. "Watch this," he says as we approach the highway cutoff. He pushes the brake pedal to the floor. The truck slows a little. "Ya don't need brakes when you got a transmission, eh?" He laughs and jams the shift lever from third to first. "If I ever think I can't make it, I take to the ditch and give the nearest farmer five bucks to pull me out before the cops show."

I ask Bill what he does when he's not shooting dogs, making hamburgers or sliding into ditches. "Septic tanks," he says, "are big business in this neck of the woods. People gotta shit, ya know. Twenty years ago, we could just pump it up, and dump it into the lake. Now you have to pay the city to dump it into the lake for you. Everyone could save a lot of money if they just shit in the lake!"

We unload the wood at the cottage and start back to Tastee Burger to pick up my car. Bill pulls around the corner at Lake and Berwick Roads. The pavement is icy, and he loses control.

The rear end of the truck slides into a snowbank. We are stuck.

"You better get out and push," he says, "my back's been real tender lately."

I get out, brace myself against the snowbank and push. Bill lights an Export and starts to rock the truck by shifting from first to third. After ten minutes of rocking and pushing, we get the truck back on the road. I climb back in, out of breath.

"Cold out there, eh?" he says.

Back at Tastee Burger, Bill pulls up the hood and opens the master brake cylinder. "Just as I thought," he says, "no brake fluid."

Anne Markey

Bob

"I was really suffering from headaches. I went to Rick's party. It got so bad I had to lie down. Next day, we came home. I made an appointment to see the doctor. He arranged for tests. They stick pins in your head with wires. They didn't show nothing. Let me see, I've got it written down here."

Bob is my brother, the youngest child and only son. He's six foot, two inches tall, twenty-one years old. Bob fumbles for his wallet and slowly unfolds a piece of paper. He covers one eye to read. The paper has dates and explanations. Bob carries the paper in case he is suspected of drug or alcohol abuse. He stumbles when walking, slurs some words, forgets others. Throughout the interview, Bob holds the paper. It gives order to the last year.

"The headaches got so bad I had to go to Peterborough. Chuck Hoag's son is a doctor there so they kept me in. It was so crowded I had to sleep on a gurney in the emergency room. They woke me up and said, 'Come on, you're going to Toronto.' They shipped me to Sunnybrook in an ambulance with a nurse and everything.

"I had several CAT scans. The dye that goes in your system made me sick. I remember I couldn't stand the light. I coloured Mom's glasses with a black marker. June 14, I was in Peterborough; June 15, I was in Sunnybrook. They set me up with the first shunt operation to remove the fluid in my brain. I presume they made tests and found I had the tumour 'cause I don't remember. So many things must have happened I don't remember.

"I forgot to say I met a lady called Kitty Wells who was scheduled to have a tumour operation too. She brought me coffee. Next morning was the day for my operation. That was June 29. We sat in the waiting room smoking cigarettes. After Kitty went to bed, I couldn't sleep. I remember I couldn't understand why everyone was so worried about me. I was supposed to be crying. I knew something was wrong. I couldn't figure out what it was. I was so out of it.

"I can still remember trying to get the doctor's shirt when I went to the operating room. I thought it was cool. The anesthetist was from Lindsay. We were talking as he gave me the anesthetic. Next thing I remember is waking up in intensive care after the tumour operation. It was strange. Half the hair on my skull was off. I had a big doughnut wad of gauze to protect the area where the shunt and tumour operations were. I kept trying to take it off because I couldn't sleep. It felt too hot in there. I think it was three or four days later I was out of bed. I'm not sure. I was in ICU for six weeks. Another shunt operation July 13. Yeah, I had another July 13. It wasn't working good enough. I had another July 25.

"It was at this point that I started feeling different as far as my health. Double vision. I had to wear a patch. Had to get around in a wheelchair. I couldn't even walk. Balance severely impaired. I couldn't go to the bathroom by myself. I had to have a sack with me. I couldn't swallow anymore. Because I couldn't swallow, I had to be fed by a tube. I lost sixty-five pounds. Went through about three dozen boxes of Kleenex putting my saliva in it. And I felt shitty about all of it.

"I realized one day why I was taken down for radiation. I had a malignant tumour. It was scary going down to the room where they did radiation. It was a big, long white corridor they pushed me down every day. It scared me because I really didn't understand why they were doing it. I found out one day.

A doctor came in and asked me if I knew what a malignant tumour is. That means it's growing. Anyway, this radiation, it made me have weird dreams. One night they said to me, 'Come on, Bob. We're going to take you to Brecker to do some treatment there.' After, we could have fish and chips. I just asked Mom if they took me there, just last week. Reason I was not told by my parents that I had cancer was I was so out of it.

"Oh yeah. How I got the tube out of me. One day I went to radiation. The nurse said, 'Off with your gown.' The tube was pinned to the top. It hurt like a bitch. She said, 'I'll get someone to put it back in.' I said, 'No. Let me try without it.' They wouldn't let me try solid food. I had to swallow liquid and sugar. That tasted like crap.

"Okay. I guess the next thing was August 21, 1982. They said I had to go for chemo. I didn't know nothing about it. They seemed reluctant to tell me anything. Doctors said I'd lose all my hair. I'd be sick, lose my appetite along with about twelve other things. The real kicker was the day they were injecting me the doctor said I would be sterile for the rest of my life. That's pretty shitty.

"I was scheduled for chemo for six months. I started October 17. Finished the day before Christmas. Lots of things they said would happen didn't. I didn't lose my hair or nothing. I lost most of it with radiation. I didn't feel really good. I wasn't sick. I felt like I was alone quite often. That's when Tammy gave me all the trouble. The second treatment was the last time I saw her. I sensed it before. She was supposed to be my fiancée. But she left when I got sick. I guess that's all you could say. She never told me nothing. I didn't need to be told. It showed she had no guts.

"Next Riverdale and rehab. I can feel myself getting better for what I'm doing. I learned to walk again, go to the bathroom by myself, and regain my balance. I have three classes: gym, remedial games, occupational therapy. Doing simple math, crossword puzzles, word searches, stuff like that. The puzzles I like to do.

"I work hard. I work hard in all of them. I find it very challenging. Next week, I start a new class called Family Lifestyles. Like trying to be on your own again. I'm trying really hard in all the classes."

Michelle Faultless
Scum

Scum lives with her fiancé, Johnny. They live in a house at Gerrard and Parliament in old Cabbagetown. I don't know Scum's real name or her age. Scum doesn't talk much about her past in Ottawa. Scum is in Toronto now. She says she's happy, and that's all that matters.

Scum and Johnny live with eight friends. They all share two bathrooms and two kitchens.

"All the people here are good shit," Scum says. She pushes her hair, bleached white, out of her face. "Griffen, one of the skinheads, causes some problems. He owed some money to the River Street boys, a local gang. They came into the house and stole all Griffen's possessions. What they couldn't move the boys slashed. They even took Griffen's dog, Rebel."

Scum doesn't worry about violence. "I'm always with Johnny if I go out at night. Then again, I'm a pretty impressive chick when I'm in full drag." She wears black cavalry boots, black leather chaps, a black leather jacket with "wild and free" written on the back and a denim vest. Scum also wears a studded dog collar and spiked hand shackles. Her hair is cut blunt and hangs to her shoulders. The bangs are longer: they fall to her waist. "Sometimes I dye my bangs pink with food colouring and braid them under my chin. It freaks people out on the subway."

The room Scum and Johnny live in is small. It contains a double box spring and mattress, a dresser and a night table. "It's better than we had before. We used to live at Sherbourne and Dundas in a basement closet. The area sucked. The heavy metal boys came down on us. I hated it."

Scum and Johnny couldn't pay the rent. Both lived off Scum's welfare. They were evicted. "Somehow we were able to survive. Johnny stayed with his mother. There was no room for me. I had to do the crash circuit for a month until we found this place. I slept on friends' couches, in hostels and back rooms of bars. My system got screwed around. I wasn't eating right. I ended up kicking smokes because I couldn't afford them, and I hated to bum."

Although Scum doesn't work, she keeps busy. "Most of the time I read: magic, the occult and demonology. I belong to Wicka, sometimes called the Pagan Circle. It is a religious group. Our purpose is to raise energy levels in the circle of people. This energy can be used to heal pains.

"One afternoon, I was lying on my bed reading and my pussycat Daisy was on my lap purring. I had a cup of tea. My man was on his way home. I realized that this was all I wanted. I love Cabbagetown and all its crazy people. I have fun. It's all that matters."

Lorraine Storr

I Love A Good Party

Saturday February 12th, 11:45 p.m. The fire has warmed the living room. Shirley, forty-five years old, has been married for twenty-five years this July. The light from the fire throws her flickering shadow on the wall behind her. A glass of rye rests in her right hand, a cigarette in her left.

"Len says I have a problem—I drink too much. We had a doozy of a fight last Thursday. He threatened to leave. Len's good that way; he'd never kick me out. He went into the bedroom and started to pack. I know he wanted me to stop him, but if he wants to go . . . fuck him. Let him go!

"He asked me if I wanted him to leave. The sad thing is that I don't care. I really don't. He says he'll give me $100,000 and leave. I don't want the money. I don't care about that. I just want to be happy.

"We were happy when we had nothing. We began in 1960 with nothing. We never knew if Santa would come, although he always did. Len made the truck body business from scratch. We worked hard. We've been through a lot. The kids came in 1960, 1961 and 1962. *We* used to have problems at work. Now, *he* has problems at work. I'm supposed to understand, but I don't. It used to be *our* business—a part of *our* life.

"He never does leave. I guess he's confused because I never beg him to stay. I know that's what he wants to hear.

"I was sitting at the kitchen table yesterday. Len comes out and says, 'Admit you have a drinking problem.'

"I mean, Jesus Christ! It's 7:30 in the morning! Here we go again, I thought. 'All right,' I said. 'I have a problem. Is that what you want to hear? I have a problem.' I figured it would shut him up. He then wants to know what I'm going to do about it. I mean, Jesus Christ.

"He says I have a drinking problem. But I don't drink during the day—never. Well . . . if I do, it's only when the housework is all done, the table's set and I'm waiting for supper to finish cooking. Maybe then I'll sit down and fix myself a drink.

"I wonder if I still love him. Do I really love him or is he just a habit? He is good to me, I admit that. I don't know what'll happen.

"The kids have it figured out. They say I'll stick around for my twenty-fifth anniversary. Well, I suppose I will. I love a good party."

Aline Burke

A Pregnant Lesbian Talks About Her Pregnancy

Sally Johnston is pregnant, and she is a lesbian feminist. I asked her about her experience as a pregnant lesbian.

"When I first decided that I wanted a baby, I was involved in a relationship. When our relationship ended, I thought, 'How can I have a baby?' Because I was not living in the couple model, I was afraid. I felt I needed the support of others to have a baby.

"Later, I moved into a collective house with other lesbians. I checked with my housemates, and they supported my having a child. One of them had lived with a child before and was still very connected with this child.

"For two-and-a-half years, we talked about what each of us would be willing to commit of ourselves to the child. It took time for us to find that everyone could trust each other's commitment. We worked it out so that people could share parenting. I would be the primary parent.

"I wanted to have artificial insemination. I did not want to know the father. I did not want the father to have legal power over me or the child. And I did not know a man that I trusted enough. Neither did I want a Sunday father.

"I was referred to a urologist by a GP. The urologist had access to sperm. When the urologist found out that I was a single woman, he took two weeks to decide whether or not he would do the insemination. Then he said yes provided I see the gynecologist of his choice. So, I agreed to his terms. This gynecologist told me, 'Having a child is no lark.' On the day before I was to get the AI (artificial insemination), the urologist said, 'No.' He gave me no explanation.

"So, I decided, 'Fuck the doctors.' I decided on a double blind method of getting pregnant. This means a friend of a friend finds a donor. My friend, Joan, has a friend, Tanya, whom I don't know and who does not know me. My friend Joan doesn't know the donor.

"He, the donor, ejaculated into a sterile container which was brought to me. I put the sperm into a syringe. Then I put the sperm into my vagina. I lay on my back with my hips raised on a pillow for about half an hour. I did this every two days during ovulation. We used friends' houses to do this. I felt good about this because these friends were so supportive.

"I do not know why men offer to be donors. The donors we used were worried that they could be tracked down and asked for child support. That's why anonymity was good for them. There were a number of different donors. Some did it for a few months until they were tired or out of town or something.

"I've been trying to get pregnant for two-and-a-half years. I have had two miscarriages.

"I feel very positive about who we are as lesbians and feminists. We have really thought about what it means to be parents since we have made such an effort to become parents.

And we have really thought about what it means for us to raise a child.

"Then there is the issue of a boy child. If we could choose, we would have a girl. Mostly though, we want a healthy child. This is what is most important to us.

"If it's a boy, I don't think that's a problem.

"People are concerned about male role models. I think the world is full of male role models. What we can offer a boy is an environment where it's okay to be nurturing, gentle, and kind—all those traditionally female qualities. So, I don't think it's a problem. I do think the boy might be angry at us because of who we are. We talked about this. We will reassure the boy that it is okay to be angry. We will tell him why we wanted a child. We will teach him how he can address his concerns. We are open to asking male friends to talk with him about his concerns.

"What we are doing challenges the traditional idea of the male/female family as the natural unit."

Diane Salter
The Ecuadorean Endurance Test

In 1976, Bill Menzo, geographer, travelled for twenty months. I interviewed him about his five-day trip into the Amazon jungle.

"Sitting in a bar in Quito, Ecuador, I overheard two travellers talk about their trip into the Amazon jungle. I thought, 'That's what I want, that's really what I want.' I bought them a beer and we talked. They told me to take a bus from Quito into the boondocks of rural Ecuador and from there to take another bus and then another bus to a village at the edge of the jungle.

"Off I went. The buses got progressively more primitive. Luggage and pigs were piled on top. Baby pigs rode inside the bus. Sheep and goats stood in the aisles. Natives don't often travel by bus and many were sick. I sat beside a woman whose child kept bringing up on me. It was a long two-day journey inland.

"I finally arrived at Misahuali, a little dirt town at the edge of the Rio Napo. I met Hector, the Indian guide, in a restaurant. He said the five-day trip cost $18.00, including food. The night before leaving, as preparation, Hector gave me *The Book of Comments*, a chronicle of one-liners written by survivors of the experience. The comments read: 'Never to be done again'; 'Definitely not for beginners'; 'Not recommended'; 'The Ecuadorean Endurance Test.' A twenty-nine-year-old man in good shape, I felt confident that I could handle the journey, but Tanis, the woman I was travelling with, was apprehensive. However, we decided to go.

"Other travellers had gathered for the trip. There was Jim, a hockey player from Vancouver, Suichi, a Japanese mountain climber and Sue, an overweight American. We questioned whether she was fit enough for the trip. She said, 'Listen guys, I will beat you through that jungle to anywhere you want to go.' She did. There was a born-again Christian from the United States, a French photographer, and two British women. After three days in Misahuali, a naive nine left with the Indian.

"We travelled on the Rio Napo for about four hours by motorized launch, a leaky old boat with a small engine on the back. It had rained for five days and the river was swollen. I had no apprehension. I had this North American mentality that adventure had built-in safeguards and that nothing could really go wrong. I soon found out there were no safeguards.

"We reached the tributary where the Auca Indians were to meet us in dugout canoes. No Indians. Hector was not concerned. I think he expected it. He said 'We walk!' I said, 'We walk?'

"I didn't have walking gear. I wore Roots shoes, blue jeans and carried a camera tied in a plastic bag. It had rained for five days and the ground was mud.

"Off we went. The Indian didn't walk. He galloped, and we were expected to keep up. The first day, we walked nine hours. My feet sank up to my knees, and at times we had to pull each other out of the mud to keep going. After four hours of mud, the soles separated from my shoes. I tied the bottoms to the tops with vines, but each time I brought my foot up, the earth came with it. The heat was unbearable. I wore only underpants and a T-shirt.

"Hector carried a butterfly net. His income, supplemented by taking *turistas* into the jungle, came mainly from gathering snakes and butterflies for North American universities. Sometimes he disappeared for half an hour at a time while our group struggled along. We crossed a large area of bog. On the far shore, Hector lined us up to scrape leeches off our legs. A five-foot-long thing that looked like a blue snake crossed our path. I asked if it was a poisonous snake and Hector said, 'It's not a snake, it's a worm.'

"We reached a river, maybe thirty feet across, and the only way to get over it was by tree trunk. Our shoes were slippery, and we had packs on our backs. I crawled over the trunk hugging it with all fours. We reached another river that we could cross only by vine. I had seen Tarzan do it. The difference between Tarzan and me is that Tarzan made it across. You take a vine, you swing across and when the vine reaches the other side at a fairly low point, you let go. I didn't let go, and I went right back up. Now I was way too high. The vine swung back out over the river. When I came back, the vine didn't quite reach the other side, so I was stuck over the river. I let go, fell in, and the current swept me to the other side.

"I'd expected animals in the jungle, but our troupe made so much noise complaining that we scared animals away. We did hear monkey and bird noises. The jungle was canopied. We saw nothing but vegetation and lots of rain. The whole trip was rain.

"We finally reached our stop for the evening, a communal thatched-roof shelter, a wooden platform built on posts. There were no walls. All night we fought off mosquitos and other jungle bugs.

"Lunch had consisted of rice with a tin of sardines mixed in. Dinner was more rice with another tin of sardines. For five days, we ate only rice and sardines. I should have known for $18 I wasn't going to get much. At dinner, I saw the American woman sneak a sardine. There was only one tin, and she ate the whole sardine by herself.

"On that first night, Tanis decided she couldn't go on; she wanted to stay in the hut until we came back. I said, 'We're in the middle of the jungle. We have to go on.' Suichi offered to carry her luggage.

"The next day was humid, I mean really humid. The combination of rain and sun turned the jungle into a steam bath. The Indian drank from the river. The river was brown. We either drink what he did or nothing. It was so hot we took off our clothes and jumped into the river. There was talk about piranhas. I was too hot and miserable to care.

"On we trudged and trudged until we arrived at the Indian village, Tayuno. Missionaries had told the Aucas that nakedness was against God's rules. There they were, in the middle of the jungle, wearing North American clothes that looked as though they came from the Salvation Army.

"There were about eighty in the tribe including lots of children. We watched the children bathe and pick lice out of each other's hair. The women slit their earlobes and hung weights from them. Stretched ears are a sign of beauty to the Aucas. The men filed their teeth into points to use as biting weapons when hunting. The hunters used blow guns with poison darts, but they also had rifles. We brought cartridges, on Hector's advice, to show our goodwill.

"We were shown to our hut, a structure built on posts, with a raised floor and a thatched roof. Our hosts were friendly. One of their customs was 'What's yours is mine.' We went to look around the village. When we came back, my shoes were missing. They had been taken by a hunter who left on a four-day hunting expedition. We complained. They chased the hunter, and my shoes were returned.

"We ate with the Indians. Breakfast was mashed bananas in river water, lunch was wild donkey meat in river water, and dinner was sardines in rice. We ate monkey meat stew and saw them kill the monkey. That night, an elderly woman, whose husband had died, chanted and wailed in mourning, a beautiful eerie sound among the bird noises and monkey howls.

"After a day and a half of village life, the Indians took us by dugout canoe a third of the way back to the Napo. We still had a day-and-a-half walk through the jungle. It was raining again. Hector started his lope.

"It took me about an hour and a half to crack. I said, 'I can't go any further. I refuse to move. I'm not going.' I sat there and saw everybody go, including Tanis. Tanis had worked herself into a psychic state where she was always moving her feet. Her legs were constantly going up and down even while standing. Her eyes were glazed as she said, 'I've got to go, I've got to go,' and off she went. I sat beside the river and heard the jungle noises. I must have been alone for about half an hour when something in me said, 'Survival is at stake here. There is no choice.'

"I thought my breaking point was at a certain level. I was wrong. The most important lesson I learned through the experience was that my breaking point was further than I ever thought possible. I sat there and realized I had to move on. I put myself into a trance, forgot about body pains, forgot about cramps, forgot about everything. There was nobody to complain to, nobody to listen. I started to move. I can't remember the return journey because I tranced myself right out of my surroundings. I concentrated only on moving.

"We reached the Napo. A Mestizo family had set up shop selling bananas, papayas and mangos. We ate and we ate. The motorized launch arrived. After an hour on the river, my bowels rebelled. Tanis said I looked green. I was sweating profusely. Others in the boat moaned. We were all going through the same process. The river was swollen and logs came downstream at us. We fought the current upstream until there were so many logs on the river and the current was so strong we were forced to pull over to the bank. Six of us rushed on shore.

"Hours later, we arrived at Misahuali and checked into a fifth-rate hotel. It had one bathroom which was locked at 9:30 at night. We couldn't get in. That night, we fought the dogs for tree space.

"The last thing we had to do was sign *The Book of Comments*. My entry:

> *People planning to go on this trip are mental, absolutely right out of their minds.*

Ted Bialowas
From Russia Without Love

I asked my father to tell me the story of his life during the occupation of Poland during World War II.

"I grew up in the small town of Ihrowica near Tornopol. My grandfather represented all the towns in our borough in government. My family was the leading family in town. With my father, mother, brother Tadeus and sister Kasia, I lived a modest existence on a large farm. All our food came from the farm.

"In September of 1939, the Russians took over the countryside. When first occupying our land, they told the Polish people stories of how they were there to help repel the invading German Nazis. Later we learned about Stalin's agreement with Hitler to split up and share Poland. Russians are like that. That winter drove me haywire. Russian soldiers were everywhere. I was eighteen years old and my future was so uncertain. Things looked bleak.

"Every day, I skied through the countryside. I wanted to know exactly what was happening. Once, I journeyed to the Carpasian Mountains on the Czechoslovakian border. There, I poled hard to make a break for freedom. I learned that crossing the range in winter would be fatal. Discouraged, I went home.

"One day in the spring of 1940, I returned home from a friend's to find Russian troops at our home. My mother's and sister's faces showed fear. The Russians were taking us away. Earlier, my father escaped through a window, thinking they only wanted the men. He was wrong. They wanted the entire family. They told us we would be leaving soon and to pack what we needed. I instructed the family to bring all the good clothes. In the attic we stored lots of ham and kielbasa. The Russians said we wouldn't need it. We brought it anyway. It saved us from starving to death.

"The Russians loaded us and our belongings into a horse-drawn cart. We trekked several kilometers to a waiting train. At this site appeared many families from the area. Russians herded us into boxcars. As the train was about to leave, my father appeared. Realizing he might lose his entire world, he gave up his freedom to rejoin his family. He looked so tired, so defeated. The door slammed shut and the train pulled away.

"For twenty-one days, we lived on the train. It stopped only to refuel, and briefly once a day to allow one family member to fetch a single pail of water. It was terrible. A hole in the floor served as the toilet. We took half-hour shifts looking out the single small window at the passing countryside. It was our only recreation.

"After three weeks, the train arrived at the Irtysh River. For three days we travelled by barge to our destination. They called it Majsh. It was situated in the desert, and there was nothing to see but sand and dunes. Cossacks inhabited the region. The Russians escorted us to our new home, a rude clay hut that housed six. Immediately they took us to work. This was a slave labour camp.

"It was an open pit mine. Men, women and children worked. No exceptions. We worked eight hours a day, six days a week. Carts holding one ton of material rolled along a track where we dug. Each of us was required to load eighteen tons a day. Eighteen carts. Our hands were our only tools. Each day I returned home and collapsed. In return for our exhaustion, we received a kilo of bread to sustain us. Work continued in summer and winter. There were no breaks in the routine. I didn't know which was worse, the hunger or the cold. Failure to work resulted in a five-year prison sentence. Once I was so sick with the flu that I missed one working day. The court pressed charges against me. Only a bribe saved me from prison. For silk stockings, the camp doctor gave me a medical certificate.

"In 1943, news spread of a newly forming Polish Army unit. A desperate Stalin agreed with our General Szykorski to allow Polish patriots to fight the threatening Nazis. I lied about my age and joined. Anything was better than this camp and these Russians.

"A group of thirty-five from Majsk was organized and, with me in charge, we set out on our own for the Polish forces' training grounds. Russian authorities refused to direct us. For months, we lived like nomads. We hopped trains, worked odd jobs and stole food. On the run, we slept in haystacks during the day and travelled at night. Freedom from the Russian oppressors at Majsk spurred us on.

"We joined the mobilizing Polish forces. This gave our lives new direction. I had a chance to fight now. I started basic training with enthusiasm and hope. The typhoid fever overwhelmed us. We suspected the Russians of introducing it into the stream we drank from. I contracted it.

"For two weeks, I lay semiconscious. Fever and delirium overcame me. I constantly imagined someone was trying to steal my new boots. Upon waking, I found myself deaf and mute. Slowly, I regained these senses. I remained disoriented. When I attempted to sit up I toppled over. I needed assistance to urinate. Soon I moved around on my hands and knees. I became physically sound, but the disease impaired my mental capacity. I couldn't think properly. In time that came back too.

"After typhoid, dysentery broke out. Fortunately, I didn't get it. Others weren't so lucky. Between them typhoid and dysentery killed many of my comrades.

"After a year, I left the camp and joined a tank battalion. It took me to Iran, Palestine, Egypt and finally Italy. The war ended. I had nothing. Leaving everything behind and losing it forever hurt the most. I lost my home. I lost my family. I had to start a new life."

Lynn MacKenzie

Innocent Victims: An Account of a Parental Abduction

Jane Morgan was thirteen years old when her father abducted her and her three younger brothers, John, Mark and Greg.

When Jane was nine years old, her parents started to fight. Her father beat her mother. Her father threatened her mother's life twice before he was institutionalized. Soon after, the courts granted Mrs. Morgan a legal separation. The decision gave Jane's mother custody. Her father was granted visiting privileges only in the presence of a guidance officer. After two years, Mr. Morgan was released, and the visiting privileges began.

The abduction happened early on a Sunday afternoon. Mr. Morgan arrived to pick up the four children for a visit. As Jane got in the car, she noticed it was packed with blankets and a cooler. When her brother asked their father about these things, the father said there had been a change of plans. They were going to meet their guidance officer, Larry, in Niagara Falls. Larry had a pilot's licence and would take them up in a plane. Jane suspected something was wrong when they drove through the border.

"We were not in or near Niagara Falls. My father then told us he was taking us away. He said my mother wouldn't let him have us, so he was taking us.

"I was very upset at first. I tried to talk him out of it, but he wouldn't listen. At the beginning, I cried nonstop. I was worried about my mother and school. I guess I wasn't rational. I kept thinking about some speech I had to write for school the next week.

"After about a week, I came to my senses. The oldest of my brothers, John, calmed me down. He made me accept what was happening."

Jane's father drove them to Mexico, where they stayed for a week. Then he drove back along the Atlantic coast to New York.

"We never knew where we were headed, and we slept in the car a lot. Being the eldest I felt like a little mother. My youngest brother, Greg, was only four. I had to clean things up when he had accidents in the car."

I asked Jane if they ever contemplated escaping.

"After seeing what my father did to my mother, we were too scared. He was very strict and had strong control over us. We never wanted to test him. We knew as long as we followed his rules we would be okay. We were always well provided for."

In New York, their father told them they were going on a plane to visit their relatives in Czechoslovakia. Jane's mother had foreseen this and had written to her sister there. In Czechoslovakia Mr. Morgan planned to regain citizenship for himself and the children. Until that happened, they would stay with his parents.

One day, as the four children played outside, Mrs. Morgan's sister passed by.

"We were playing out front when this strange lady approached us. She knew our names, but we didn't know who she was. I guess we were brainwashed at that point. We were afraid of being in trouble, and we knew our dad wouldn't be pleased. So we ran inside and wouldn't answer the door.

"That was about two months after we were first abducted. We had become allied with our father. My father's family was very supportive. He was very influential, and they had every reason to go along with him."

Mrs. Morgan's sister reported seeing the children to Jane's mother. She contacted the Canadian Embassy in Czechoslovakia, and the embassy sent people to get the children.

"They came without any warning. We were playing outside when we saw the car pull up. Four strange people got out: one woman and three men. They spoke English, and they said they were taking us home. Luckily for them, nobody else was around. We were afraid to go with them. At that point, I had doubts about going home. I didn't know if we were normal, or if people at home were the same. I wondered if everyone would think we were weird.

"My dad wasn't around to say goodbye to, so they let me write a letter. I was sad. The people were nice, but they were not relatives. My brothers were more ready to go with them. My brothers did whatever they were told.

"My biggest worry was going back to Mom. I didn't know what she would be like. When we saw her at the airport, she looked so worn out and aged. We didn't know how to react to her. We couldn't run up and hug her right away.

"At first, we were testing each other out. It was a relaxed transition stage. My brothers and I couldn't believe at first that we were home. But after that everyone was so warm to us. It was so overpowering that it erased three months of hell."

Today, Jane attends the University of Toronto. She is completing her final year of graduate studies in the Master of Social Work program. Mr. Morgan no longer has visiting privileges. The court ruled that he must never contact his wife or children again. Neither Jane nor her brothers speak much of the abduction. Jane intends to become a social worker after completing her studies, and she plans to devote her attention to victimized children from broken homes.

Laura Szostak
Carl, An Ex-Gambler

Carl sucked in the last breath of his cigarette. He pushed the play-button on the cheap tape recorder. His eyes teared as he heard his own voice.

Carl is fifty-five. His life has withered him. Carl was an alcoholic and a gambler. He has conquered both problems. He has since remarried and leads "a happy, dry life."

"I guess I've always been attracted to the risks in gambling. You can really meet some interesting people, people who have so many problems that you tend to forget your own. Bails was one of those characters. His real name was Bailey. He thought that sounded too feminine. Yeah, Bails. What a guy. It's funny how everything comes back to you so clearly detailed. Even after all these years.

"I used to think that to gamble meant to sin. A mortal sin. I was smart then. I guess I was the opposite of most people. I was wise in my youth. I was dreadfully stupid in my adult life. I should have walked right by The Hide. That was the nickname of our favourite place to drink. It was at The Hide that I first gambled. I loved the thrill of it. I loved the excitement when I thought money was mine.

"It really wasn't so bad then. A few bucks here and there. It's too bad I didn't stay there. I wouldn't have lost so much if I had. The only good thing that came out of The Hide was Dale. She worked as a waitress. She was beautiful. You could never find a better woman. I married her. She had no idea of my favourite hobby. She would never have condoned it.

"There was one time I could have been a millionaire. I was within reach of that money. I was at this horse race. I picked

Black Jet. I had an inside scoop on her. I put down all I had on her. I remember how I stood on top of my chair. I rooted for her. She was ahead of every single horse. My heart pounded as she neared the finish. I thought that this was it. I still don't see how that other bastard won. Glenda's Girl was that horse's name. What a stupid name. I hated that horse.

"It didn't take long for Dale to figure out what had happened after that. I was clever. I was able to cover for the few hundred. I lost that earlier. There was no escape this time. We lost everything. Dale left me forever. I'll never forget her face. I loved her. I still do. The kids were young then. She told them I was dead. She felt they'd be better off. What could I do? My entire family left me alone. I've never seen them since. It hurts.

"It was then when I met Bails. He just appeared at The Hide one day. I liked him immediately. Bails had a few debts. But he was in better shape than myself. Bails and I roomed together. He was a truck driver. I got a job as a dishwasher. I hated it. We saved a couple of dollars between us. We decided not to gamble anymore. It didn't last long. I think we lasted a month. Bails was the first to start. I wasn't far behind.

"I lived at the YMCA for a while. I think the head housekeeper liked me. She never charged me for my bed. She always saved me a piece of toast for breakfast. Bails had gotten worse. He had become an alcoholic. That was something we kidded about. Bails drank anything. He stole a lot too. He stole from me, his best friend. I saw a side of Bails. I didn't like it. He said he was sorry. He even cried. I couldn't forgive him.

"I remember the winter of '65. It was a snowy February. We broke our friendship that night. He was drunk. He sang loudly. He didn't have a bad voice. Bails laughed and joked. He didn't see the car. He lay there so helplessly. I later learned that he died instantly. I remember how I held his head in my lap. I forgave him. I told him everything would be okay. He was dead. That bastard wouldn't even let me forgive him.

"I don't remember what happened the week after that. I think I was drunk. I was so smashed. I can't remember. I gambled a lot more. I lost a lot more too. I lost everything again. Everything didn't amount to much this time.

"I got a job at some stupid button factory. I worked the night shift. I started at eleven at night. I worked through to nine in the morning. My pay cheque wasn't much. What could I do?

"I met this kid. Brett was his name. He reminded me of Bails. Brett had a good sense of humour. We talked for a long time one night. I saw that Brett was like me. He already gambled a bit. I told him about myself. It didn't seem to affect him. I hope he's on the right track.

"After I heard myself talk to Brett, I did something different. I wrote my story down. Every word. I read it over and over again. I cried all night. I fell asleep. I slept for a long time. I knew what had to be done when I woke up.

"I called the hospital. They told me about Gambler's Anonymous. I got a lot of help there. They know how to listen and respond. Bails never thought he needed this place. I knew better. I wish it wasn't too late for him. He would have made it this time.

"It has been eighteen years. I haven't drunk or gambled. I feel good. I never thought I could do it. Here I am. A fifty-five-year-old ex-gambler. I feel the urge sometimes. No way. If Dale could see me now. I wonder how the kids are."

M. Nakamura

Mr. William Long

Mr. William Long was born in Toronto on November 23, 1896. As a young boy, he worked in a factory that produced electrical fixtures. He travelled west, slept on the "Boards" and worked on harvests. At nineteen, he joined the army and was sent to France, where he fought in World War I. He was injured in October of 1918 and recovered in England.

He returned to Toronto, married and became a firefighter. He has three children, ten grandchildren and two great-grandchildren.

I asked him to tell me about his war experiences.

We were going over the top to attack the Germans. I was at the front line and got shot. They told me not to move because I had a serious wound, but the Germans were counterattacking with their tanks. In those days tanks were great big clumsy looking things and I didn't want to get run over so I rolled over and tried to get up and walk. I had a bullet in my leg and one in my stomach, but I walked to a sunken road where the Divisional Machine Gunners were setting up their machine guns to stop the counterattack.

One of the fellas there knew me and said, "What's the matter Bill?"

"I've got a bullet in my stomach!"

One of the officers told me not to get up, that he would have some men carry me across. So they carried me to an old blown-out house being used as a dressing station.

The next thing I remember was being put into an ambulance. Everybody was pretty badly wounded and they were calling the poor driver every name they could think of because he was hitting shell holes in the road.

When we arrived at our destination—I don't know where it was—I kept passing out and coming to again. I was lying out in this big field. I looked around and I could see nothing but stretchers.

Two stretcher bearers came along, looked at my tag and said, "Take this one in first." So they took me into the tent and I passed out again.

Well, then I came to again and a fellow with a big pair of scissors had started at my putties (feet), cut all the way up both sides, and pulled the clothes right off of me. They carried me into the operating tent where the nurse was.

She said, "I want you to take a deep breath."

They put chloroform over my head. I took about two whiffs and I was gone. When I came to I was in the tent and the nurse was sitting beside me.

She said, "I've had an awful time with you!"

I asked her, "Why, what happened?"

She said, "You wanted to kick all of the patients out of the ward. You were hollerin' and I told you to keep quiet because there were more people in the ward than you. You said, 'Well, kick them out!' "

They had my knees up and my feet sat on something. Two guys, orderlies, about sixteen came and rubbed my legs to get the circulation going.

All they could give me to eat or drink was champagne and I hated it. It came in little bottles. There was no refrigeration, and you had to drink this little bottle three times a day to keep your strength up. They didn't want anything to go to my bowels because my abdomen was punctured. I used to crab like anything to this nurse over this crazy champagne. She said, "You're the first Canadian I've ever met who has refused a drink."

So I said, "Well, when I get better you can bring in lots of it!"

One day, this nurse said to me, "You'll be going on a long trip on the train to England and it's not good riding. I'll give you a good drink of brandy for the trip. I can't give you much else."

Time came to go, and I was on my stretcher. She came, but do you think I could even look at that brandy? No sir, I didn't want anything to do with it!

They put me on the train and, oh, the train was awful. Some of the guys were in such terrific pain, hollerin' for the nurse every minute. The poor nurse ran up and down to different coaches.

I arrived at the hospital in France. There was an Irishman who came from Toronto in the bed next to me. He was what we used to call a weepin' Irishman because he talked as though he was crying all the time. He was missing a leg, but he was as witty as ever. When they took the leg off, they used to peel the skin back like an orange, in four pieces and leave a pad there. Sometimes they used chloroform to peel it back, to keep it clean. My brother had both his legs off, and he said that sometimes you get an awful feeling as though your leg is still on.

One night, this Irishman starts hollerin' because of his leg. I was laughing at him. He said, "All right, when I get back to

Toronto and I'm selling shoelaces at Queen and Yonge, you won't buy any."

So I said, "I certainly won't!"

The nurse said to me, "Look, I want you to quit laughing. You're going to break that wound open. I don't know what we'll do with you then."

So this night, the Irishman started on me again and I started to laugh. I rolled over in bed and open came the wound. I put my hand down to the bandage and I thought I felt blood so I hollered for the nurse. She came and felt down to the wound holding her lantern above me to see. The doctor came and put his lantern together with the nurse's. They saw that the wound had broken open and that pus was running out of me like water out of a tap.

"Boy," said the doctor, "You're a lucky one that broke open. If that had gone through your system, you'd be dead: it was all poison."

So I thanked the Irishman for making me laugh. In the first World War, they didn't have antibiotics. Of those who had stomach wounds, only ten percent lived. I was lucky.

Karin A. Treml

Love and Guns

Derek Cranston (not his real name) is a powerful man. A Canadian who volunteered for duty in the Vietnam war, he is now a member of a major police force. I got to know Derek through my Karate club where he was my instructor. I asked Derek if I could interview him about his work for the Crisis Task Force. He consented, but once we sat together in his office, our talk turned to the private passions that underlie Derek's public service.

I met with Derek on a dark, rainy Wednesday afternoon in October at the Crisis Task Force building, which looked like nothing more than a warehouse. A sign on the front door stated that this was a police special detachment building and that in case of emergency help could be sought by ringing the bell at the side door. I walked around to the side and rang the bell. Derek came to the door. We walked along a barren corridor, heels clicking until we came to Derek's office.

Derek's office was gloomy. The dark curtains were drawn and a solitary lamp lit the room. Derek offered me one of two chairs beside an old metal desk. I looked around.

Above me, on a wooden shelf, sat a Ruger semi-automatic, propped up in its own stand. One wall was covered with bracket-mounted shotguns. Several pistols lay on Derek's desk. A cabinet beside me contained two Uzis, one dismantled to show its parts. Sniper rifles, strategically hung, pointed at me from each corner. Derek saw me looking and, without my asking, explained several guns. He handled them with tenderness and passion.

"I love them. Guns possess an orgasmic quality for me. I learned how to shoot when I was seven. I fell in love then too. It was a twelve-gauge shotgun and it knocked me on my ass. I was awed I guess you'd say. I couldn't believe the power it had. After that, I always bugged my dad to let me shoot. That twelve-gauge set me on my ass with a bruised shoulder time after time, but I remember the first time I didn't get knocked down by it. I felt like I was on top of the world. I felt like the strongest kid out of all the kids at school.

"After that, my dad bought me a rifle. I was about ten I guess, and I went hunting with my dad. I'd shoot and miss and shoot and miss. I got pissed off. I was almost thirteen when I finally shot a deer. Talk about a rush. My dad patted my shoulder, and I felt ten feet tall.

"That night, I cleaned and polished my rifle like never before. I began target shooting every day after school. I was obsessed with becoming a perfect shot. Every time Dad took me hunting and I killed something, I loved it. I felt so powerful, like I could control anything."

"You volunteered for Vietnam. Why?"

"I wanted to fight a war. I was put in the Rangers, a highly trained seek-and-destroy paratrooper regiment. They trained us to find the enemy intelligence troops, kill them, then search the bodies for documents. It was neat."

"You enjoyed it?"

"Yeah. There's something about hunting humans that excites me. It's the butting of minds with the enemy. It's unreal. They have troops doing the same thing. They're hunting us while we're hunting them. It's a strategy game with high costs. It makes winning a rush. Seeing their faces just as you shoot is fantastic. They realize they're goners. We cut off their right ears and strung them on a fish line so that, at the end of each mission, we knew how many we'd killed."

"Did this ever get to you after 'Nam?"

"No. Should it have? It was a war. We made the best of it. We fought, we killed, we won. Why should it get to us?"

"What effect then did Vietnam have on you?"

"It made me aware of my strength. I was in fantastic physical shape. I worked my reflexes and my other senses until I was tight, sleek and deadly. I had a strong mind. I felt powerful.

"I came back from 'Nam knowing I wanted to continue my training. I wanted superior mental and physical strength, and I wanted top-notch combat skills. I learned Karate and Ju Jitsu. I joined a gun club and perfected my marksmanship with a lot of different guns. I'm forever training."

"To what end?"

"Power. Strength. Control. I want to be the superior of the superior. I need to know I can kill with my bare hands. I need to see each muscle."

"Tell me about your job, Derek."

"I like the work. When I started with the cops, I knew I wanted to be in a special unit. After five years on the streets, I went to Drugs, then Vice, then Homicide, and now the Crisis Task Force. This is the best.

"Every call I go to deals with guns. I train the gun unit here. It is, again, butting wits with the other guy, but you know that when you're on the inside perimeter surrounding the gunman, you had better get it right. Usually he's got a hostage; he's got the advantage. All I have is forty-five coppers with .38's, a ton of tear gas and about fifteen highly trained CTF guys with any combination of weapons. With these odds, I negotiate. Usually, in fact ninety-nine percent of the time, the gunman gives up. We've killed four guys in twenty years here at CTF. We've never lost a hostage. It's a war of the wits, and I love it."

"Have you killed anyone in the line of duty, Derek?"

"I've been involved in two duty-related shootings. In case you want to know, no, they didn't bother me. Maybe all of this seems to you like mindless killing, or whatever you call it. As a copper, I wouldn't ever shoot without a damn good reason, but don't think I'd give a second thought to killing someone if I had to. I like the adrenalin rush of shooting something or someone. It doesn't scare me. It doesn't bother me.

"I have to go now, but I'll leave you with a parting thought. Have you ever thought what it would be like to shoot someone and then watch the last twitches of their dying nerves?"

Three days later, I read through the transcript of my interview with Derek. I was stunned by the things he had said. I wondered whether Derek had ever lost his sense of strength and control. I debated whether or not I should phone him and ask. Our interview had been tense. One week later, I phoned.

"Derek, one more question. Have you ever felt powerless?"

"Yeah, when my dog Buck was hit by a car and lay dying in my arms."

"How did you feel?"

"I wanted to die with him. I cried for hours. There wasn't a thing I could do. I was devastated."

Chapter Ten

Arguments

Write an argument, a piece designed to enlist support for your point of view. Choose an issue important to you now.

Diane J. Salter
Trouble in Paradise

The bird is a problem. Bill and I merge our financial resources, divide household chores, take eight-month trips together, but we cannot agree on what to do with the bird. As I sit in bed writing, Bill sits beside me reading. The bird sits on his big toe and looks at me. I don't like the bird, and the bird doesn't like me.

Joy Tweety the Second is Bill's friend. They have been together for two years, ever since Joy Tweety the First was eaten by a cat. Joy is a cockatiel. Bill learned about these birds in New Zealand where he met a lighthouse keeper with a cockatiel named Captain. Captain and his keeper lived on an island off the north coast. Captain was nationally known through his TV appearances. Captain talked: "Good Morning, this is the Captain speaking." Captain whistled tunes, "Good King Wenceslaus" and "Blow the Man Down," when the lighthouse keeper conducted by waving his finger in front of the bird's beak. Bill decided he wanted a cockatiel.

Bill thinks a bird is the perfect pet. He's had birds since 1971, birds that sat on his glasses and ate out of his mouth, birds that woke him up in the morning by crawling on the bed and pecking his nose. Now Bill has Joy who whistles when he hears Bill's key in the front door. They sing together, they play together. Joy whistles to accompany Bill when he plays the guitar.

I like birds—outside of the house. When I enter the room, Joy swoops at me. Bill says, "Go for the eyes, Joy!" When I go near his cage to feed him, he hisses and tries to bite my fingers. Bill insists that the bird fly free. He doesn't think it's fair to have him locked in a cage. Neither do I. I think birds should be free—on trees, outside.

Because Joy flies free, we have to keep newspapers on the floor. According to Bill, you have to take a bird as it is. Joy can't be toilet trained. I object to the papers and what Joy does on them. I've asked Bill to change them daily. He agreed to change them twice a week. He does it every two weeks, if reminded. I complain that I don't like newspapers spread over the carpet when we're having company. Bill suggests that I change my friends and invite only people who like birds.

The mess bothers me, but Bill doesn't notice it. When we first met, he kept Joy in his kitchen. The perch was over the tea towels. I avoided eating there.

When Bill moved in with me, the bird took up residence in our bedroom. After the first night, I moved Joy to the living room. Now he lives in the basement.

Bill says Joy needs company, that it is unfair to keep him in the basement alone, that we need another bird. Twice the noise and twice the mess. I imagine living in a house filled with newspapers and birds flying free, and I don't like the image. I tell Bill it's not Joy that I object to, it's what Joy does. Then I feel guilty for wanting him to give up something he loves. If we can get a larger cage that the birds can stay in, I'll consider keeping them. Bill says that might be okay, although cleaning a big cage will be more work. We need a change.

I finish writing and move back the covers. Joy flies from Bill's toe to the top of the bedroom door. I complain that now he's going to make a mess on top of the door.

Bill says, "That's okay, it's out of sight."

"Yes," I say, "but not out of mind."

Brian Cartwright

House #39 and Why I Should Get Into It

Early one November evening, Bob Morton stabbed Richard Simon's pillow with a butcher's knife. The knife went through the pillow and into the mattress. It said something of Bob and Richard's relationship.

Bob and Richard and I and three others lived together in one of Erindale College's residence townhouses. Richard moved out at Christmas and was not replaced. The Erindale Housing Department did not send anyone new because of

Bob's medical condition. Bob has a new disease, a product of twentieth-century technology. It is called variously "the ecological disease" and "the twentieth-century disease" and "total allergy syndrome." People who have this chronic condition are allergic to almost everything. They are allergic to all food, so they must eat foods they are the least allergic to in rotation. They are allergic to all chemicals. This means no cleaners, no paint, no plastic, no fresh ink, no artificial fibres or freshly bought clothes.

Bob's reactions take many forms. I've seen him shiver as if with intense cold. I've seen his skin discolour. I've seen him with migraines and severe cramps. I've seen him so confused that he forgets how to count. I've seen his wild mood swings; anyone who didn't know him might think he was schizophrenic.

The knifing took place during one of his hyperactive phases. Richard was the one of our five who refused to alter his lifestyle to accommodate Bob's allergies. Richard insisted on the right to use hair spray—not an unreasonable demand, except that prolonged exposure to it could put Bob in a coma. The fault was not Richard's. He never should have been put into this situation without being informed. None of us should have. The Housing Office failed to recognize the implications of putting a person with Bob's problem in with five other people. They made no provisions to deal with him and gave none of the rest of us the opportunity to opt out.

Bob's problem increases with the number of things he's exposed to. More exposures mean worse health, and living with more people means more exposures. These are inevitable, no matter how careful his housemates are. The answer, then, is to have fewer housemates. For this reason, Housing did not replace Richard, and Bob was grateful to them for it. However, five is still a problem. Bob has requested that Housing allow him to live in house #39, residence's only two-person house.

Paul Lepan, the head of Erindale's Housing Department, has agreed. The selection committee, students who allocate housing, has not. Mr. Lepan has no control over them, but he has asked. They agreed to consider the request but were not enthusiastic.

Their position is this. They traditionally select the residents of house #39 from fourth-year students by lottery. The lottery is popular because many students are tired of five-person residences, and they have a strong friend they want to live with in the two-person house. This is a special privilege.

I have lived with Bob for seven months. I know what it is to live with him. I've given up normal things like drugstore soap and shampoo. I've given up cleaning the house with anything other than baking soda. I've dealt with his moodiness. I've dealt with not being able to bring friends in because they are wearing or using something that is a threat. I've done all these things and I'm used to them. I've adjusted to this fashion of living and I don't mind it anymore. Bob and I are good friends with similar interests, and we want to live together next year.

It may seem that Bob provides me a convenient way of getting a sought-after privilege. I would enjoy living in a two-person house as much as anyone. However, the real issue here is fairness to Bob and fairness to those who might be asked to live with him. It is unfair to put anyone but me in with Bob next year, just as it was unfair to put the four of us—we had no warning about what we were getting into—in with him this year.

It may be unfair to tell the fourth-year students that house #39 will not be available for this year's lottery. We have to weigh that against natural compassion for Bob's condition and our respect for his right to an education.

Ed Ogibowski
Police Power

Police officers have the authority to charge people they believe have committed offences. Once charged, a person makes a court appearance where guilt is decided. This is efficient. However, when an officer misuses his or her authority, the judicial system is weakened because our faith in it weakens. This misuse of authority can also threaten the innocent.

A friend of mine recently had an experience with the police. Doug is twenty-one years old, married, and has two young children. He was mistaken for a bank robbery suspect. While on the way to his grandmother's house to pay his rent, Doug realized he was being followed by a police cruiser. After six blocks, the cruiser flashed its high beams. Doug pulled over. The officer yanked Doug's car door open. Doug was ordered to get out with his hands on his head. The officer pointed his gun at Doug. Five more cruisers arrived. So did CITY TV news cameras.

Doug answered questions for an hour in the back seat of the police cruiser; then he was told why he had been stopped. To verify Doug's explanation of his whereabouts, the police escorted Doug home. They questioned his wife. The detectives were finally satisfied that Doug was innocent. No charges would be laid. The detectives kidded young Officer Smith, the officer who stopped Doug, about his mistake and told him to drive Doug back to his car. The police were doing their job.

Then Officer Smith charged Doug with careless driving—an offence that brings six demerit points on the licence and a maximum $500 fine. When Doug protested, Officer Smith warned him that he was lucky not to be charged with trying to evade a police officer. Further complaints to the police department received no results. Doug was worried. He did not have money for traffic fines and possible car insurance increases.

Doug took a day off work to appear in courtroom 54 at 9:00 a.m. He brought his lawyer, Mr. Woods, to represent his case. Middle-aged, short and overweight, the lawyer wore a dark blue suit, white socks and black shoes. Mr. Woods asked Doug to repeat his story quickly before the trial started; since their meeting in the lawyer's office, Mr. Woods had forgotten what the case was about. They sat through the first three cases hoping Officer Smith wouldn't show up. That way the case would be dismissed.

As the fourth case began, Smith walked in. He grinned at Doug as he walked to the back of the crowded courtroom. Mr. Woods briefed Doug, and then the lawyer took his position at the defence counsel's table. Smith tiptoed over and asked Doug to step outside.

Smith wanted to know why Doug had brought a lawyer. Doug answered that he didn't want to "get shafted" in court.

Smith insisted that a lawyer wasn't necessary and that if Doug had phoned him the whole thing could have been settled easily. Doug told Smith he didn't like being charged in the first place.

They returned to the courtroom after five minutes, just as their case was called. Mr. Woods entered a plea of not guilty. Smith whispered to the crown attorney, who stood up and asked that the charges be dropped. The judge ordered the case dismissed. Doug was relieved.

Mr. Woods' fee was $150. Doug paid it.

Chapter Eleven

Evaluations

Write an evaluation of something or someone by presenting details of your experience with the subject.

Julia Compton

Chief Elison

Our platoon stood to attention in front of Chief Elison, the drill instructor. Five foot, eleven inches, 170 pounds, Chief Elison had short brown hair, blue eyes, horn-rimmed glasses and false teeth he got two years ago when he had his crooked original teeth pulled out. He wore his green dress jacket, shirt, pants, peaked cap and black boots. His boots shone. His uniform, as always, was wrinkleless and spotless. He was the instructor for this part of the junior leadership course.

I needed the course to get my promotion to Master Wren—the navy-rank equivalent to master corporal. This was the first session. The second session would be at Albert Head, a camp in the woods, twenty minutes from Victoria, British Columbia.

In this session we had to learn to drill a platoon. Chief Elison took half an hour in class to teach us the theory. He felt the best way to learn was to practise what he taught.

"Leading Wren Compton," he bellowed.

I came to attention. "Yes, Chief."

"Fall out!"

Oh, no! Why did he pick me first? I turned right, fell out of the platoon, and marched to halt in front of him. I turned to face him. He looked at me.

"Compton, I want you to march the platoon around the parade square. You know the theory. Apply it."

"Yes, Chief." I wanted to tell him that I was not sure what to do. I knew it would do no good.

"I want to be able to hear you at the end of the parade square," said Chief Elison.

"Yes, Chief."

He marched away. His boots clicked on the deck. He had taps on them. He halted at the end of the parade square, turned, stood at attention and waited.

I took a deep breath. Calm down, I told myself. Do the best you can. I turned to face the platoon.

"Let's go, Compton!" yelled the Chief.

"Platoon," my voice squeaked out.

"Louder!" bellowed the Chief. "I can't hear you."

I became angry. I'll show you, I thought.

"Platoon," I yelled, "Right turn."

My voice echoed through the parade square. They turned. It amazed me. It worked.

"Platoon! By the right, quick march!" They stepped off. Twelve pairs of feet marched in unison.

"Platoon, left turn!" I commanded. I remembered to call the left turn on the right foot.

They approached a wall. How do I turn them on the march? What foot do I call the about-turn on? They got close to the wall.

"Platoon!" I yelled.

Quick, think of something. It was too late. They marched into the wall. They continued to march on the spot, up against the wall. I stared at them.

"Platoon, halt!" boomed another voice. It was Chief Elison.

"Turn them around, Compton. I want you to march them down here and about turn them again."

"Yes, Chief." I knew my face was red. I turned the platoon around. My friend, Catherine, who was in the front rank of the platoon looked at me and smirked.

I reviewed in my mind how to do an about-turn on the march. I know what to do, I consoled myself. I just panicked. I forgot to say anything. I began again.

"Platoon, quick march!" I ordered. They stepped off.

"Platoon . . . about turn!" Feet shuffled. Confusion broke out. Half the platoon did an about turn; the other half marched off in the opposite direction.

"Halt!" bellowed Chief Elison. "The about-turn starts on the left foot. You called it on the right foot, Compton."

I said nothing.

"I'll do it for you once," he said. "Fall back in properly," he commanded the platoon. "Watch what I do. I want you to do the same thing."

When he finished, he asked if I understood.

"Yes, Chief," I replied. I did not want to say no.

"I want you to practise until you get it," he said.

For the next fifteen minutes, I marched the platoon around the parade square until I satisifed the Chief that I knew my drill.

The next general parade was on Wednesday evening at 19:40. Chief Elison put me in charge of the communications platoon for the parade at colours and sunset. I knew what to do.

Jo-Anne Timmins
Fun In The Sun

Classical Economic Models (ECO 204) is required for the economics programme and the prerequisite for most third-year courses. I took the course last year every Tuesday and Thursday. I was always late for ECO 204, a 9:00 class. This was the first time I had had a 9:00 class. It didn't matter what time I got up; I always arrived late. Professor Anderson usually arrived after me.

The first class after reading week was no exception—9:15 and no professor. I turned to the girl beside me.

"Hey, Grace, do you think class will be cancelled?"

"It wouldn't surprise me," she said. "Anderson hasn't missed a class in over three weeks. It must be time by now."

"No such luck. Here he comes," I said.

Professor Anderson took his spot in front of the class. He started his lecture.

"Assume a shift-share analysis of employment structure has been undertaken for the set of regions described by Friedman. Now posit a classification of these regions using the taxonomy proposed."

My mind wandered. I wrote down his words without hearing them. I thought about next weekend. My parents were leaving town on Friday. I decided to have a party on Friday night. Who should I invite? Nice people. I don't want the house destroyed. I made a list. I looked it over. No good. I needed a few rowdies. I added Paul and Rob to the list. If I invite them I have to invite Glen and Sharon, maybe Daryl. No; last party I saw Daryl at, he puked on the carpet. Grace interrupted.

"Jo-Anne, look at Anderson when he bends over. He's going bald."

I looked. Grace was right. Anderson had a bald spot about two inches in diameter on top of his head. I never noticed it before. Anderson was so tall I never saw the top of his head unless he bent over.

Anderson noticed us talking. He glared at me. I shut up and tried to concentrate. I took notes without listening for the rest of the class.

"Bye, Grace. See you Thursday." I hurried out of the room.

I arrived for class at 9:15 on Thursday. Anderson was not there. A note on the door said, "Class Cancelled." I found a similar note on the door the following Tuesday. I didn't bother going to class on Thursday. I returned to class the next Tuesday. We had an assignment due on the following Thursday that I had not even looked at. I was hoping for some clues.

Anderson was not in class. The TA was. He told us Anderson was sick and that class was cancelled for another week. The TA said we didn't have to do the assignment. Anderson had told the TA to give us a mark based on the average mark of our previous assignments. I was relieved. The assignment was worth fifteen percent of our final mark. Grace was mad. She had done the assignment.

A week later, I went to class. Anderson arrived at 9:15 and took his position in front of the class. He was tanned. He bent over to pick up his notes. His bald spot was peeling.

Chapter Twelve

Murders

Write a short piece from the point of view of a murderer. Base details, except for the murder itself, on situations you know well. Push everyday events to absurd extremes.

Bruce Parker

Sergeant Banks

"Goddamn maggot!"

Private Walker's face turns white.

"You got GD creases in your GD trousers!" yells Sergeant Banks. "Defaulters parade 0-five-thirty."

Private Walker mutters, "Yes, Sergeant."

"I can't hear you!"

"Yes, Sergeant!"

Each morning is the same. Up at five. Shit, shave, shower by five-thirty and inspection by six. Then we stand at attention while Sergeant Banks torments us. "There's spiders in that rifle Rollet!" "You sleep in that uniform, Clair?" "Shave Rogers? Next time, use a GD razor!"

Sergeant Banks finishes his inspection and looks as if he's swallowed piss. "You're disgraceful!" he bellows. "This morning, we're going to the ranges. With the condition your rifles are in, the targets will get the GD day off!" He pauses for effect. "Course . . . Attention . . . Move to the right, right . . . Turn, quick march!"

We march down the laneway, past the barracks and out to the road. Dust fills our noses and covers our spit-shine boots. Today, the hottest of the summer, Sergeant Banks marches us to the range. Sergeant Banks marches ahead. "Shut your spouts!" Sergeant Banks marches behind. "Arms shoulder high!" He sneaks up on Harrigut. "Head up! Look proud, you little shit!"

"Right wheel!" We turn onto Amiens Range. The road shimmers and the baked grass crunches under our boots. Dark patches of sweat soak through our uniforms.

We stand to attention as Sergeant Banks talks to the officer at the ammo truck. At least, he's not yelling at us.

"Each of you will cover off a target, from one to twenty-five. The RSO will give you instructions so you know what to shoot at. Keep your weapon safe unless you plan to use it. Is that clear?"

"Yes, Sergeant."

"I can't hear you!"

"Yes, Sergeant!"

"Bellies in the dirt at the hundred-yard firing point!" I lie beside my weapon. Down range are twenty-five large signs, each a different colour with a large white number on it. A red flag flies in the centre. My target is number 17. I pick up my rifle.

"Put that GD rifle down, and don't touch it till you're told!"

A private walks down the line and hands everyone a magazine. Sergeant Banks tells us we've been given seven rounds. We are to fire two into the butts and the remaining five into the target.

"Try not to miss, it's only four feet square!" he sneers.

I pick up my rifle, load the magazine, release the breech and put it to my shoulder. I sight the target. I aim. I breathe. In...Out...Hold. I squeeze the trigger. The rifle punches my shoulder. My ears ring. I squeeze again and again. I can't remember how many rounds I've fired.

"Cease fire!" yells Sergeant Banks.

I put my rifle down. The red flag at the target starts to go down, but tangles. The green flag doesn't go up to indicate safe. Sergeant Banks mumbles. The flags don't move. Sergeant Banks swears.

"GD privates can't even work the GD flags!"

He runs down the range. His figure shimmers as he trots to the flagpole. His arms are waving as he chews up the private working the flag.

I look around. I look at my rifle. The action is closed. I pick it up and aim at my target. I shift and move the sight towards the flagpole. I centre on Sergeant Banks. His arms flap like a bird's wings.

I hear his last words: "GD...Red flags...maggot!"

Karen Bush
The Bridge

"Karen, hurry up! Dad will be here any minute!" Murray yells up the stairs.

I think I might throw up in the toilet I'm leaning over and scrubbing. My knees ache and sting. After I finish cleaning the third bathroom, I have to vacuum two staircases. I need to shower. I smell like ammonia.

"Karen, are you almost done? You still have to iron my shirt," Murray yells again.

"I would be if you helped for once!" I yell back.

"Women's work. Ha! Ha!" His voice trails off down the hall. At fifteen, Murray is already a sexist.

I stand up and flush the remaining soap. This sucks! I look at the list in my bedroom: dusting—check; laundry—check; bathroom—check; staircases—tomorrow. Sean—shit! Mom works Saturdays, and I have forgotten to pick up Sean!

"Murray, can you pick up Sean at Stevie's? I forgot to get him an hour ago!"

"No, you're the one who forgot. You can pick him up!"

I put on my shoes and slam the front door. "What about my shirt?" Murray screams down the street.

Stevie lives two blocks away, but Sean is only four. Sean follows me back to the house. He doesn't seem to mind that I'm late.

Home again, I lay out clean clothes for Sean. I stand in the hall and look at my watch, myself, the list, and the mess I still have to clean.

The list is supposed to be divided three ways. Sean is too small, so I don't mind doing his share, but Murray is three years older than I am! It isn't fair! But I do Murray's share 'cause I don't want Mom to come home to a mess and get upset. Mom tries so hard since Dad left.

"Karen, are you just going to stand there and do nothing all day?"

Murray stands a foot away and glares. I feel like hitting him, but he is bigger and stronger than I am. I know what would happen if I tried.

"Hurry up and press my shirt! God, you stink, Karen. When's the last time you had a shower?" Murray turns and trips on the telephone cord.

"That's the third time I've done that today," he says to Sean. I laugh. Murray doesn't hear me.

I shower and dress in a hurry. Downstairs, I lace Sean's shoes. The doorbell rings. The three of us run out and climb in the back of Dad's Honda. I look at Murray's wrinkled shirt and smile. He sees me and punches my leg.

Dad says, "Today, we're going to see the new Sky-Way bridge my company has been working on. It's almost finished." Dad looks at us in the rear-view mirror. There is silence the rest of the way to Burlington.

Dad drives up to the edge of the construction site. The security guard lets us go past the gate. We get out of the car. "First female on the new bridge," Dad says. He looks down at me. We walk out as far as we can, out to where the centre span of the bridge is being built.

"This part will be finished next week," Dad points to a three-foot gap. "Not too close, kids. I don't want to lose any of you," he says laughing.

Murray and I look at each other. Murray laughs too.

Dad and Sean turn back. Why not, I think. Murray steps closer to the edge for a better view of the water below, and I take a step closer to Murray. He doesn't see me. I look at Dad and Sean walking back to the car.

I place both hands on the back of Murray's hockey jacket. I push. I watch my footing. I step back again. Murray doesn't even scream.

I scream for him.

Dad and Sean run over to me. I hold Sean. Dad looks down at Murray's ant-sized body, floating limp on the water hundreds of feet below.

First female on the new bridge. I don't even have to clean up the mess.

Mandy Irvine
Another World

"Cute kid. How old is she?"

"Four."

"*My* sister is five—a real brat and nothing but hassles. I can't control her. She controls me."

Melissa sits up straight on the edge of the chesterfield across from my friend Christine. She crosses her legs and folds her hands on her lap. Her blond hair is in a bright red bow on top of her head. Pearl buttons and lace frills decorate her crisp cotton dress. She wears white ankle socks and shiny black shoes.

Christine finishes her tea, gets up to leave, and I see her to the door. Melissa smiles and giggles. She acts shy and won't say goodbye. Christine says, "You're lucky to have a quiet one."

I rush back into the living room to return to my soap. Steve, on *Another World*, kisses Rachel's cheek. He moves to her neck. I edge my way back into Dad's armchair without lifting my eyes off the television. Melissa dashes around me and jumps into the chair. She reaches over and presses channel 29 on the TV converter. The *Tom and Jerry Show* flashes onto the screen. The squeaky theme song breaks the romantic mood. "I'm watching TV now," Melissa says.

"Melissa," I begin. "You know Mom does not allow you to change the channel when someone else watches a program." I press channel nine. Steve whispers to Rachel, "Oh, my darling . . . ." Tom and Jerry flash back. "Melissa what do you think you're doing?" I yell. "Turn it back!"

"No! You're not my mother. I can do anything I want."

I grab her scrawny finger off the button and turn the channel back. Steve lifts Rachel into his arms and carries her toward the bedroom. The music softens. The camera focuses on Rachel's eyes. Melissa slides her hand over to the button. "Don't you dare," I warn. I move to the end of the chesterfield to be closer to the television. Steve and Rachel embrace and kiss. He whispers to her as Melissa begins to sing, "I'm telling. I'm telling. You're going to be in trouble. Hah." She repeats it over and over.

"Shut up!"

"Ahh . . . now you're really in trouble."

The phone rings. I throw the cushions on the floor and run towards the kitchen. Melissa jumps up and races after me. I'm in front of her until the end of the carpet. She turns the corner cleanly. My socks slide over the polished tile. Melissa picks up the phone. I fall against the counter.

Melissa talks to my father in her sweet-and-innocent voice. "Daddy, you know what. . .Miranda won't let me watch TV.— Okay, Daddy. Bye. I love you." She drops the phone onto the dishwasher. She sticks her tongue out of her mouth and runs to the television. I talk to my father.

I know what he will say before he says it. "Let the child watch the television. She is much younger than you."

I refuse to be pleasant.

"Is the lasagna in the oven?"

"Yeah."

"At 325 degrees?"

"Yeah."

"I'll be home at six."

"Yeah."

I slam down the receiver. I lean against the counter and brood. I have to know if Sandy and Blaire's relationship will last. I want to see if Mac Corey interferes with Rachel's new love.

Melissa walks into the kitchen. "Move," she commands. I watch as she takes three Oreo cookies out of the cookie jar. Her stringy blond hair hangs around her face. She glares up at me. Her grin is wide with satisfaction.

She goes into the living room. I stay in the kitchen.

I pull down the blinds in the kitchen window and lock the back door. I put on Mom's Playtex rubber gloves and Dad's chef hat and apron. I stuff a spoon and a can opener into my pockets. I take down the box with the Phillips electric knife inside.

Melissa comes into the kitchen for more cookies. I stand against the side of the fridge. I wait until she returns to the television.

I jump out from behind the rubber plant in the living room five minutes later. "So you win do you? We'll have to fix that." I pull out the cords for the electric carving knife and hand mixer. We struggle but I get her down. I secure her legs to the sides of the chair.

Melissa squirms and yells. I pull the can opener and a can of Heinz Baked Beans from the pocket of the apron. Melissa hates baked beans. I dump beans in her mouth every time she opens it. She chokes and coughs. I eat her Oreos.

I change the channel to see my second soap, *Texas*. Justin kisses Rina. Melissa cries. "One more word, and you're dead, kid."

She moans. I wait for the commercial. The Glad Man advertises his new "stronger than ever garbage bags." I go to the kitchen, open the cupboard and take out a Glad bag. This one will have to be "stronger than ever," so I put one inside the other and another inside those two and Melissa inside all three. I put her out front with four bags of dead leaves. At 2:45, the garbage truck picks up the bags. The soaps are over at 3:00.

I have time to clean up the beans before Dad gets home.

Sylvia Stiglic
As I Stand Here...

As I stand here in the corner, I wonder what month it is. I know it's spring but I can't remember what month. I think it's April. I don't even care so I don't look at the calendar on the inside door of the broom closet.

I go into the broom closet because the closet is small and private and dark and it has just enough room for me. I step inside, me and my mind and my knife. I like it in here in the closet. I feel like it is my mind.

I take the knife and put it under my white, turtleneck sweater and against my stomach. I feel the cold, big blade, sharp and fine, reach down past my belly button.

I hold it flat against me. I don't want to cut myself. The knife is part of me. I wonder if the knife is a baby. What would it be like to give birth to a sharp, sharp knife? It would cut me as it pushed out of my body. It would cut the doctors' hands as they tried to take it out of me.

I wait here for him. I love him so much. I gave myself for him. I give for him. I feel tired, useless. I want him bad. Why does he make me so happy and so sad? He has me and he has her. I don't ask him to leave her because she is his. No, he is hers because she is so selfish and won't let him alone.

So I am tired. I don't like running. I am sick, my mind is tired, I want blue ocean life calm and natural and . . . if I take him and kill him then I will be able to be happy with my real husband who loves me so much and has no idea. I just have got to stop—STOP. If I kill him, then my husband will not be cheated as I do cheat him. I will give him double love because he will get love I always give the other one.

He will come here tonight, and I will kill and clean up the mess, and I will do it neatly so there will not be much to clean. I will wear gloves so there are no fingerprints. I will throw the body in the dump. They set that place on fire every couple of weeks. I only have to worry about someone finding the body before then, but they will not. Then, me and my husband will be happy because we are happy now but with him gone there will be a lie erased and we will be truly rich and happy. Not rich, I don't know why I think rich. I want happy.

I feel stifled. All of a sudden. I open my eyes which were always open, but they must have been closed because now I see behind my body a man's, his body. I must have eyes in the back of my head or maybe my eyes are in my hands. It is his body against mine pressing because I know this is my goodbye to him. I'm so sorry, I think. I have to, honey.

But then I feel him grab me around my waist and hold me but he squeezes too hard and I am stifled and scared. I cry out loud a word and I open the door and rush out of the closet. Then I think he really isn't there and I think my eyes were closed so I really didn't see. He is not there.

Oh my God, the front door opens and I hear hello and I am surprised but I know what I have to do. I just feel heavy. My head feels so heavy. I am afraid my neck will break with the weight, and I set my head against the china cabinet's cool glass so that my neck will not break. He cannot see me but I see my hand grow bigger and bigger and I am sure he sees my big hand because my hand is going crazy and growing longer and longer. My hand is as big as my head. But he doesn't see my hand. I almost laugh because these eyes of mine always see things his eyes don't.

God, I can't remember walking here. But my legs did it. I am behind him but he doesn't even know because he is reading the newspaper.

"Boo," I say.

He laughs and turns. I don't even see his face. I just see my hand move and my hand is big and weighs a lot and pushes the knife slowly into him but maybe it's my eyes that are slow because he would grab the knife if my hand went so slowly. My big hand sticks that knife in again right near his heart and I think this must be what it feels like to stab a pig.

It's done. He is quiet, eyes closed with a sad look inside them, I am sure. So easy and my knees are shaking and my hands shake and my stomach is not there and I forget and I am not nervous but feel everything is surely okay. So I roll the body in the floor rug it is already dead on. I feel better because I am doing something.

I have a garden rope I got at Canadian Tire and I tie the rug four times on both ends and twice in the middle. I drag that damn rug down two stairs, out the open door, into the garage and into the van.

God, I am driving and at the dump, it's all going so smoothly and I am not even thinking as I drag the rug out of the van and roll it down the hill so it lands on all the other shit in the dump. I throw the stupid string in too. I throw in the kitchen garbage I brought along because I was coming here anyway. On my way back, I think, tire tracks. I go to Canadian Tire. I am shopping like a normal person, not like someone who just killed him. I am smiling but acting normal, not silly or sad but I mind my business.

I go to the shop department and say I need new tires and the service man is helpful. I can tell he finds me attractive. I think, "Don't be an asshole 'cause I can kill." So the tires get changed. He asks if I want to trade-in the old tires and I say no because they keep records, so I tell him these are going to be put on another truck. I will get rid of these tires another time.

I can't remember anything because I just tell myself not to remember and I don't. When I get home I wash the floors like every Saturday and feed Kitty. I wash my stupid white turtleneck and put it in the dryer. I go to bed because now I am suddenly tired.